THE CRUEL SKY

A HEAVY BOMBER GROUP IN WORLD WAR II

ROBERT THOMPSON

WESTHOLME
Yardley

Facing the title page: Aircraft of the 451st Bomb Group over Ploesti, Romania, May 31, 1944. (*National Archives*)

Westholme Publishing, LLC
904 Edgewood Road
Yardley, Pennsylvania 19067
Visit our Web site at www.westholmepublishing.com

ISBN: 978-1-59416-441-5
Also available as an eBook.

Printed in the United States of America.

In loving memory of my father, HAROLD THOMPSON, who flew fifty combat missions as a B-24 aircraft commander in the 727th Bomb Squadron of the 451st Bomb Group, July to November 1944.

CONTENTS

Maps and Plans

PREFACE

With the generation that fought World War II now fading into memory, the story of how that war was fought and, perhaps even more importantly, the experiences of those who fought that war, have also begun to fade into the fog of history. While many historians have battled valiantly to ensure the war and the many lessons learned from it are not forgotten, one part of the war's story is deeply important to me—the American daylight precision strategic bombing of Nazi-occupied Europe. While much has been written about the American effort to destroy Nazi Germany's war-fighting ability from the air, I felt the need to tell the story of one American bomber group, how it was formed, what it was like to fly its planes, and the personal experience of those who flew some its most dangerous and challenging missions. I do this so younger generations can have some understanding of what this part of the war was like. The unit I chose to write about is the 451st Bombardment Group (Heavy) of the Fifteenth Air Force, also known more commonly as the 451st Bomb Group.

One of my reasons for choosing the 451st was its unit awards. President Franklin D. Roosevelt created the Distinguished Unit Citation (now called the Presidential Unit Citation) via Executive Order

9075, which he signed on February 26, 1942. The order specified that the citation would be awarded to units of the armed forces of the United States for extraordinary heroism in action against an armed enemy on or after December 7, 1941. To receive the award, a unit had to display the sort of gallantry, determination, and *esprit de corps* in performing the mission that set it apart from other units participating in the same campaign.[1]

During the American strategic bombing campaigns in the European and Pacific Theaters during World War II, only two heavy bombardment groups of the US Army Air Force received three Distinguished Unit Citations, the highest number of awards issued to any heavy bombardment group: the 95th Bomb Group of the Eighth Air Force and the 451st Bomb Group of the Fifteenth Air Force. The 451st's missions for which it received the citation included targets at Regensburg, Germany, on February 25, 1944; Ploesti, Romania, on April 5, 1944; and Markersdorf, Austria, on August 23, 1944.

My motivations for writing this history are also personal. I spent much of my professional life as an officer in the US Air Force, including several years as a B-52G navigator, radar navigator (the equivalent of a bombardier on the bombers of World War II), and bomber tactics instructor. Therefore, I am naturally interested in how these men and their aircraft operated during World War II. Far more compelling, my father, who passed away in March 2023 at age 100, was a twenty-one-year-old pilot and aircraft commander in the 451st who participated in the Markersdorf mission. If you find the idea of someone only twenty-one being in command of an aircraft carrying nine other men that delivered several tons of bombs on targets in Nazi-occupied Europe somewhat astonishing, you are not alone. I feel the same way, and even more so because I realize that so many of my father's comrades in the 451st and the other American bomber groups fighting in World War II were barely in their twenties—many were still teenagers. In fact, the "old man" on my father's B-24 crew was only twenty-seven.

Further, many were like my father who came from rural America, and before they entered the Army Air Force had seldom or never traveled outside their home states. In that sense, they were truly innocents thrown into a world of which they had little first-hand knowledge and into a war that was the worst in human history. But many, like my father, did not wait for the military to draft them. Instead, they volunteered for many reasons. However, while they may have gone to war for different reasons, once in it, almost all seemed to develop a grim determination to see it through.

Moreover, they all paid a price in one way or another. Many gave their lives—more than 27,000 were killed in the skies over Europe—and thousands more were wounded or spent years as German prisoners of war. Almost all of them lost close friends they had made in their units, while others suffered grievous physical wounds. Even more, however, suffered emotional wounds that took years to resolve, if ever. No one had defined post-traumatic stress syndrome in those days, but it was as prevalent in the veterans of World War II as it is in more recent combat veterans. When my parents were first married four years after the war ended, my father would leap out of his chair at the sound of any loud bang, and like many of his fellow veterans, he suffered from horrific nightmares in which he would loudly call out the clock positions of attacking German fighters, yell that another airplane was on fire and going down, or shout that one of his plane's engines was on fire and the propeller needed to be feathered. After writing this book, I can see why he and other veterans in the 451st had those nightmares, and you may come to understand that as well.

Another reason that makes the 451st an ideal subject to represent the American heavy bomber experience in World War II is to redress some historical oversight that started during the war and has been prevalent since. The Eighth Air Force, "The Mighty Eighth," as some call it, has consistently received the lion's share of the historiography of the American strategic bomber campaign. Flying mostly Boeing B-17 Flying Fortresses from bases in Great Britain beginning in 1942, it was the first of the Army Air Force's numbered air forces to undertake strategic bombing operations. Naturally, this meant that the Army Air Force's publicity efforts related to the American strategic bombing began with reporting on the missions of the Eighth Air Force. The April 1944 documentary *Memphis Belle: A Story of a Flying Fortress,* was the first film to present the heavy bomber campaign to the American public. It became a mainstay in war bonds drives, cemented the Eighth Air Force in the popular imagination, and gave the B-17 legendary status. Meanwhile, when the Fifteenth Air

Force—of which the 451st was a part—began its operations out of Italy in November 1943, it was more than a year behind the Eighth Air Force's publicity campaign. As a result, it always lagged in terms of media reporting and exposure.

After the war, the Eighth Air Force continued to dominate popular presentations of the war effort from the air, including motion picture productions such as Metro-Goldwyn-Mayer's *Command Decision* in 1948, 20th Century Fox's *Twelve O'clock High* in 1949, and Warner Brothers' *Memphis Belle* in 1990 (a remake of the wartime documentary), as well as the 1960s television series *12 O'clock High* and, more recently, the Apple miniseries *Masters of the Air* in 2024. This singular attention is also manifest in hundreds of histories written about the American bomber campaign. Recently, a few historians have helped to redress this problem with books about the Fifteenth Air Force, such as Stephen Ambrose's *The Wild Blue* (2001), Kevin Mahoney's *Fifteenth Air Force against the Axis* (2013), and Barrett Tilman's *Forgotten Fifteenth* (2014). The Fifteenth Air Force's missions were just as crucial to the outcome of the war as those flown by the Eighth Air Force, and the experience of the crews, ground personnel, and support services were equally terrifying, exhilarating, and tragic. So by writing about the 451st, I can bring the shared reality of the heavy bomber campaign while exploring a lesser known unit.

In deciding how to tell that story, I felt I needed to provide some context before discussing the unit's combat operations. Otherwise, the details of those missions and the experiences of the men who flew them would make little sense to a casual reader of history who likely has no knowledge of bomber operations during World War II. Therefore, I first describe how the 451st came into being, how the group trained and organized its initial members, and how they deployed overseas. Then I discuss the design and technical features of the Consolidated Aircraft Corporation's B-24 Liberator, which, while it may seem a crude piece of aerospace machinery now, at the time was one of the most sophisticated and complex bombers in the world. It had a reputation for being exceedingly difficult for pilots to master. Some aspects of that reputation were well deserved but others were not. Therefore, I will try to cover the many features and aspects of the plane and how its young, inexperienced crews were trained to fly and operate it in combat.

The next element in providing context is the tactics and operational methods used to employ heavy bombers in combat. When the Army Air Force began its heavy bomber operations in Europe in 1942, it asked the crews of the B-24 and the B-17 Flying Fortress to perform a mission that had never been undertaken: daylight strategic precision bombing. The operative word there is "daylight." The British had tried daytime bombing operations and quickly abandoned them in favor of nighttime attacks because the losses they suffered were prohibitive. But the Americans were convinced they could pull it off. While they eventually succeeded, it took a lot of work on the right blend of tactics and aerial technology. By the time the 451st began its bombing operations in early 1944, much had been learned about employing heavy bombers. Most of that education involved significant losses in aircraft and men. However, their first two Distinguished Unit Citations involved missions that still relied on relatively immature tactics. But their attack on Markersdorf in August 1944, after which they were awarded their third Distinguished Unit Citation, employed the latest techniques. However, as will be seen, no matter how good the plan or how solid the defined tactics might be, the mistakes made by human beings can lead to near disasters.

In addition, I felt it was also necessary to describe the tactics and weapons employed by the German Air Force, the Luftwaffe, that defended Nazi-occupied Europe against the Allied bombing campaign. I discuss its deadly antiaircraft artillery and its employment, as well as its excellent fighter aircraft and aircrews, who smashed into American bomber formations repeatedly in an attempt to stop them from reaching their targets. All these often led to terrible American losses in heavy bomber groups, which was true for the 451st.

With this baseline providing the needed background, the book recounts the missions to Regensburg, Ploesti, and Markersdorf. I describe each mission in as much detail as the available supporting historical data allows. As is always the case when researching historical topics, I discovered some gaps in the available information and conflicting views on events. However, I did my best to close and resolve these. To this end, I searched for additional supporting material and closely analyzed areas where different accounts of events did not tell the same story. For example, I found a few accounts of the Regensburg mission that portrayed the 451st's route to the target going to north-eastern Italy near Udine and then over the Brenner Pass into Austria. However, when I plotted the locations of the group's downed aircraft, they were nowhere near that route, with almost all being in modern-day Slovenia, well to the east of the Italian border. Luckily, I found a detailed account of the lead bomb group's route to Regensburg, and it correlated with the locations where the 451st lost aircraft. I also found what I believe is the source of the apparent confusion. The route taken that day went over Fiume in present-day Croatia, and some authors must have mistakenly believed the route crossed over Fiume Veneto, Italy, which is northeast of Venice.

Readers may also note that much of the narrative about each mission covers the aircraft lost and the experiences of the aircrews onboard those planes. This is because one of the most information-rich sources related to these missions is the Missing Air Crew Reports, or MACRs. Many of the stories in these MACRs are both dramatic and heartbreaking and deserve to be told. These reports, which the National Archives and Records Administration maintains today, include the MACRs filed by the 451st immediately following each mission. These reports contain complete information on the aircrew members onboard that day and any eyewitness statements from men in nearby planes. Furthermore, they also contain statements made after the war by surviving crew members. There are also, in many cases, copies of official German records that Allied forces found after the war. This invaluable source of information provides important data about the capture, recovery, and disposition of each aircrew member. Combined, these sources provide a compelling narrative.

Lastly, I fervently believe that one must talk about the people who made this story. While history is undoubtedly about events, it is even more about the people who were part of those events. In this case, that means the privates, sergeants, lieutenants, and captains who served and fought in the 451st must be the most critical players in the story, and that is what I have attempted to present in this book.

B-24 heavy bombers parked on the ramp at Fairmont Army Air Field, Nebraska, during a blizzard in November 1943. (*National Archives*)

Chapter One

Creating a Heavy Bomber Group

In preparation for flying his B-24H, named *Lamplighter*, to North Africa, Captain Lloyd Ryan studied the planned route closely. In the 1940s, flying an aircraft thousands of miles with much of the route over open ocean was not a trivial matter, so Ryan wanted to be certain he thoroughly understood the demands of each leg of the flight plan. On November 30, 1943, he and his crew of ten, along with four passengers, started a journey that would take them from their staging base in Lincoln, Nebraska, to Florida, Puerto Rico, Trinidad, Brazil, French West Africa, Morocco, and, finally, Algeria. The first leg of the flight to Morrison Field in West Palm Beach was uneventful. The crew and passengers stayed there for two days to ensure everything on the aircraft was in good working condition before they started on the remaining legs, many of which would be over water or dense jungle without emergency airfields.[1]

Unlike most other pilots in the 451st Bomb Group, Lloyd Ryan was older and more experienced. He was twenty-six when the 451st began its overseas deployment and had flown for Trans Continental Western Airlines before the war. Ryan had enlisted as an aviation cadet a month before Pearl Harbor. He had trained at Lubbock Army Airfield, Texas, where he met and married his wife in June 1942.[2]

Ryan, his crew, and passengers arrived at Borinquen Field, Puerto Rico, on the afternoon of December 2. They were to leave the following day, but in addition to Ryan having a head cold, one of the propellor governors failed when he started the engines, so he decided to wait at Borinquen until his cold cleared and ground crews could fix the governor. It took three days to make the repairs, and Ryan's cold finally resolved. So they resumed their journey on December 5. From Puerto Rico, they flew to Waller Field, Trinidad, which was nothing more than an airfield carved out of the jungle where the mosquitoes were so bad one had to sleep under netting. On December 6, the *Lamplighter* roared into the air for a 1,200-mile trip to Belem, Brazil. This part of the flight was mainly over the dense jungles of French and British Guiana, which had no landing strips for hundreds of miles. But luckily, the *Lamplighter* "ran like a charm" with "never a sputter."[3]

While the arrival at Belem was uneventful, the airfield was not where Ryan wanted to stay very long. He later recalled it was "awful—hot, murky, poor food and barracks not too sharp." So, the *Lamplighter* took off for Natal, Brazil, the next morning rather than lay over in Belem. Upon arrival, Ryan requested a complete aircraft inspection since the next leg of their journey would involve a 2,000-mile flight over the Atlantic to Dakar in French West Africa. The inspection and poor weather at Dakar caused a delay until December 12. During that time, the crew and passengers of the *Lamplighter* spent their days laying on the beautiful sand beaches, swimming in the warm ocean waters, and dining on mangoes and papaya.[4]

In the early morning of December 12, the *Lamplighter* took off from Natal and began what Ryan called their "big hop" to Dakar. The flight took almost twelve hours, covering a distance far greater than the plane's crew had experienced up to this point. Of all the crew, Lieutenant John Robinson, the navigator, faced the most significant challenge during this long overwater leg. The flight to Dakar meant having to guide the aircraft without the aid of landmarks on the ground, which, with the technology available in 1943, was usually the surest way to keep the aircraft on course. However, with nothing but two thousand miles of water to see below, Robinson and all the other group navigators had to guide the aircraft the same way as mariners on the open seas had for centuries—via celestial navigation. Since the *Lamplighter* was flying during daylight, Robinson would take measurements of the sun's height and azimuth using the "astrodome"[5] above his position in the nose of the plane to view the sun through a handheld sextant. Robinson would draw the resulting "sunline" on this chart, compare it to his estimate of the aircraft's position using dead reckoning (a position based on a combination of elapsed time with estimated ground speed and heading), and make his best guess as to their position. Given the potential inaccuracies in this process, it was easy to make errors involving dozens of miles in each celestial-based estimate, which could compound over time. Until one made sight of land, there was no way to know where the aircraft really was.

The only other navigational tool Robinson had was the automatic direction finder. However, this only worked once you were within about fifty miles of a shore-based transmitter, a nondirectional beacon. Once they were within range of the beacon, the navigator checked his automatic direction finder receiver and suggested Ryan turn the aircraft slightly to the north. But Ryan elected not to do so because he recalled that during their predeparture briefing at Natal, they were told the Germans were operating a secret transmitter in southern Morocco that was broadcasting false signals designed to send Allied aircraft off course. Luckily, Robinson's celestial navigation proved accurate, and they soon saw the African coast near Dakar. They adjusted the *Lamplighter*'s heading toward the airfield and made an uneventful approach and landing.[6]

The landing was interesting, however, for one reason—it was the first time Ryan had landed an aircraft on a runway built using pierced steel planking, or PSP. Popularly referred to as Marston Mat during the war, PSP had been developed by the army just before the war to rapidly construct airfield runways, and it became a standard fixture for Allied runways throughout the European and Pacific Theaters.[7] Therefore, this would not be the last time Ryan and the other pilots in the 451st would land on a PSP runway because all their operational airfields throughout the war were constructed using this steel material.

The *Lamplighter* remained at Dakar until December 17, when it departed for Marrakech, Morocco. The only thing Ryan later noted about Marrakech was that it was "freezing cold," a considerable change from the tropical locations they had visited on their journey. The city had little to offer them regarding tourist interest or food. Ryan took off the next morning, and after a five-hour flight across the barren desert of Morocco and Algeria, he landed the *Lamplighter* at Teleghma, where the aircrews of the 451st would wait before making their final journey to war.

Headquarters Second Air Force established the 451st Bomb Group, formally known as the 451st Bombardment Group (Heavy), by issuing General Order No. 58 on April 22, 1943. The new bomber group activated nine days later, on May 1, at Davis-Monthan Field near Tucson, Arizona. It consisted of four new bomb squadrons, the 724th, 725th (of which Ryan and his *Lamplighter* were part), 726th, and 727th. By late May, the initial nucleus of ten staff officers arrived at Davis-Monthan to begin organizing the new group. However, given the evolving conflict dynamics in Europe, the Army Air Force's plans for the 451st quickly changed.[8]

The original plan for the 451st was to serve as an Operational Training Unit, or OTU, to provide the final training phase at Davis-Monthan for new pilots and crews flying the B-24 bomber. But before the new group's officers could even finish unpacking and start their work, new orders were issued on June 4, 1943, transferring them, all other officers and enlisted men en route, and the group's headquarters to Dyersburg Army Air Base, Tennessee. The move meant the 451st would no longer be an OTU. Instead, it would organize as a combat unit and prepare for eventual deployment overseas when all crews and support personnel had been assigned and thoroughly trained.[9]

Once the staff had assembled at Dyersburg, they were given a small space in the headquarters of the 346th Bomb Group before moving to the corner of a building used by one of the 346th's squadrons.

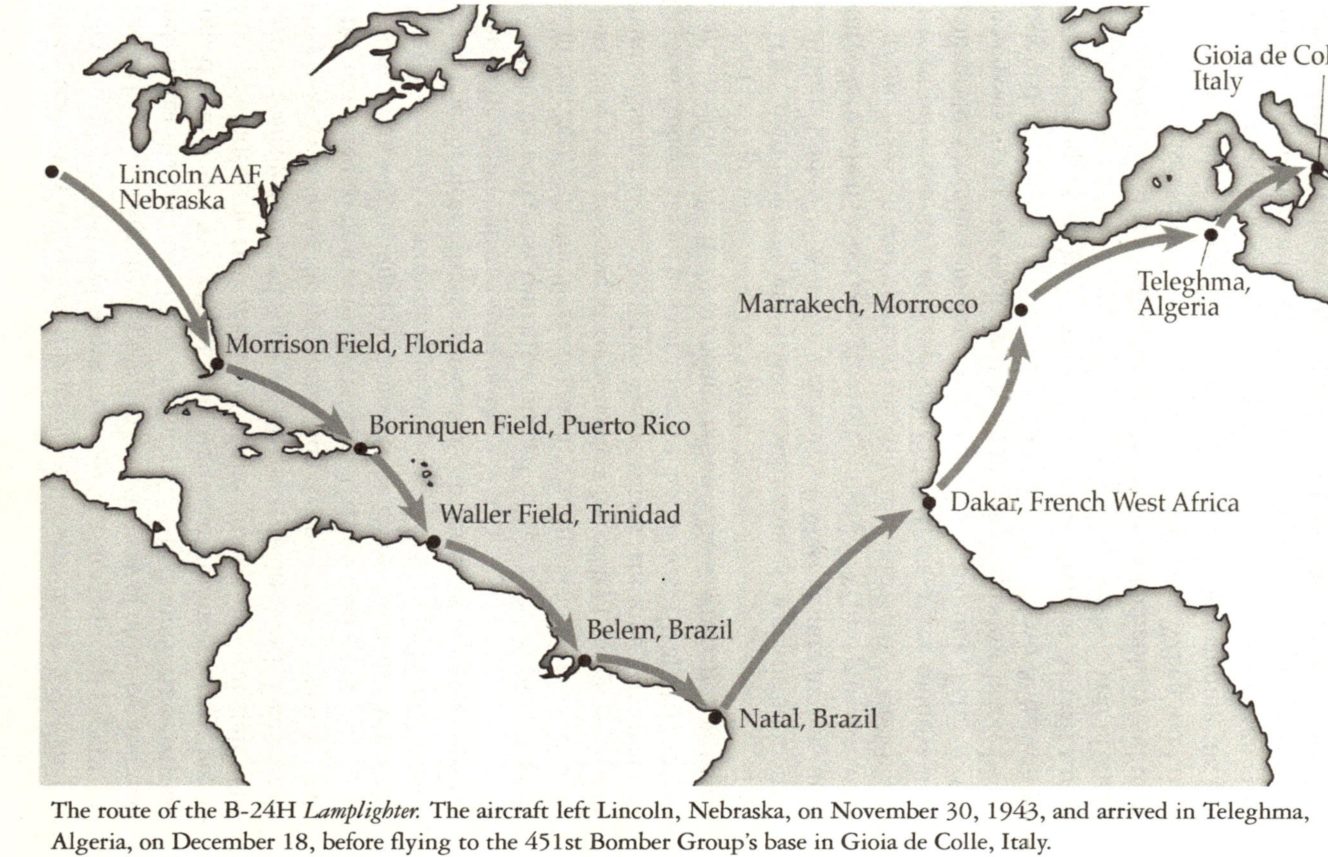

The route of the B-24H *Lamplighter.* The aircraft left Lincoln, Nebraska, on November 30, 1943, and arrived in Teleghma, Algeria, on December 18, before flying to the 451st Bomber Group's base in Gioia de Colle, Italy.

There, the newly arrived staff began rapidly working on a shoestring. They quickly started their work by preparing the required paperwork despite having a tiny office space, little in the way of office equipment, and an insufficient number of administrative personnel. As newly assigned men began to arrive in more significant numbers, their population included the first members of the group's medical staff. The doctors managed to steal some office space in the 346th Dispensary. They began checking the immunization records of all the new arrivals who continued to flow into Dyersburg. The base had a regulation requiring all newly assigned personnel to be examined daily during the first ten days for communicable diseases, such as measles and scarlet fever. The medical officers scheduled this series of examinations for every officer and enlisted man in the 451st.[10]

Officers were now quickly assigned to key roles in the S-1 (Administration), S-2 (Intelligence), and S-3 (Operations) staff, as were those who were to serve as commanders for each of the group's four flying squadrons. While all this was occurring, the group commander, Colonel Robert Eaton, had yet to arrive. Eaton was still at Davis-Monthan, attending the B-24 Standardization School, where he was being trained and qualified as a B-24 pilot.[11]

One man from the group described Eaton as "a charismatic, natural-born leader."[12] A 1931 graduate of West Point, he was only thirty-four when he became group commander. While initially commissioned as an infantry officer, the army sent him to be a student officer in pilot training at Randolph Field, Texas, three months after graduation. Once he completed his initial flight training, Eaton served three years in Hawaii with the 4th Observation Squadron before being assigned as the operations officer for the 5th Bomb Squadron at Mitchel Field, New York, where he flew the Douglas Aircraft Company's B-18 bomber. That tour of duty was followed by a year of study in meteorology at the Massachusetts Institute of Technology and then duties as a base weather officer at Scott Field, Illinois. When war broke out in December 1941, Eaton served as a major, commanding the 7th Air Base Group at Scott. The following month, he was promoted to lieutenant colonel and sent to Patterson Field, Ohio, to be regional control officer for the Second Weather Region. He continued working in meteorology as chief of the Weather Central Division in Washington, DC, in December 1942. Still, the Army Air Force decided to move him back into flying operations in June 1943 by assigning him as the new 451st Bomb Group's first commanding officer.[13]

Once he finished his B-24 coursework at Davis-Monthan in June 1943, Eaton finally joined the group, but he did not join it at Dyersburg. Instead, he traveled to Orlando, Florida, where those who were part of the 451st's air echelon had been ordered to attend the Army Air Forces School of Applied Tactics, or AAFSAT. AAFSAT incorporated all the information the Army Air Force had learned about bomber operations since the first B-17s were deployed to Great Britain a year earlier. Not surprisingly, the training at AAFSAT seems to have been especially important to Eaton. Once he arrived, Eaton gathered the forty-four officers and sixty-nine enlisted men sent there from Dyersburg and presented his thoughts on the importance of the upcoming training. That initial address to the men was apparently quite fiery, and one man recalled it as being a stern lecture on "how the cow ate the cabbage."[14]

The first ten days at AAFSAT were spent in the classroom. But after that, everyone moved to Pinecastle Army Air Field, which served as an auxiliary airfield to the main base at Orlando. The work at Pinecastle was intended to simulate combat conditions as much as was practical. It included a series of overwater mock-bombing and navigational missions designed to prepare the group's air echelon for operations overseas. The men were housed in tents, and a larger tent was erected along the flightline where the aircraft were parked and serviced to provide an operations and intelligence worksite. Initially, four B-24s were provided for the training, but three were found badly in need of replacement. So they were sent back to their home base at Biggs Field, Texas, while Eaton and his men waited for replacement aircraft, which delayed their training.[15]

Finally, three new aircraft arrived, and once they were serviced and found ready for flight operations, the combat training began. Simulated orders for each training mission arrived by teletype. Once they were pulled from the machine, the operations and intelligence staff broke them down and deciphered the detailed mission requirements. They then developed a plan for accomplishing each mission, compiled the required operations and intelligence data, and prepared a presentation for the aircrews who were to fly the mission. Just as it would eventually be done in a combat theater, the aircrews gathered about two hours before the scheduled takeoff time to receive the presentation. During these briefings, Colonel Eaton would outline the objectives for the mission, its importance, and what had to be achieved for AAFSAT to judge the mission as a success.[16]

Even though the men of the 451st had moved past the issue of insufficient aircraft for their training, the summertime Florida weather was not cooperative. It rained every day but one, and it frequently rained more than once a day. Maintaining and servicing the aircraft was also a challenge. However, as the ground crews always seemed to do, they found a way. The maintenance personnel on the flightline only had three crew chief kits; usually there would be at least one kit per aircraft. These kits contained all the essential tools needed to repair and maintain the B-24, such as a socket wrench set, adjustable and open-end wrenches, screwdrivers, high-speed twist drills, ball peon hammer, rubber mallet, valve repair tool, and two flashlights. With a severe shortage of personnel and the necessary tools, keeping the aircraft ready for each training mission meant the ground crews worked all night, every night.[17]

Despite the difficult conditions at Pinecastle, the men of the 451st worked diligently to complete their training missions and achieve the objectives required for each to be graded as a success. Eaton or his deputy commander, Captain Linnan Blackmon, personally accompanied each formation, ensured that cameras were onboard to record mission activities, and used the resulting photographs as evidence of objective completion. Each mission required the group's leadership, the aircrews, and the enlisted men to work closely together, getting to know one another as they labored long hours in central Florida's summer heat and dampness, ate poor food, and lived in challenging conditions. In the end, the group successfully completed seven out of a possible eight missions, a feat only one other bomb group had achieved. In fact, some groups had only been able to complete two or three missions out of the eight scheduled.[18]

It was time to move on to the 451st's next step in preparing for war. When the group sent to AAFSAT had received its orders, they specified that once training in Florida was complete, it was to head for Wendover Field, Utah, to join the rest of the 451st. The men who had remained behind at Dyersburg, including many new arrivals, were told to board trains that would take them "somewhere out west."

When they reached Wendover, most of the men referred to it as "God forsaken." While the ground echelon traveled by train, Eaton and the air echelon departed Pinecastle in the four B-24s they had used for training.[19]

Located 111 miles directly west of Salt Lake City on the Nevada-Utah border, Wendover Field sat on a barren, grim desert plain, far from the prying eyes of anyone who might want to learn more about American bomber operations. It was little wonder, then, that the base was later chosen as the location where the crew of the B-29 *Enola Gay* would train to drop the first atomic bomb on Hiroshima. If the natural conditions were not challenging enough at Wendover, the army made things worse for the 451st. When Eaton entered his new headquarters there, he found the base's personnel engaged in an urgent phone call to his ground echelon staff back at Dyersburg. They told the staff at Dyersburg that the training for an earlier group at Wendover had not yet been completed because of some likely screwup at higher headquarters. As a result, there were insufficient provisions and quarters for the 451st. But Eaton was undeterred—his men would still leave Dyersburg for Wendover as ordered and on time.[20]

The base's personnel immediately began setting up temporary living and work quarters to house the 451st. They erected a tent city to provide group headquarters and living quarters for the enlisted men. While their efforts were valiant, they still proved inadequate to the 451st's needs. The tents could house four hundred men, but the group brought more than twice that number to Wendover. More tents were erected at another end of the field for squadron staff activities, and a single building was earmarked to house the group's operations and intelligence staff. As carpenters and workmen hammered and drilled inside the building to create the required office spaces, the group's staff officers began their work undeterred.[21]

The weather at Wendover was also a constant issue. In the first days of operations, the winds were so high that many tents collapsed, including those that housed the four squadron staffs. As workers tried to raise the tents, the staff was forced to work outside. This, naturally, led to papers and records being blown about by the wind, creating administrative chaos at times. Throughout their time at Wendover, the men of the 451st were either plagued by high winds or torrential rains that made the field a muddy, shallow lake.[22]

Meanwhile, late July saw the influx of men from the ground echelon accelerate. One of those men was Karl Eichhorn, assigned to maintain the B-24's armament. Eichhorn was nineteen, from Belmont, Ohio, and had enlisted in Akron right out of high school in February 1943. His enlistment records indicate he was five feet six inches tall, weighed 140 pounds, and possessed photographic processing skills.[23] Eichhorn trained at Buckley Field and Lowry Field outside Denver, where his classes covered seemingly everything involving the armament equipment on the B-24, from bomb racks and releases to gun turrets and sights. He completed his training on July 4, 1943, and headed for Wendover via Salt Lake City on July 15. Eleven days later, he and a group of other men bound for the 451st loaded onto army trucks and began the journey to Wendover at 5:30 PM. The terrain they passed through was unlike anything young Karl had seen growing up in Ohio. As the trucks rumbled into the night, he noted, "We passed along the Great Salt Lake and then across a bleak and desolate desert. It was like a moonscape." The trucks drove through the gates at Wendover around 11:30 PM. They dropped off the men, who were then assigned to various areas where pyramidal six-man tents containing cots awaited them. After placing his blanket on a cot, Eichhorn unpacked some of his gear and "wearily went to sleep."[24]

When Eichhorn visited the flightline the following day, he was probably somewhat dismayed at what he found. As had been the case at Pinecastle, the ground crews had to fight poor weather while trying to service the group's growing fleet of B-24s despite lacking the tools and equipment they needed. But here, as in Italy later, the maintainers and their leadership demonstrated their keen organizational and technical skills and labored mightily to overcome any obstacles. Later, Colonel Eaton noted that he thought the poor conditions on the flightline at Wendover proved beneficial because they required the officers and men to use all their ingenuity and fortitude, which later paid off in combat conditions.[25]

Eichhorn and some other men were also disappointed to be working on B-24s. At that time, the B-17 Flying Fortress was the most famous and even "sexy" aircraft of the American bomber fleet. It had received almost all of the media coverage and was seen as far more glamorous than the B-24, which Eichhorn noted looked "a bit awkward on the ground." However, he would soon see the venerable bomber in a different light, saying, "But, like pelicans, though looking clumsy on the ground, B-24s were a thing of beauty in the air, and I very quickly came to love them."

While trying to prepare the aircraft to begin training activities, the ground crews had to construct their own work areas. They built frames for the needed tents and erected them while constructing equipment storage cabinets, workbenches, and storage racks. Eichhorn said of this work, "I quickly became a fair carpenter if not a cabinet maker." The armament maintenance crews also built their own firing ranges while fighting the wind-blown desert sands that seemed to find their way into everything.[26]

The winds were consistently so destructive that the men began referring to Wendover as "Windover."[27] The worst of those winds came on August 28—forever remembered by those who were there as the "Night of the Big Wind." While the winds had blown down tents here and there before, this windstorm was of gale-like proportions. Sweeping in from the desert, the winds blew down tents like "ten pins, crashing down wooden supports, flopping, full of salt and sand and dirt, over sleeping men, who thought they were perhaps being bombed." The winds soon were so strong they produced a nonstop howl, while "bed and belongings were playthings before the wind." Eventually, more than 100 tents fell to the winds that night.[28]

Meanwhile, the winds also played havoc on the flightline. Lieutenant Eli Zinn, the engineering officer for the 727th, was supervising a crew of men accomplishing an acceptance check on a B-24, a task they had completed a few days before on another aircraft in about twelve hours. When the gale began, Zinn allowed the men to return to their tents so they could save or salvage their belongings. When they arrived, they found all their tents in ruins, their personal effects blowing away across the base. Seeing nothing they could do, the men returned to the flightline to continue the acceptance check. Under Zinn's leadership, they finished the check well within the twelve-hour limit they set for themselves before heading back to the tent area to "retrieve what was retrievable."[29]

Of course, the group was at Wendover to train, and as soon as the aircraft and personnel were ready, that training began in earnest. Practice sorties were planned and executed over the nearby bombing range. While aircrews practiced navigation and bombing, the group's medical staff carefully evaluated every officer and enlisted man to ensure each was fit for overseas duty. At the same time, the engineering, communications, armament, operations, intelligence, and weather sections performed their duties, and a series of ground school classes were held under a schedule prescribed by the Second Air Force, which was responsible for the overall training of heavy bomber units. All the training, both in the air and on the ground, was conducted in two phases, and no bomber group could proceed to the second phase until all the training objectives for Phase 1 were met. The 451st successfully concluded Phase 1 on August 17 and began Phase 2 the next day.[30]

Although the 451st was destined to fly the G, H, and J models of the B-24 in combat, all the aircraft at Wendover were the earlier D and E models. As a result, the training aircraft did not have an automated gun turret in the nose, just a manually operated fixed gun that protruded from the glass in the nose section. Karl Eichhorn and his comrades in the armament maintenance section had to wait to learn how to maintain the nose turret later. Most of the time, the ground crews worked on the aircraft outdoors on the ramp. But when the weather was nasty, or the aircraft required major maintenance such as an engine replacement or structural repair, the aircraft was towed into one of several large hangars that had recently been built on the flightline. Eichhorn was curious about the large sliding doors at the entrance to the hangars. Each set of doors had two smaller sliding doors in the top center that extended from the top of the regular doors almost to the roof line of the hangar. This created a larger opening in an inverted T-shape. Karl thought this looked like the extra doors might be there to accommodate the vertical stabilizer of a large aircraft, one much bigger than the B-24. Years later, he found out his guess was correct—the hangars had been built for the B-29s that were still in a testing phase and would not arrive at Wendover until late 1944.[31]

One of the issues encountered in trying to effectively train at Wendover was the qualifications, or rather the lack of qualifications, of the newly arriving air and ground crews. Under the Army Air Force training system, the aircrews arriving at Wendover were supposed to have completed the first phase of training so that the 451st would not have to provide a "catch-up type training." But this was often not the case. The squadron commander for the 724th, Captain James Beane, said, "This was a problem that existed during the entire time of our training because as we went into second and third phase, we were supposed to get crews who had completed that phase of training. Unfortunately . . . this was not true. We got crews who had had little or no training in the B-24."[32]

Meanwhile, the ground crews arriving at Wendover should have completed various school training courses in their assigned specialty. While most had when they arrived at Wendover, there were enough of them who had not to cause problems. For example, armaments maintenance personnel like Karl Eichhorn were supposed to be able to perform all the required maintenance and repair activities for both the machine guns and gun turrets on the B-24. However, some arrived who had officially completed their training course but had actually spent much of their time performing tasks such as kitchen patrol or KP. It was a classic US Army tactic—have the student do whatever duties you wanted, pass them off as qualified, send them on their way, and let them be someone else's problem. As a result, the only thing many of them knew about a .50-caliber machine gun "was that it had one end that the bullet came out of and another end that the bullet went into."[33]

The Army Air Force training process called for each bomber group to complete its two phases of training at one base and then move to a new base to continue training so another group could arrive for its initial training. As a result, as the 451st's Phase 2 training approached completion in early September, rumors began to circulate that the group would soon relocate, but no one seemed to know where. The rumors were, in fact, correct. On September 5, Colonel Eaton and some of his key staff flew to Sioux City, Iowa, before going on to the site of the 451st's final training location—Fairmont Army Air Field, which was in central Nebraska about fifty miles southwest of Lincoln. They inspected the facilities and determined how to place their men, equipment, and aircraft. Eaton and his staff quickly returned to Wendover and made final plans to move to Fairmont.[34]

On September 8, the move began when the ground echelons for the 724th and 725th Bomb Squadrons departed for Fairmont in two trains carrying 673 men. Three days later, on September 11, the ground echelons for the other two squadrons left by train, and the entire air echelon of ninety-three officers and enlisted men took off for Fairmont in eleven aircraft, arriving there around 5:00 PM. The first ground echelon was waiting for them, and they quickly began servicing the aircraft and getting them ready to commence the next training phase. The second ground echelon group arrived on September 13 and began setting up its own operations at Fairmont.[35]

The facilities at Fairmont turned out to be remarkably different from those at Wendover. Construction on the new base started in September 1942 and used more than one thousand workers from all parts of the country. One of their first projects was to build a rail spur from the main rail line that passed through the town of Fairmont to the site for the base so construction materials could be delivered directly. In laying out and building the base, the Army Air Force installed a "maze of concrete runways" that formed a triangle, with one of the runways built to be seven thousand feet long. More than two hundred buildings were spread across the 1,980-acre base, including hangars, storage buildings, and even one for celestial navigation practice.[36]

Compared to Wendover, Fairmont was a luxurious palace that would prove far more comfortable than what awaited the group overseas. Gone were the flimsy tents of Wendover, replaced by gleaming new barracks and office buildings. While the buildings were the typical wood-frame, tar-paper temporary structures built by the thousands across the United States during the war, they were a vast improvement over what the men had experienced in Utah. The large, roomy hangars on the flightline allowed the ground crews to work undisturbed by weather.[37]

On September 17, thirty-four new crews arrived and were distributed among the four squadrons. By the end of September, eighteen new aircraft had arrived, including the group's first seven B-24H aircraft. These B-24Hs were called flyaway planes because they would accompany the group when it headed overseas. Unlike all the other twenty-two aircraft the group now possessed, these B-24Hs had the new Emerson nose gun turrets installed. These were so new that armament maintainers like Karl Eichhorn had not even heard of them, much less been trained to maintain them. Therefore, he and the others in his squadron studied the Technical Orders and explored all the turret's mechanisms.[38]

The arrival of October signaled fall was coming to Nebraska as the weather began to cool noticeably. At the same time, excitement and anxiety began to build as a deployment to some overseas location moved ever closer. The most significant sign of this impending event was a series of rigorous inspections, all designed to prepare the 451st to pass the Preparation for Overseas Movement, or POM, inspection, which had been scheduled for November.[39]

On October 1, Colonel Eaton started the inspection process by reviewing the POM Manual with his key staff so each person could understand how the inspection would impact his department. Throughout the month, inspectors from the 2nd Bomber Command, Army Air Force Headquarters, and the War Department traveled to Fairmont to review the group's progress and readiness for the POM inspection. Overall, they deemed the group's readiness as "satisfactory" but the inspectors' reports provided items that could stand improvement and fine-tuning. Special attention was made to ensuring all the aircrews would complete the training requirements for overseas movement. This included meeting training objectives such as a minimum of twenty hours of formation flying above twenty thousand feet, dropping at least twenty bombs on a precision target from above twenty thousand feet, and completing a one-thousand-mile navigational flight.[40]

One of the complications some squadrons encountered as they fought to complete the required training by the time the inspectors arrived was properly preparing their aircraft. This meant the aircraft had to be sufficiently maintained to meet the demanding training schedule, which required the necessary supplies and spare parts to be available. Sadly, more often than not, those supplies and parts were not available to the ground crews at Fairmont. So the 724th commander, Major Beane, went to his ground crews and asked them what they needed, and one enterprising sergeant gave him a complete list. To get these items, Beane ordered an aircraft to be ready, bought a case of whiskey, and flew off to one of the major B-24 depots. Once there, the sergeant used the supply of whiskey to negotiate for everything he needed. At the end of the day, the aircraft had been loaded, and Beane flew back to Fairmont with the sergeant and a treasure trove of tools and spare parts.[41]

At the same time, the enlisted men were prepared for overseas deployment. Each man was issued a steel helmet, firearm, cartridge belt, ammunition clips, and a checklist of required clothing to pack. Private Eichhorn recalled: "At a 'show-down inspection' in late October, all of our gear was checked for proper size and condition. Anything that was even slightly worn was turned in for salvage and replaced with new items. Dog tags, shot records, and pay records were all carefully checked. We stood retreat in full equipment, with packs and steel helmets, and were lectured on personal security and censorship. Time was moving quickly."[42] At this point, no one knew precisely where the 451st was headed. Still, the cold weather gear they received caused many to believe Great Britain and the Eighth Air Force were their final destination. The men were also subjected to physical fitness tests, including chin-ups, push-ups, and running three-hundred-yard dashes.[43]

The other notable event in October was the continuing arrival of new flyaway B-24H aircraft. By the end of the month, fifteen of these planes had arrived, which meant a great deal of work for the ground crews. Every new aircraft had to be inspected, serviced, and "broken in" to ensure it met all the Technical Order standards. For Eichhorn and the armament maintainers, these activities included removing, cleaning, lubricating, and checking each of the aircraft's six machine guns before reinstalling them. The B-24H's four gun turrets also had to be thoroughly inspected, and the plane's bomb racks and gunsights were inspected and repaired or recalibrated as needed.[44]

In some cases, the ground crews found the aircraft to have left the factory in less than pristine condition. The usual culprits among the aircraft's shortcomings were faulty electrical circuits, missing parts, and systems that "simply did not operate properly." In Eichhorn's experience, Ford Motor Company's Willow Run Plant aircraft suffered from poor quality control. In contrast, those from aircraft manufacturers like Consolidated and Douglas seemed to always be in good condition. In his mind, this was because auto manufacturers like Ford "never really understood quality control." In addition, some of the aircraft arrived from the factory without incorporating the latest modifications. In those instances, the ground crews would make the modifications themselves and ensure their work met the latest Technical Order specifications.[45]

October 1943 was also a month of intense flying training, emphasizing the tight formations needed in combat to protect against enemy fighter attacks. Colonel Eaton flew on as many of these missions as possible and proved to be a harsh taskmaster. During the missions he flew, the aircrews could hear him bellow instructions over the radio. He would constantly shout, "Tighten it up," or, "Low flight, you're too low," or, "Lead flight, you're too fast . . . 35 inches manifold pressure!" His frustration with the formation flying sometimes would lead to sarcastic statements such as, "Look at us! We're spread all over the goddamn Nebraska countryside!"[46]

On one occasion, Eaton was flying with the crew of a plane they had christened *The Jolly Roger*. As *The Jolly Roger*'s formation got together and began its flight to the bombing and gunnery range, the aircraft's number two engine (left inboard) caught fire. The pilot pulled the throttle back while the copilot feathered the engine's propeller, and the flight engineer cut off the fuel flowing to that engine. *The Jolly Roger*'s radio operator and waist gunner, Sergeant James Atkinson, immediately scrambled to prepare his parachute for a potential bailout. He stored his parachute under the radio table, and only one thing stood between him and the parachute—Colonel Eaton. Atkinson, a twenty-year-old from Mississippi who had played football for East Mississippi Junior College before enlisting, lowered his head and lunged toward his parachute as though he were crashing through the offensive line, lifting Eaton off his feet. The colonel "landed on the flight deck in a heap," looking up sheepishly at the sergeant who was clipping the parachute to his harness. Once they all realized the emergency had passed, Atkinson helped Eaton to his feet, and the group commander said nothing further during the flight.[47]

Afterward, however, Eaton debriefed with all the aircrews who had flown that training mission. He mentioned the need for tighter formations and the usual training discrepancies. Then he paused before saying, "Today, men, I flew with Lt. Williams' crew. We had an engine fire emergency on one of the older D models, and I would like to commend Lt. Williams, his copilot, and his flight engineer on their handling of the emergency. I would also like to suggest that if any of you have any problems accessing your parachute during an emergency, you should consult with Lt. Williams' radio operator who will allow nothing to stand between him and his chute, including me!"[48]

Sadly, October also brought the group's first deaths. On October 10, three officers and three enlisted men from Crew 42 of the 726th Bomb Squadron were flying a routine training mission. After an early morning takeoff, they climbed to high altitude and flew toward

Wayne, Nebraska, about 113 miles northeast of Fairmont. As the aircraft proceeded toward a simulated bombing run over the range near Stanton, Nebraska, all seemed well. Then their aircraft suddenly plunged to the earth, exploding on impact. No cause was determined for the accident, which took the lives of all six men onboard. The group was still mourning their loss when a second accident occurred on October 25. In this accident, two aircraft from the 724th Bomb Squadron collided during a formation training flight and crashed near Milligan, Nebraska, just fourteen miles southeast of Fairmont. Seventeen aircrew members died in the accident, and one man managed to parachute to safety.[49]

By November's arrival, all the flight training requirements were complete, and the group made the final preparations for the POM inspection. At the same time, flyaway aircraft continued arriving, and the ground crews worked diligently to prepare them. By the time the POM inspection arrived in mid-November, the 451st had a complete complement of sixty-two B-24H aircraft. The group assigned sixteen each to the 724th and 725th Bomb Squadrons, while the 726th and 727th Bomb Squadrons received fifteen each. The last act before the POM inspection was conducted on November 11 when the group flew a practice POM mission. The entire group participated in the mission, which was to include dropping bombs from twenty thousand feet over the Stanton Bomb Range. However, complete cloud cover over the target prevented the planes from releasing their bombs. The arrival of brutally cold weather and the fact that some emergency landings were made between takeoffs made the mission more challenging.[50]

On November 16, the POM inspection team arrived, and all went well. The group flew a five-hour mission to drop practice bombs at Stanton, and it went off without a hitch. The POM inspectors deemed the 451st ready for deployment, and the next day, orders arrived telling the group to pack up and get ready to move. The orders included routing for the group's aircraft, indicating that the rumors about going to Britain were wrong. The flights would start on November 18 with a short trip to Lincoln Army Air Base, Nebraska, and continue for five days. After a brief staging period at Lincoln, the aircraft would fly to Morrison Field in Palm Beach, Florida. From there, they would proceed to Teleghma Field in Algeria via Borinquen, Puerto Rico, or Waller Field in Trinidad; Atkinson Field in British

Guiana; Belem, Brazil; and finally, either Natal or Fortaleza, Brazil, which were the jumping-off points for the perilous two-thousand-mile flight across the Atlantic to Rusisque Field near Dakar, in what was then French West Africa. From there, the aircraft would fly to Tindouf, Algeria, or Marrakech, Morocco, before flying the final leg to Teleghma Field.[51] The flight covered just over nine thousand miles and presented a formidable challenge, especially for new, inexperienced navigators who had never flown anything remotely like this routing, requiring them to use every navigational tool available.

On the morning of November 18, 1943, the 451st Bomb Group began its journey to war when eleven aircraft from the 724th took off for Lincoln. Colonel Eaton was on the first plane, and each was crammed with luggage for ten crewmen and four passengers. The group repeated the process for the next five days until the ramp at Fairmont was empty, and only the ground echelon remained at the base. The ground and air echelons would not reunite until January 20, 1944.[52]

The aircraft remained at Lincoln until November 26, when the first aircraft from the 724th, piloted by Lieutenant Claude Vail, departed for Morrison Field. From there, it left the continental United States on November 27, landing at Dakar on December 3. By January 4, 1944, all sixty-two aircraft had arrived at Teleghma. For the most part, the flights went smoothly, with one exception: The aircraft flown by Captain Sidney Winski lost three of its four engines over the ocean between Morrison Field and Waller Field in Trinidad. With seventy miles left before landfall, the aircraft steadily descended. Winski ordered the crew and passengers to throw everything loose overboard, including baggage, guns, and parachutes, hoping they could remain airborne a little longer. He also ordered everyone to prepare to ditch in the ocean, a dangerous prospect since the B-24 was notorious for not being a suitable aircraft in which to ditch. Luckily, though, as the aircraft broke through the cloud cover over the Caribbean, the crew saw the island of San Lucia with the airstrip at Beane Field just ahead. Winski landed the aircraft there safely.[53]

While the air echelon was moving to North Africa, the ground echelon made its own journey, which was not as simple as that experienced by the aircrews. As soon as the last aircraft had departed for Lincoln, the ground crews and staff worked to rapidly complete packing and preparing to move out. Rather than moving by air, the ground echelon made its path to the war by train and then by ship. On November 26, the ground crews boarded a train in Fairmont that took them on a two-day trip to their port of embarkation at Newport News, Virginia. After a Thanksgiving dinner at Camp Patrick Henry outside Hampton Roads on November 28, the men made their final preparations for the transit across the Atlantic, which included more immunizations, lectures on various topics, and the issue of additional clothing. On December 1, the ground crews from the 725th and 726th Bomb Squadrons began boarding a Liberty Ship at Newport News called the SS *John Pillsbury*.[54]

The loading process on the *Pillsbury* and the three other Liberty Ships that would carry the ground crews continued for two days, consisting of a forty-minute train ride from Camp Patrick Henry to the docks at Newport News, where they were met by women from the American Red Cross who greeted them with hot coffee as an army band played patriotic music, which must have been intended to raise one's spirits. Each man then began walking up the gangplank that led into the ship. This proved a precarious exercise because each man had to carry a fully loaded musette bag, a large duffle bag, a weapon, a steel helmet, and a blanket roll wrapped around the pack. Karl Eichhorn later wrote about the walk across the gangplank into the *Pillsbury*, saying, "We carried the duffel bags on one shoulder, which made for a high and unstable load. As we walked towards the gangplank, one of the men in the front lost his balance on the way up the gangplank and almost fell into the water. He did drop his duffel bag into the water and was saved by the quick action of a seaman who grabbed him as he almost went through the rope." It was not an auspicious start for a long journey across the Atlantic.[55]

Once the ground crews were loaded aboard their respective ships, they sailed out of Newport News on December 3 as part of an eighty ship convoy. The pace of the journey was agonizingly slow. After all, the ships had to maintain the same speed as the slowest vessel, which turned out to be the *Pillsbury,* because it could only manage a top speed of six knots due to bad engine rings. Karl Eichhorn described the men's quarters in the hold of the *Pillsbury* as being nothing more than bunks made from canvas slings mounted to the steel hull and stacked six bunks high to the ceiling, allowing the housing of between seventy-five and one hundred men in each of the ship's passenger holds. Eichhorn said of these quarters, "There was a rumor that we were sleeping over tons of ammunition, but no one really believed 'they' would do that! We were to learn later that 'they' would and did!"[56]

Conditions aboard the *Pillsbury* were those that almost any enlisted man who shipped out overseas on a Liberty Ship would find painfully familiar. No hot water was available for bathing, so the men had to make do with cold salt water and a product of dubious cleaning value called "salt water soap." The officers, meanwhile, had an aft hold all to themselves, which the enlisted men could not enter, where they enjoyed hot water and could eat in the ship's officer's mess.[57]

After waiting for the rest of the convoy to arrive, the ships set sail as part of the largest convoy to leave Newport News up to that time. In addition to the various freighters and tankers, the convoy's escorts included a Wasp-class aircraft carrier, two cruisers, American and Canadian destroyers, corvettes, and a US Navy dirigible, which followed the convoy during the first day before returning to land. Within twenty-four hours of setting sail, about three-fourths of the men in the enlisted holds were seasick, and most remained so for the entire voyage. Luckily for Karl Eichhorn, he bedded down in a top bunk, which protected him from being deluged by vomit from the sick men below him. Soon, of course, the mess and smell caused by so many seasick men became almost overwhelming, and efforts to keep the holds clean were essentially in vain. In fact, conditions became so bad that Eichhorn decided to sleep on deck, where he found a relatively comfortable spot between a couple of crates and a ventilator. Of course, he had to contend with cold wind and ocean spray, but he could remain warm and dry by curling up in his blanket and overcoat. Eichhorn's primary concern was the prospect of a large wave washing him overboard while sleeping. To combat this danger, he found a large piece of hemp rope, looped it around his waist, and tied it to a deck fitting.[58]

As the convoy set sail on December 3, those on the *Pillsbury* still did not know where it was headed. However, two days out into the Atlantic, the group executive officer, Major Raymond Marshall, told the men their ship was bound for Algeria, and the trip would take three weeks. From that piece of information, most of the men figured out that Italy was their eventual destination because they knew they could not effectively execute bombing missions against Germany from bases in Algeria. Of course, the men were right.[59]

The convoy made its way through the Strait of Gibraltar early on the morning of December 21 before anchoring that night offshore along the North African coast. The next day, the ships carrying the ground echelon split, with the men from the 725th and 726th docking in the harbor at Oran, Algeria, while the other two squadrons went on to dock in the harbor at Naples. The men from the 725th and 726th briefly camped near Oran, while those from the 724th and 727th departed their ships on December 27 for quarters at a college outside Naples. A few days later, the ground crews near Oran reboarded the ship and went to Naples. But on January 2, 1944, all the ground crews received orders to move by train and truck to the new base at Gioia del Colle, about 135 miles east of Naples. When they arrived at the base, there were no quarters for them, so they had to make the most out of nothing. Those leading the ground echelon assigned areas for each squadron, and the men erected tent cities for both quarters and mess halls throughout the base.

As it turned out, Gioia del Colle was not the best place to locate a base for heavy bombers like the B-24. The airfield had been an Italian Air Force base, but it only needed a short grass field for its operations, not a five-thousand-foot runway. As a result, the airfield boundaries were too small to build a runway that long. So, in order to lay down a long Marston Mat runway, the Army Corps of Engineers had to extend the airfield limits into a low, boggy area. To make it suitable for the runway to be laid down, they filled it in with earth and then packed it down.[60]

However, once the 451st's aircraft arrived, it was discovered that their weight caused the runway to sink about six to eight inches. This would not have been an issue except that January to February 1944 was the worst winter in southern Italy in twenty-five years, with torrential rains. The heavy rainfall turned the low-lying part of the runway into a lake about six inches deep that the B-24s had to plow through when taking off or landing. Worst of all, when the bombers took off, the water and mud would spray onto the bomb bay doors and then freeze once the aircraft climbed into the frigid skies at eighteen thousand to twenty-five thousand feet. When that occurred, the bomb bay doors would not open, and the aircraft could not release their bombs on the target.[61]

The rainy January weather and the resulting deep, sloppy mud that covered the base also did not help the ground echelon in completing its work. One report about conditions at the field said Gioia del Colle "became a sea of mud and water as the weather continued to go from bad to downright unbearable. The steel matt runway had almost sunk out of sight." But the men persevered because their officers and NCOs told them all had to be made ready for the impending arrival of the air echelon from Algeria and the commencement of combat operations.[62]

However, the arrival of the air echelon was delayed slightly by a new requirement for the aircrews to complete seven practice missions in Algeria before moving on to Gioia del Colle. The group's aircrews flew these missions out of Teleghma, and each sortie included bomb runs using practice bombs on an assigned area in the desert. On January 16, after discussing the situation at the new base in Italy via telephone, Colonel Eaton decided that enough progress had been made in the construction at the new base to allow the aircraft to move there. On January 20, 1944, the air echelon arrived at Gioia del Colle, and the 451st began its final preparations to go to war.[63]

A B-24 H Liberator. (*National Archives*)

Chapter Two

The "Flying Boxcar"

Having completed aviation cadet training at Brooks Field in San Antonio, Texas, in November 1943, Harold Thompson moved on to begin the first phase of flight training at Bruce Field, which was in the small west Texas town of Ballinger. At this point in becoming a full-fledged aviator, he did not know what aircraft he would fly once he completed his training; all he knew was that he would first fly the Fairchild Aircraft PT-19 *Cornell*, a single-wing monoplane with an open cockpit. The PT-19 was designed to do nothing more than provide a solid, basic platform for initial pilot training. It did not even have an intercom system. Instead, the instructor and student used a crude communication device called the Gosport Tube. This device consisted of a hollow tube similar to one in a stethoscope into which the instructor could speak directly to his pupil.[1]

During his training, Thompson occupied the front seat of the cockpit, while his instructor sat behind him. At Bruce Field, like many other Army Air Force primary flight training bases, the instructor pilots were civilians. The reason for using civilian instructors was simple—at this point in the war, the Army Air Force did not have enough qualified pilots to spare any to serve as instructors for this initial phase of training. In this case, the instructors at Bruce Field were employees of the Fred Harmon Flying School.[2]

Many of his fellow trainees were nervous about finding out if they had what it took to fly an aircraft, but young Thompson was very confident.[3] As soon as he turned sixteen, he used the money he had saved from repairing the tractors and machinery on farms near the one owned by his family to take flying lessons. So as he went out onto the flightline to take his first training flight, he was filled with the confidence he had gained during five years of experience flying light aircraft.

He met his instructor, and the two men shared a brief conversation. The instructor was likely trying to learn a little about his new student and gain a feel for who he was. When he asked Thompson if he had ever been in an airplane before, the new student pilot proudly informed him that he not only had been in an aircraft, but he also had his pilot's license and had been flying since 1938. The instructor smiled at hearing this and gave Thompson a knowing nod of the head. Thompson saw this as a good sign, but little did he know that his instructor had heard this before. The instructor knew from long experience that training a new pilot was not a task made easier if the student had previous flying experience. Rather, it meant that he would need to first correct numerous bad habits gained from flying in an undisciplined environment before getting down to the business of teaching the basics of good flying.

From his experience, the instructor also knew that the best way to start the process of "unlearning" bad habits was to shock the student into a keen understanding of just how much he did not know about flying an aircraft. On this day, the instructor's approach to shocking his new student started when he told Thompson that their first flight would be a simple trip to familiarize him with the local area. The instructor told Thompson that he should just relax during the flight and that he did not even need to tightly fasten his seat belt. So after climbing into his seat in the cockpit of the PT-19, Thompson followed the instructor's recommendation, clicking the fastener on the seat belt closed but barely doing anything to tighten it across his waist.

After the instructor lifted the aircraft off the runway, he climbed to about five thousand feet and began casually meandering around the Ballinger area, speaking through the Gosport Tube as he identified key local features on the ground below. Once he was sure his new student had relaxed completely, the instructor suddenly pulled the aircraft controls sharply to the right until the plane was upside down. With his seat belt lying loosely across his lap, Thompson suddenly found himself perilously hanging below his seat almost in midair. He grabbed the belt desperately with his hands, trying to hold on lest he hurtle out of the cockpit to the ground below.

The instructor then rolled the aircraft back upright as his new student thought the man completely insane. But the instructor picked up the Gosport Tube and calmly told Thompson that maneuver was intended to let him know that he did not really know anything about flying and its inherent perils. He added that it would now be time to forget everything he had ever been taught about flying and learn to fly the Army Air Force way—with discipline and professionalism.

It was a lesson Harold Thompson never forgot.

Almost every pilot assigned to fly the B-24 had the same impression the first time he saw the aircraft on the flightline ramp during training: it was a monster. Unlike the graceful B-17, the B-24 was squat and ungainly, and it seemed so complex he could never hope to learn to fly it, much less become its master as an aircraft commander. One new pilot later remarked that the B-24 "was a god-awful looking aircraft on the ground," and another pilot he knew "described it as a pregnant salmon with wheels on its belly and a wing with engines attached to its top dorsal fin."[4]

The process of reaching the point where he would learn to fly the B-24 was the same for every trainee. Each man entered the Army Air Force via the aviation cadet program. However, since thousands of men were enlisting to be aviation cadets, it could take months to begin training from the time one enlisted to going on active duty.

One twenty-year-old who enlisted as an aviation cadet and later became an aircraft commander in the 727th Bomb Squadron in July 1944 successfully completed his initial examinations in July 1942 but did not complete his basic cadet training until November 1943.[5]

After aviation cadet training, each pilot candidate would begin learning how to fly the army way. This process began with primary flight instruction, which was typically conducted by civilian flight instructors at one of dozens of small rural airfields hastily built by the army. The Army Air Force had realized in the late 1930s that it would have to drastically expand its pilot training capacity should war come in Europe. The largest shortcoming in its training system was the initial or "primary" training phase. So it began hiring civilian flight training firms to conduct that phase in 1938. When France fell to Nazi Germany in June 1940, the Army Air Force upped its annual pilot production goal from a mere three hundred men to seven thousand. But it soon realized this would not be enough to meet true wartime demands.[6]

In response to the need for pilots, the Army Air Force began a massive project to build primary training bases and hire civilian flight schools to run them. This led to an expansion in the number of primary flight training bases to forty-one by the time of the Japanese attack on Pearl Harbor, with a maximum of fifty-six schools operating at any one time by 1943. From a prewar goal of producing 7,000 pilots per year, the Army Air Force rapidly increased its goal to 75,000 by 1942. With all the new primary flight schools in place, annual pilot production peaked at 102,000 in 1943.[7]

During primary flight instruction, the recently graduated aviation cadets were introduced to flying in an open cockpit primary trainer such as the single-wing Fairchild PT-19 or the biwing Boeing PT-17. Here, the Army Air Force would determine if each man had the hand-eye coordination needed to fly and the required mental and emotional makeup. The latter was the reason for dismissal from the training program more often than not, and many men found themselves being sent for a different type of military training because of what was called "manifestations of apprehension."

Once they had mastered the primary training aircraft, the pilot candidates would move on to a larger base to fly a basic trainer, usually the Vultee Aircraft BT-13. The BT-13 had a far more powerful radial engine than the primary training aircraft. One B-24 pilot said of the BT-13, "When you opened that throttle and started down the runway, that plane just fairly jumped." With its additional power, the BT-13 had more speed. That same pilot commented, "It brought you definitely to a different level of flying. It required considerably more skill to handle."[8]

After basic flight training, each potential B-24 pilot moved on to advanced training in either the Curtiss-Wright Aircraft AT-9 or the Cessna Aircraft AT-17. This training required each man to master the intricacies of flying a multiengine aircraft, prove they could manage instrument flying in day and night conditions, and fly the aircraft in formation with others. Once this training was successfully completed, the men were commissioned as second lieutenants in the Army Air Force, requesting the aircraft they would like to fly on active duty and receiving their notice of what aircraft they had been assigned to fly.[9]

It seems almost no one requested an assignment to the B-24. This was probably because it was physically unattractive and had a reputation for being exceedingly challenging to fly. Some did not want an assignment to the B-24 because they had heard "all these gory stories about the B-24s blowing up."[10] When Lieutenant Walter Baskin was told he would be flying the B-24, he wrote to his parents, "I have been assigned to a B-24. That's just about as far from what I wanted as anything could be, but I can still hope."[11]

After moving on to the base where they would be trained to fly the B-24 and seeing one up close for the first time, the new pilots were confronted by a sight some characterized as "bewildering." Up to now, they had flown aircraft that, while the cockpits increased in complexity as they progressed through each training level, had relatively simple flight controls and instruments. However, when they first climbed into the cockpit of the B-24, they saw a panel with twenty-seven gauges and twelve levers to control the throttle, turbocharger, and fuel mixture. The wheel they would use to control the aircraft was called a "yoke" and was as large as the ones installed in large trucks. There were also more than a dozen switches and brake and rudder pedals. In fact, the Army Air Force B-24 training manual had a photo of the cockpit that indicated the pilot and copilot had seventy-one controls, levers, switches, and instruments to master.[12]

Training for the B-24 took place at bases such as Liberal Army Airfield in Kansas and Maxwell Field in Alabama. However, the training was the same regardless of where the pilots were assigned. Each man learned to fly what was, at the time, a complex, high-performance aircraft while also acquiring specific flying techniques, knowledge about all aircraft systems, the duties of each B-24 crew member, and their responsibilities as both a pilot and aircraft commander. The gravity of the latter was powerfully described in the Army Air Force training manual for the B-24:

> Here's where they separate the men from the boys. You can be one of the best B-24 pilots ever trained and still fail as an airplane commander. In addition to qualifying yourself as a top-flight pilot, you have the job of building a fighting team that you can rely on in any emergency. Failure of any member of the crew to do the right thing at the right time may mean failure of your mission, unnecessary loss of life and possible loss of your airplane.[13]

One pilot who would go on to fly a B-24 in combat from Italy commented that learning about all the aircraft's systems was something akin to learning about the human body. He later wrote that like a human being, the B-24 "had to be fed oil and gas; it had an oxygen system, an electrical system (nerves), a hydraulic system (muscles), and a system of cables extending to the tail and out to the ailerons (tendons), which controlled its movement. It even had a skeleton frame and was covered with a protective aluminum skin. The automatic pilot is the brain."[14]

Once transition training into the B-24 was completed, the new pilots were told whether they would be a pilot or copilot based on the skills they demonstrated during their recent training. Then they would go to combat training at places like Tonopah Army Airfield in Nevada or Davis-Monthan Field in Arizona. This final phase involved more formation flying and added combat skills, including bombing from high and low altitudes. In some cases, this was where pilots first met some of the crew members with whom they would fly in combat. Once this training was complete, it was off to a port of embarkation and the final journey to combat in the B-24.

The official history of the Army Air Force during World War II says, "The B-24 represented one of the earliest products of President Roosevelt's intervention on behalf of air power in the autumn of 1938." General Henry "Hap" Arnold, the Army Air Force's commander, took advantage of the authority given to him by the White House for the development of a new heavy bomber. On February 1, 1939, he issued Type Specification C-212 to Consolidated Aircraft of San Diego, California, to develop and produce a four-engine bomber with a three-thousand-mile range, a top speed of three hundred miles per hour (mph), and a service ceiling of thirty-five thousand feet, while carrying a bomb payload of eight thousand pounds. The army already had the B-17 *Flying Fortress* in its inventory, but these new specifications exceeded many of its capabilities, and the Army Air Force hoped that a "superior plane" might be the result.[15]

The design produced by Consolidated was designated Model 32. It incorporated some of the new design features Consolidated had employed on its Model 31, the XP4Y-1 flying boat. One of these was an oval, twin-tail design. However, the most notable design feature borrowed from the Model 31 was the "Davis Wing."[16]

The Davis Wing, also called the "Davis Fluid Foil," was a unique design. The wing was not truly a specific wing. Instead, it was a "mathematical formula for creating high-aspect, low-drag airfoils." Initially created in 1931 by engineer David Davis, the Davis Wing was a laminar flow airfoil that passed through the air by placing the thickest part of the wing as far as possible from the leading edge, consistent with maintaining lift. In 1938, Davis proposed his design to Consolidated. Initially, the company was not impressed by the design, which had already been rejected by one aircraft manufacturer. While it "flew in the face" of the airfoil design principles developed by the National Advisory Committee on Aeronautics, Consolidated's chief engineer, Isaac Laddon, found Davis's design intriguing enough to make him believe they should at least test it.[17]

It took some effort for Laddon to persuade Consolidated's president, Reuben Fleet, to give Davis's design a try, but Fleet eventually agreed to pay the costs to test the Davis Wing at the California Institute of Technology's new wind tunnel. The results were remarkable—the drag coefficients were so low the engineers at the wind tunnel decided to run three tests to ensure the data they were seeing was accurate. Their report to Consolidated characterized the wing's performance as so incredible that they left it to Fleet, Laddon, and Consolidated's engineers to determine if the results were "an aberration or remarkable." After viewing the test results, Fleet decided to risk the Davis Wing design on the XP4Y-1 and the B-24.[18]

While experience would show that the Davis Wing had outstanding aeronautical performance, it tended to fold up when enemy fire led to significant structural damage. The army's official description did not tell pilots that distressing information but instead said of the wing, "The B-24 wing is an internally braced, skin stressed type, tapered, with a high aspect ratio. It is considered one of the most efficient airfoils ever developed and was a radical departure from airfoils in use when the *Liberator* was designed. Its unusual efficiency accounts for the combination of high speed, long-range, and great load-carrying qualities of the airplane."[19] However, some of those who would fly the B-24 in combat initially had misgivings. One veteran pilot later said, "When I first saw the B-24, it looked like a boxcar held up by toothpicks. I couldn't believe those tiny things could lift that big fuselage."[20]

Once the B-24 was fielded, it received official and unofficial nicknames. When some of the first models were delivered to the Royal Air Force, or RAF, the British Air Ministry called Reuben Fleet to ask what it should call the aircraft. Fleet told them the B-24 was to be called the *Liberator*, adding, "We chose the name *Liberator* because this airplane can carry destruction to the heart of the Hun, and thus help you and us to liberate those millions temporarily finding themselves under Hitler's yoke."[21]

Of course, the unofficial nicknames ranged from complimentary to insulting. Some who admired the B-24 called the bomber the "Flying Boxcar" because it was big enough to carry B-17s overseas. Those nicknames that were less complimentary included "New York Harbor Garbage Scows with Wings," "Spam Can in the Sky," "Banana Boat," "Flying Brick," "Pregnant Cow," and "The Old Agony Wagon."[22] However, while its looks when on the ground did not inspire anyone, that changed once the B-24 was airborne. The official history of the Army Air Force during the war states, "An ungainly looking ship on the ground, it had a grace of its own in the air."[23]

As the plane entered service, it garnered a not entirely undeserved reputation of being the most challenging American bomber to fly.

The B-17 was "easier to take off, easier to fly, easier to land, and had other advantages, such as it didn't break up or sink when it crash-landed in the sea." One historian characterized the B-24 as "a man's airplane," adding, "It could be sternly unforgiving. It always required, and sometimes demanded, almost superhuman strength to fly." One B-24 pilot later recalled, "You could never trim the son-of-a-gun and had to horse it around constantly."[24] This characteristic would lead to some saying you could always tell who a B-24 aircraft commander was because his left arm would be oversized from constantly struggling to keep the aircraft from rolling to the right.

However, critics and fans of the B-24 could agree on one thing: it was extremely tough. The Army Air Force official pilot training manual said the B-24 "proved itself capable of delivering tremendous blows against the enemy over extremely long ranges, under unfavorable weather conditions and against heavy enemy opposition. . . . [It] has everything—speed, climbing power, carrying ability, and above all, guts. The B-24 can take it and dish it out."[25] The manual quoted one pilot, "She'll take you there and bring you back." It went on to relate that he had seen B-24s so badly shot up by enemy fire "it seemed impossible that the airplane could stay in the air." Some B-24s returned to their home bases with half the rudder controls shot away, propellers shot off, engine supports blown off by enemy fire, both ailerons gone, and no ability to control the elevators on the horizontal stabilizer.[26]

During a mission to bomb the Osterreichische Motor Works and marshaling yards on October 13, 1944, Lieutenant Harold Thompson, now a twenty-one-year-old aircraft commander, was flying a B-24J from the 727th Bomb Squadron and was approaching the bomb run. Suddenly, an 88mm antiaircraft artillery (AAA) shell smashed the cowling and propeller for the number two engine inboard on the left wing. The shell, which did not explode on impact with the engine, continued on, blowing through the pilot's left-side window, cutting Thompson's oxygen hose in half before exiting through the cockpit ceiling. The impact knocked the aircraft into a ninety-degree right bank, but Thompson managed to get the aircraft back to flying straight and level. The plane maintained formation until they had released their bombs on the target and completed the bomb run. However, as the aircraft exited the bomb run, the number four engine outboard on the right wing failed because of damage from shrapnel, leaving the aircraft with only two usable engines, and even they had sustained damage. This, in turn, resulted in a steady descent of about one hundred feet per minute despite full power being applied to the two remaining engines. But even though the aircraft was severely damaged, it got its crew home to their airfield at Castelluccio, Italy.[27]

The manufacturing and production required to field enough B-24s to meet wartime needs posed a particularly daunting challenge for planners. Even before the United States entered the war, it quickly became apparent that Consolidated could not produce the number of required B-24 aircraft on its own. Therefore, the Army Air Force decided to create a group of manufacturers who, along with Consolidated, would build B-24s based on Consolidated's design, selecting Ford Motor Company and Douglas Aircraft for the work. Consolidated would manufacture the aircraft at its existing San Diego plant, and it would build an additional B-24 factory in Fort Worth, Texas. At the same time, Douglas would build a new plant for B-24 production in Tulsa, Oklahoma.[28]

Ford took on its part of the job with particular enthusiasm. Under the leadership of Charles E. Sorenson, Ford built a new factory at Willow Run, Michigan, which incorporated everything Ford had learned about assembly-line manufacturing. The new facility was 3.5 million square feet and employed thirty thousand. The first B-24 came off the Willow Run line in May 1942, and by June 1945, Ford had built 8,685 B-24s, which was 47 percent of all the *Liberators* produced during the war. The assembly line at Willow Run built 234 aircraft a month, or about eight per day, resulting in one B-24 being completed in three hours. In total, this consortium of manufacturers built almost 18,500 B-24s by the end of the war, the largest number of any single aircraft type produced by either the Allied or Axis nations during the war.[29]

A fully loaded B-24 at takeoff weighed in at 55,000 pounds, with 2,750 gallons of high-octane aviation gasoline and an 8,000-pound bomb load, which was carried in two bomb bays that had rollup doors instead of those on other bombers that opened out into the slipstream. This unique design eliminated buffeting caused by standard doors opening down into the plane's airflow. The bomb load could consist of four 2,000-pound bombs, eight 1,000-pound bombs, twelve 500-

pound bombs, or twenty 100-pound bombs. Later in the war, improvements allowed the B-24 to carry as much as 12,800 pounds of ordinance. Further, it could carry its bomb load and crew up to 2,850 miles at speeds of between 255 and 355 mph, depending on the aircraft's gross weight.[30]

Like many other aircraft built during World War II, the B-24 received numerous modifications that resulted in different models of the bomber, five of which were flown by the 451st Bomb Group. While the group's inventory of B-24s consisted entirely of the H model when they first arrived in Italy in January 1944, it also received a total of twenty-two earlier model B-24Gs as replacement aircraft during the war. The first B-24G arrived on April 1, 1944, and the last was delivered on July 17, 1944. The feature that distinguished it from previous versions resulted from earlier B-24s not being able to adequately defend the aircraft from frontal attacks by enemy fighters, a preferred tactic of the Luftwaffe. As a result of this issue, the design of the B-24G replaced the fixed, moveable machine gun in the nose with an Emerson A-4 gun turret.[31]

The 451st's inventory during the war eventually totaled 115 B-24Hs, with the last H model being delivered to the group on Christmas Day 1944. This version of the B-24 was remarkably similar to the B-24J, except that the tail gun was replaced by an improved Emerson A-6B gun turret. Later models of the B-24H had a Martin A-3D top turret that incorporated what was called a "high-hat" design that provided the gunner with improved visibility, a clear glazing that enclosed the waist gun windows, and an improved nose gun turret, the Emerson A-15.[32]

The next model flown by the 451st was the B-24J. The group inventory included ninety-two of these aircraft, delivered between March 17 and October 11, 1944. More of these aircraft were built than any other version of the B-24, a total of 6,678. So many of the B-24Js were built that there were not enough Emerson A-15 gun turrets to meet the demand. So, many of them used a Consolidated version of the Emerson A-6. The other changes in the B-24J model included an improved version of the Pratt & Whitney R-1830 engine, a new model of the Norden bombsight (the Norden Mk. XV), an improved autopilot, and electronic regulators for the superchargers. The B-24J design also replaced the deicing boots on the wing and tail surfaces with the Thermal Ice Preventative System, which used hot air from the engines to prevent ice buildup on the wing and tail leading edges.

The final two versions of the B-24 flown by the 451st were the B-24L and B-24M. Although the B-24L was like the B-24J, it incorporated design features intended to reduce the plane's weight. Because fighter escorts were generally available when the L model was produced, most weight savings came from the aircraft having less defensive armament. In this case, the tail gun and ball turret were removed, saving over one thousand pounds. The B-24M, meanwhile, reinstated the Consolidated A-6B turret in the tail, and some also had the ball turret in the lower fuselage. The 451st flew thirty-five B-24Ls but only twelve B-24Ms.[33]

Further, a total of twenty-eight B-24H, B-24J, B-24L, and B-24M aircraft flown by the 451st were specially configured to serve as "Pathfinder" aircraft. These planes had the AN/APS-15 or H2X "Mickey" radar system installed in place of the ball turret to provide a capability to bomb targets despite heavy overcast. The Mickey radar was based on an earlier British design, the H2S radar, which had been developed by engineers at the Massachusetts Institute of Technology. The radar, which weighed three hundred pounds and had eighty vacuum tubes, was operated by a technician who sat at a console behind the copilot's seat and directed the bombardier to his release of the bomb load.[34]

Like many combat aircraft of the era, consideration of human factors, much less human comfort, was not part of the design process. For the most part, the B-24 was "built like a Mack truck" with few, if any, refinements. New crews first discovered this when they tried to enter the aircraft. The bombardier, navigator, and nose turret gunner had to squat almost to their hands and knees and crawl forward to their stations through the plane's nose gear. They then squeezed themselves into the "cramped" nose compartment. Once in place, the bombardier sat on a small seat behind the nose gunner's turret from where he could hunch over the bombsight. The navigator, meanwhile, sat on a tiny retractable stool beside the navigator's table, where his maps and equipment were located. When the navigator looked behind him, he could see the pilot and copilot's feet over the bulkhead that separated the nose compartment from the cockpit.[35]

The remainder of the crew entered the aircraft by crawling through the bomb bay doors about three feet off the ground and onto an eight-inch wide catwalk that connected the forward part of the aircraft to the rear sections. The pilot, copilot, radio operator, and engineer would carefully walk forward to the cockpit and radio compartment, which was just behind the cockpit. While the two pilots climbed into their seats, the radio operator would sit at a small desk where his radio sets were installed. The engineer would stand just behind and between the pilot and copilot during takeoff to help monitor the engines and then sit down directly behind the pilot until it was time to operate the top gun turret. Then he would climb into the turret by standing on a metal bar just inches from the radio operator's head.[36]

The waist gunners, ball turret gunner, and tail gunner would go from the bomb bay catwalk to the rear of the aircraft. The waist gunners would stand at open windows to operate their guns while being subjected to fierce winds blowing through the plane and freezing temperatures that led to their guns being covered in frost. But if the waist gunners' positions were uncomfortable, the ball turret gunner had the one place on the plane that was the most miserable. This gunner was usually one of the smallest men on the crew, and for good reason, given that the ball turret was exceedingly cramped, with only enough room for the dual machine guns, their ammunition belts, and the gunner. The ball turret gunner would climb down into the turret once the plane was airborne, and the waist gunner would lower the turret into position on the bottom of the aircraft using a hydraulic system. As a result of the ball turret's limited space, there was no room for the ball turret gunner to wear his parachute. If the crew were ordered to bail out, one of the waist gunners would raise the ball turret back into the fuselage, help the ball turret gunner out, and get him into his parachute. Given this, one had to hope there was sufficient time during an emergency for this process.[37]

In addition, the B-24 was not pressurized, and there was no heating system to combat the temperatures at altitudes that were often as cold as twenty-five degrees below zero. The Army Air Force had developed electrically heated flight suits, and the crews of the Eighth Air Force's bombers in Britain all had them. However, the 451st and the other bomber groups in Italy only had these suits for the waist gunners. Harold Thompson recalled that this decision had apparently been made because it was warmer in Italy than in Britain, even though it was twenty-five degrees below zero at twenty-five thousand feet no matter where one was based. As a result, when he flew missions, he would have one hand on the yoke and sit on the other to keep it warm, changing hands every half-hour.[38]

If crew members needed to move between the bombardier-navigator or flight deck compartments to the rear fuselage compartment during flight, they had to navigate the treacherously narrow catwalk across the bomb bay. This act was performed with great care because the bomb bay rollup doors were made of light aluminum and only had a capacity of about one hundred pounds. If a crew member walking across the bomb bay fell, he would break through the doors.[39] Given that no one donned their parachutes until an order to bail out was given, this would be a fatal accident.

Naturally, the crew was the critical component in the B-24 performing its mission.[40] While each crew member had a specific set of tasks, coordination and trust among the ten men was crucial. The Army Air Force, however, saw the pilot assigned as aircraft commander as the man who would play the most critical role. The B-24 pilot training manual told pilots, "It is your airplane and your crew," and they were responsible for the safety and efficiency of the crew at all times, not just in flight. The manual also stated, "Your crew is made up of specialists. Each man—whether he is the navigator, bombardier, engineer, radio operator, or one of the gunners—is an expert in his line. But how well he does his job, and how efficiently he plays his part as a member of your combat team will depend to a great extent on how well you play your own part as the airplane commander." Further, the manual reminded pilots that the lives of their crews and the success of each mission were mainly in their hands—quite a responsibility, given that many of the aircraft commanders were only in their early twenties.

That same manual also went to great lengths to reassure pilots about the challenges of flying the B-24. "The B-24 airplane is not difficult to fly," it said, adding, "It has no vicious characteristics and when the Pilot learns the difference in 'feel,' due to its size, weight, and speed range, flying it is no more of a problem than flying a trainer." However, it also pointed out that the B-24 was a "highly complicated" aircraft that contained numerous systems, and they, as aircraft commanders, must do all they could to learn about each system. "Learn your airplane," the manual said, "study the functional operations of the several systems and the mystery of imagined complexities will become surprisingly simple." This, it added, would allow pilots to understand the fundamentals that made the B-24 "tick," which would "pay amazing dividends in psychological reaction and peace of mind." Finally, it communicated an essential message: "Master the airplane, don't let it master you, but never lose respect for it."

The copilot, meanwhile, was described as the aircraft commander's executive officer and his "chief assistant, understudy, and strong right arm." He not only had to know all his duties and functions as copilot but also needed to be familiar enough with the pilot's duties to take over, if necessary, in combat. Like copilots on most large aircraft of that time, he was responsible for closely monitoring the engines' performance and fuel status while maintaining a comprehensive log of performance data. The copilot also needed to be able to fly the aircraft in formation when climbing through overcast so the pilot could watch the rest of the formation. Most importantly, however, the copilot had to be capable of taking command of the aircraft, completing the mission, and getting the crew safely back home if the pilot was killed or wounded. Therefore, the aircraft commander was responsible for doing all he could to prepare the copilot to perform the job of aircraft commander.

As for the navigator, his job was to guide the aircraft and direct its course of flight from takeoff to landing. To perform this task, he had been trained in navigation using what was called pilotage, dead reckoning, radio, or celestial navigation. Celestial navigation was primarily used for overwater flights, such as when the aircraft flew across the Atlantic during their initial deployment, and radio navigation only came into play during combat when the aircraft approached its home base. Therefore, pilotage and dead reckoning were the primary navigational tools for combat missions.

Pilotage involves determining the aircraft's position by looking at the ground below for key landmarks and matching them to the navigation maps and charts. The Army Air Force stressed that this process had to be performed with precision. The goal was pinpoint accuracy, not merely guessing the aircraft's vicinity. The pilot training manual stated, "The exact position of the airplane must be known not within 5 miles, but within ¼ of a mile." As anyone who has performed pilotage can say, this is not easy. It required the navigator to determine the aircraft's ground speed by timing the passage between known points and calculating the speed while constantly monitoring his maps and charts. Dead reckoning, meanwhile, involved determining the aircraft's position by maintaining a log of the track and distance flown and estimating the required heading and speed to stay on course.

The bombardier was responsible for the "accurate and effective" delivery of the B-24's bombs, which meant that the ultimate success or failure of each mission depended on his performance during the short interval required for the bomb run. Whenever the bombardier took control of the aircraft's course using the controls on his Norden bombsight, he was effectively in command of the aircraft. As the B-24 pilot training manual said, the bombardier would tell the aircraft commander what he needed to do during the bomb run, and until he said "Bombs away," his word was "virtually law." The bombardier had to be thoroughly familiar with the critical aiming point for the target, how to operate his bombsight, and how to load and install fuzes in his bombs.

Arming bomb fuzes was a hazardous job, especially on the B-24. This was done in flight in the bomb bay, which, as described earlier, had aluminum rollup doors that would not support a man's weight if he were unlucky enough to fall on them in flight. But the process of installing the fuzes was also fraught with danger.

Each bomb fuze was installed on the ground by the armorers on the ground crew.[41] The fuze contained an extremely sensitive train of explosives designed to detonate the bomb. Before installation by the armorer, the fuze was in a "safe" condition, as each fuze had a small propeller at the end that was locked into a safe mode via a removable safety pin that was much like a cotter pin. Once the aircraft was in flight, the bombardier had to make the perilous journey back into the bomb bay and remove each bomb's safety pin. To ensure that each bomb had been properly armed, the bombardier was required to bring pins back from the mission and have the armorer for his aircraft verify the number of pins matched the number of bombs loaded onboard before the mission.

Once the bomb was released from the aircraft, the airflow around the fuze would cause its propellers to rotate rapidly. After a set number of revolutions, the fuze was armed and ready to detonate the bomb upon impact. The armorers adjusted the fuzes before takeoff to be either instantaneous or have a time delay set so the bomb did not explode immediately. This was useful if you did not want the bomb to explode until it had penetrated inside a building. The fuze time delay could also be set so that the bomb did not detonate for several hours. In these cases, the fuzes were referred to as "booby-trap" fuzes because they would not explode until they had been buried in the ground long after the bomb had landed and, thus, might kill enemy personnel returning to make repairs.

The bomb fuzes also had one other unpleasant feature involving two ball bearings with tapered tracks on opposite sides of the fuze. When the armorer was screwing the fuze into the bomb, these ball bearings recessed into the deep portion of the tracks so they would not cause any interference. However, if someone tried to disarm the bomb by removing the fuze, the ball bearings would jam against the threads in the tracks, penetrate the walls of the fuze, and instantly detonate the bomb. Even the armorers could not remove the fuzes safely once they had been armed, so whenever an aircraft had to return with unused bombs, the bombardier would drop them into the ocean.

Behind the pilot, the radio operator sat in his compartment and managed and monitored the plane's radios, of which there were many. The job might have seemed simple, but it was quite complicated. The radio operator had to know his equipment thoroughly and be able to troubleshoot in flight. He also had to understand the communications plan for each mission and what radio and frequency were critical to every phase.[42]

The engineer sat in the same compartment with the radio operator and was required to know more about all the B-24's equipment than anyone else on the crew. He had to "know his airplane, his engines, and his armament equipment thoroughly and know how to strip, clean and re-assemble the guns." His responsibility was serving as the aircraft commander's "chief source of information concerning the airplane." Given his critical function among the crew, he had to be a man the aircraft commander could rely on. One B-24 engineer refined his duties down to one critical task—starting the two-cylinder hydraulic system, which he said was no more than a glorified "lawn mower, putt-putt" engine. However, he said this single job filled him with anxiety on every mission because this one system was "designed to generate pressure to raise and lower the landing gear and activate the brakes once the plane touched down." His concern about this little engine was expressed by a series of questions that ran through his mind every mission. He thought, "Will the damn putt-putt start? What can I do if it doesn't start? We couldn't land without disaster; it would mean the brakes won't work! Disaster! Fire! Explosion! We're ruined!"[43]

Finally, there were the gunners, the men responsible for defending the B-24 against German fighters. There were two categories of gunners on the B-24: turret gunners and flexible gunners. The power turret gunners had to possess mental and physical qualities like those needed to fly the aircraft "since the operation of the power turret and gunsight are much like airplane operation." Meanwhile, the flexible gunners who manned the waist guns had to have a "fine sense of timing and be familiar with the rudiments of exterior ballistics." All the gunners had to know the effective coverage areas provided by their gun position and be experts in aircraft identification. They also had to be able to quickly clear any jams or stoppages in the guns and properly "harmonize" the sights with their guns.[44]

Naturally, one of the most critical things every B-24 aircrew member had to know was the designated bailout locations and the proper method for bailing out. Every crew member had an assigned place from which to bail out, although the necessities and circumstances dictated by combat sometimes required crew members to use alternative bailout locations. Therefore, everyone had to know where every available bailout exit was and how to use it. The navigator, bombardier, and nose turret gunner were to leave the aircraft through the nose gear door hatch one after the other, facing the front of the ship, crouching near the opening with their hands placed on each side and then rolling out headfirst. Back in the waist compartment, the tail turret and left waist gunner were supposed to exit through the camera door hatch on the belly of the fuselage by crouching down, facing the direction of flight, and then rolling out through the hatch headfirst. However, while the aircraft manual said the ball turret gunner and right waist gunner were supposed to bail out from the rear part of the bomb bay, experience later proved that most of the time, they went out the camera door hatch with the other gunners in their compartment. Finally, the flight engineer/top turret gunner, radio operator, copilot, and pilot were to use the bomb bay for bailout by crouching on the catwalk facing the direction of flight.[45]

The engines that drove the B-24 through the air were four Pratt & Whitney R-1830 Twin Wasp engines with seven cylinders each and a combined 4,800 horsepower. The first time a crewman flew on a B-24, he saw a change once the throttles for all four engines were pushed forward. The aircraft went from "waddling" along the taxiway to rushing down the runway with so much power that you were pushed back into the seat. One new pilot said the power used for takeoff "sent tingles through every nerve." Control of the engines involved a complex dance that included throttle setting, fuel-air mixture, propeller pitch, and turbine supercharger settings. Takeoff required 2,500 revolutions per minute, and climb power required 2,400 revolutions per minute.[46]

The turbine superchargers were also a unique feature of the B-24's engines. They were centrifugal compressors, one for each engine, powered by the engine's exhaust. The engine exhaust gas went into a nozzle box and was directed against buckets on the turbine wheel of the engine. The idea behind them was related to the power of the engines decreasing as the pressure of the charge entering the cylinders lessened due to the atmospheric density decreasing as the aircraft gained altitude. Therefore, the function of the supercharger was to overcome this loss of power by supplying air to the engine at or above sea level pressure from sea level to a critical altitude of twenty-five thousand feet. This allowed the B-24's engines to maintain their power and performance no matter the aircraft's altitude.[47]

Among the engine controls were the switches that would "feather" an engine should it have to be shut down because of damage or some other malfunction. Feathering meant the propeller blades of the selected engine would have their pitch angle increased until the blades were parallel to the airflow going through them. This allowed the propeller blades to slice through the air and not keep spinning like a windmill or become frozen entirely. This was an essential function because if the engine could not be feathered, it could not only cause significant drag on the aircraft but also cause vibrations so severe the pilots could not read their instruments.[48]

After a pilot and copilot started the four engines while parked on the flightline, they watched the gauges to ensure they reached the proper operating temperature. Only then would they start to taxi the aircraft toward the runway. This process required slow, smooth turns since sharp maneuvers on the ground would grind rubber off the tires and cause severe stress to the nose and main landing gear. Pilots were also instructed to use their engines to steer the aircraft so they would save wear and tear on the brakes, which needed to be in good shape to stop the plane when landing.[49]

Another unique feature of the B-24 was its tricycle landing gear, which had one wheel under the nose and two main landing gears under the wings.[50] Until pilots began training on the B-24, every other aircraft they had flown during training had two main landing gear under the wings with a small wheel located under the tail, which was why these planes were called "taildraggers." This tricycle landing gear required different techniques for takeoffs and landings than taildraggers, but this did not pose a significant challenge for most new B-24 pilots.

Once the aircraft had reached the runway, the pilots would run up the engines, check the magnetos, adjust the propeller controls, and set the superchargers based on the Pilot's Check-Off List. Then they would open the cowl flaps, which were used to help cool the engines, to one-third open, lower the wing flaps to one-fourth, and head down the runway into the wind. As the aircraft sat at the end of the runway, the aircraft commander advanced the throttles slowly until they hit the stops and held the brakes until the manifold pressure for the engines reached twenty-five pounds in inches of mercury or Hg. Then he released the brakes, and the aircraft would accelerate down the runway at full engine power. The copilot would take control of the throttles, holding them tight against the stops and adjusting the superchargers, as the calculated takeoff data required. The aircraft commander would focus on steering the aircraft using the rudders to maintain control until the plane reached a safe minimum takeoff speed, usually between 110 and 130 mph. At that point, the aircraft would easily come off the ground with the nose wheel lifting into the air first, followed immediately by the main landing gear.[51]

Once the aircraft achieved a positive climb rate, the landing gear was raised, the aircraft accelerated to 130 mph, and the wing flaps were raised before the aircraft reached 150 mph, which was the best climb speed for the B-24. The copilot monitored the engine temperatures during the climb and adjusted the cowl flaps to maintain the proper operating temperature. At that point, the aircraft continued climbing as it approached the planned cruise altitude.[52]

As the aircraft first reached the cruising altitude, the aircraft commander would execute a maneuver that was another unique aspect of flying the B-24. This maneuver, which was called "Going over the Hump," called for him to continue climbing until the aircraft was about five hundred feet above the planned cruise altitude. Then he would push the aircraft into a shallow dive until the plane reached the cruising altitude. During this dive, the B-24 would accelerate until the aircraft commander reduced the power to achieve the needed cruising speed, which was called getting "On the Step." If this procedure was not followed, the B-24 would fly in a slight tail-down aspect that increased drag and made the aircraft "mush along," handling sluggishly and laboring to maintain the correct cruising speed, which would only get worse based on how much of a fuel and bomb load the aircraft was carrying.[53]

Once the mission was complete and the aircraft approached its home base, the two pilots ran through the Pilot's Check-Off List for approach and landing, slowing the aircraft to 150 mph. They also turned on the auxiliary hydraulic power in case it was needed to lower the landing gear and apply the brakes, turned on the engine booster pumps, lowered the landing gear, and checked for the green light indicating the gear latches were locked. The bombers usually flew what was called a "downwind" leg that ran parallel to the runway on an opposite heading in trailing formation until they reached a point past the runway's end when they would turn toward the runway and fly a short "base" leg on a heading that was ninety degrees from the runway heading.[54]

As they made a final turn to the runway heading, they slowed to 140 mph and lowered the wing flaps to one-half before slowing to a final glide speed of 110 mph and fully lowering the wing flaps for landing. The final descent was usually made at a rate of four hundred to six hundred feet per minute. Once the aircraft was safely over the runway threshold, the aircraft commander would completely close the throttles and have the copilot hold them to prevent them from creeping forward. As the aircraft approached the ground, the aircraft commander held the nose up slightly, allowing the main landing gear to touch down on the runway first before lowering the nose so the nose gear touched the runway. As the aircraft commander applied the brakes, the cowl flaps were fully opened, the wing flaps were raised, and the aircraft was slowly taxied to its assigned parking space.[55]

Despite its many complexities, the B-24 would prove to be a reliable weapon of war. As those flying it in combat with the 451st would learn, the trick was finding a way to survive in the hostile skies over occupied Europe where the enemy would try desperately to kill you. Overcoming that threat and living to go home would require a combination of tactics, skill, and luck.

Chapter Three

War in the Air

Operations, Tactics, and Strategy

The most crucial time of every mission flown by the 451st Bomb Group—or any bomb group—was the bomb run. All the planning and tactics employed, as well as the work of the entire crew and the group formation, came down to this crucial period of five to six minutes. If the bombs did not hit the target, everything done up to this point would have been meaningless. In one way of thinking, the procedures employed for the bomb run were the penultimate tactic for every American bomber (returning to base safely being the ultimate), and their success rode on the shoulders of one man—the bombardier.

As soon as the navigator notified the crew that they had arrived at the initial point or IP, the bomb run began. The navigator told the pilot to turn to the bomb run heading. Once the pilot completed the turn, he switched on the autopilot and told the bombardier over the intercom, "Your aircraft." From that moment until after the bomb release, the bombardier steered the aircraft using his Norden bombsight.

Before the bombardier leaned down in his seat to place one eye over the eyepiece in the bombsight, he placed his hands around the eyepiece to warm it, which would help ensure it did not fog up when he placed his face near it. Then he looked down through the bombsight. As soon as he could clearly see the ground, the bombardier began looking for the critical checkpoints on the ground along the bomb run that the group bombardier had provided to him and the other bombardiers before the missions. These might be large, distinctive buildings, major road or rail intersections, bridges, or easily recognizable terrain features such as a large lake or a bend in a river.

Whatever they might be, the bombardier should be able to see them through the bombsight if the plane was close to its planned route to the target. As he identified them, the bombardier adjusted the bombsight's line of sight to the target using the turn knob. Next he used the drift knob to turn the airplane into the wind to kill any drift caused by the winds blowing around the formation. As he did this, the Norden bombsight automatically solved for crosswinds and steered the aircraft on its proper course, upwind of the target.[1]

While this was happening, the bombardier had to maintain his focus on the task at hand. This was not easy because, as the B-24 formation approached the target area, they usually encountered heavy German antiaircraft fire, often called "flak." This meant that as the bombardier tried to find the target and guide the aircraft toward it, gray-black explosions filled the skies around the formation, sending deadly shrapnel flying in all directions, some of which could be heard smashing into the fuselage and wings of the bomber with a sickening thud. At the same time, the bombardier had to overcome the distraction caused by his fellow crew members calling out that they had seen other aircraft hit by the flak, some of which might be on fire and leaving the formation as they looked for parachutes of any crew members who might be trying to escape their burning ship.

As the target came into sight, the bombsight solved the point of release for the bombs by automatically computing the required dropping angle based on ballistic settings the bombardier had dialed into the bombsight before the bomb run. The bombardier kept the target in sight through the eyepiece via an optical system that included a telescope and mirror. The mirror would rotate the exact amount needed to maintain the correct line of sight as the B-24 approached the target.[2]

As the bomber closed in on the target, the bombardier searched for the exact aimpoint he had been provided before the mission. Once he had found it and ensured it was the correct place to aim his bombs, the bombardier would adjust the bombsight to place the crosshairs directly over the aimpoint. When he had locked the crosshairs in position, the bombardier turned to the Bombardier's Control Panel, which was mounted on the side of the fuselage to his left and flipped the Master Switch to "On." Then he reached down to his immediate left, where the Bombardier's Control Stand was mounted, and pulled on the handle that opened the bomb bay rolling doors. The bombardier next glanced at the control panel to make sure the bomb bay door open light was illuminated, telling him the roll-up doors were fully open. Now he flipped the switches on the same panel to select all his bomb racks for release before looking back into the eyepiece to ensure the crosshairs were properly tracking the aimpoint and made any needed adjustments. At this point, the aircraft was prepared for an automated release of the bombs once the Norden bombsight determined it had reached the desired release point.[3]

When the aircraft reached that release point, the bombs would begin to drop from the racks in the bomb bay, and the bombardier would call out over the intercom, "Bombs away!" He then monitored the bomb release by watching a set of twenty-four lights on his control panel. There was one light for each bomb, and as they successfully fell from their bomb racks and out the bomb bay doors, those lights would illuminate one after another. As soon as the panel indicated all the bombs had been released, the bombardier closed the bomb bay doors and gave control of the aircraft back to the pilot by saying over the intercom, "Pilot, your aircraft." The pilot then disconnected the autopilot and, as the navigator gave him the required heading to the "rally point," he turned the B-24 away from the target area. As the plane turned, the bombardier took one last look through the bombsight to see where his bombs struck the target. If all went well, he would see signs of multiple explosions and heavy smoke rising from the enemy target below.[4]

Mission accomplished—all that was left to do now was for the crew to get themselves and their aircraft safely back to their home base.

During World War II, the United States and its Army Air Force were committed to the daylight precision strategic bombing concept. This involved attacks on key enemy infrastructure targets by large formations of heavy, long-range bombers that would drop hundreds of bombs on those targets with great accuracy. Even before the war began, a group of American officers based primarily at the Air Corps Tactics School, or ACTS, at Maxwell Field, Alabama, studied this concept of warfare with a dedication and fanaticism that created an almost cultlike atmosphere. Very few in the War Department paid attention to their work, and until just before the outbreak of war in Europe, senior officers in the army were not really aware of the scope and detail of the intellectual exercises being conducted in the isolation of south-central Alabama. However, when war did come, this group of ACTS faculty members were ready to act, and they burst out into the open to exercise significant influence on American war planning. Little wonder, then, that they became known as the "Bomber Mafia." While that label was not intended as a compliment, the ACTS faculty enthusiastically accepted it, thinking the label that saw them as outcasts "quite suited them."[5]

In 1941, the Army Air Force began drafting its part of Rainbow 5, the primary war plan for the coming global conflict, and it called on four officers from ACTS to write it. The result was Air War Plans Division Plan No. 1, or AWPD-1. The entire document came directly from the work the Bomber Mafia had been doing for almost ten years. It described in "exacting detail" how many aircraft, pilots, and tons of bombs the country would need to execute a continuous bombing campaign against the "German national infrastructure, industry—especially the aircraft industry—and the Luftwaffe," the vaunted German Air Force.[6]

Some of the earliest work at ACTS was conducted by officers like Lieutenant Kenneth Walker, who was an almost fanatical advocate of daylight precision strategic bombing. In 1931, Walker gave a lecture based on an article he had written in the *Coast Artillery Journal* in October 1930 that outlined the fundamental premises behind the concept. He argued to a receptive audience at the school that "a well-armed and well-motivated offensive bomber force can penetrate and strike its target in the face of enemy defenders and without the aid of air cover." He postulated these bombers would make their attacks in formation at altitudes above ten thousand feet. Furthermore, their formations would be designed to provide defensive machine-gun fire from the bombers' gun positions that was "superior to that which may be brought against" them by enemy fighters. Walker also believed this formation would provide a "measure of security against antiaircraft fire" from the ground.[7]

Walker stated that the formation used by the bombers needed to be able to accommodate up to forty aircraft in an area about five hundred feet wide and one thousand feet long. Using this approach, attacking fighters would have great difficulty making successful attacks from either the front hemisphere of the formation or its flanks. If they attacked from below, the fighters' airspeed would be so drastically reduced in the climb that they would be highly susceptible to defensive machine-gun fire from the bomber formation. Therefore, they would have to concentrate on attacking from the upper rear hemisphere. That was why Walker proposed a narrow formation that would make a "coordinated, concentrated attack" by enemy fighters very difficult. In Walker's mind, as well as those of the other faculty members at ACTS, even if forty fighters equipped with two machine guns each could deliver a simultaneous attack against the bomber formation, they would be "bringing but 80 machine guns into action against either 160 or 240 guns mounted on 40 bombardment airplanes." He also pointed out that at that time, fighter aircraft guns, which fired through the propeller just as they had in World War I, had a firing rate less than half that of the flexible machine guns on bombers.[8]

Thinking like Walker's was accompanied by a fallacious belief regarding the ability of American bombers in these mass formations to drop their bombs with great precision. In the 1930s, it became popular in American aviation circles to claim Army Air Force bombardiers could drop a bomb in a "pickle barrel" from high altitude. Moreover, in 1940, Theodore H. Barth, president of Carl L. Norden, Inc., the firm that built the Norden M-4 bombsight used in World War II, said, "We do not regard a 15-foot square . . . as being a very difficult target to hit from an altitude of 30,000 feet," provided the bombardier was using Norden's bombsight.[9]

However, once the shooting started in Europe, the realities of a modern, mechanized war quickly proved that men like Walker and Barth were operating on concepts that did not hold up during practical application in combat. Since Walker gave his lecture in 1931, the capability of fighter aircraft had increased exponentially, far beyond what he and the others in the Bomber Mafia could have imagined. German fighters like the Messerschmidt Bf 109 and British fighters like the Supermarine Spitfire had engines capable of propelling them to high speeds that allowed them to rapidly sweep through bomber formations, even if they made their attacks from below. Further, their primary armament no longer fired through a spinning propeller. The modern guns on fighters were mounted in the wings and were capable of rates of fire as high as or higher than those defending the bombers.

Moreover, AAA guns were now deployed en masse near potential targets. These guns, such as the German 88mm 8.8cm Flak 18, the preeminent German AAA weapon in Europe during the war, could fire fifteen to twenty shells per minute against targets as high as 34,770 feet using either a manual sighting device or radar.[10] As a result, Britain's RAF Bomber Command learned quickly that attacks made during daylight led to prohibitively high losses. Therefore, in summer 1940, they switched totally to nighttime bombing, when German fighters and AAA were less capable of inflicting damage.

The RAF also learned that precision bombing of specific targets at night was almost impossible with the technology of the time. So it switched to broad-area carpet bombing intended to inflict damage on military targets while impacting the morale of German citizens. Still, while observing what was happening to RAF bombers, the American Army Air Force clung to the belief that it could achieve accurate, precision bombing of specific targets in the daytime. Again, a part of the belief continued to rest on the "bomb in a pickle barrel" myth. But the actual statistics on practice bombing by American bombardiers during 1940 told an entirely different story. At that time, the average score for bombardiers dropping practice bombs indicated a circular error of four hundred feet. Worse, those bombs were dropped from a mere fifteen thousand feet, not the twenty-five thousand to thirty thousand feet proposed in American war plans.[11] Apparently, if you repeat a myth often enough, it takes hold, and even accurate statistical data cannot overcome its claims.

However, the ACST faculty who wrote AWPD-1 were not fooled by the "pickle barrel" stories. In their planning, they used data from training and practice bombing that indicated a heavy bomber dropping bombs from 20,000 feet using the Norden bombsight had a 1.2 percent chance of hitting a 100-square-foot target. That meant it would take about 220 bombers to achieve a 90 percent probability of destroying that 100-square-foot target. Those estimates led them to believe the United States would need 251 bomber groups to conduct AWPD-1. But once American bombers were flying in combat, accuracy results made while the enemy was shooting at them were even worse. In 1943, the average circular error for the Eighth Air Force's bombers was 1,200 feet, which meant 16 percent of the bombs struck within 1,000 feet of the aiming point. One historian pointed out, "Rather than dropping bombs into pickle barrels, Eighth Air Force bombardiers were having trouble hitting the broad side of a barn."[12]

However, the issues surrounding precision bombing seemed to pale in light of the casualties suffered when American bombers began operating in Europe. During the early months of strategic bombing in late fall and early winter 1942–43, the American bomber crew casualty rate exceeded 80 percent. As raids continued into late 1943, matters did not improve significantly. The worst day in the history of the Army Air Force was October 14, 1943, when Eighth Air Force B-17s attacked the ball-bearing factories at Schweinfurt in Bavaria. On that horrific day, sixty bombers were shot down, with the loss of 600 crew members either dead, wounded, or captured—a 21 percent casualty rate. In addition, 17 more bombers returned to Britain but had to crash-land, resulting in them being unsalvageable, while 122 other aircraft required significant repairs.[13] It was clear that the ACTS faculty had sorely underestimated the abilities of the Luftwaffe's fighters and AAA batteries to inflict severe damage on the heavy bomber formations they advocated so strongly.

At first, the Luftwaffe's fighters were responsible for most of the American bomber losses. Still, by June 1944, German AAA was shooting down ten times more Eighth Air Force and Fifteenth Air Force B-17s and B-24s than its fighters. While the Germans fielded eleven types of AAA guns during the war, ranging in caliber from 20mm to 150mm, the 8.8-cm Flak 18 88mm gun was the most heavily deployed. While the Germans referred to it as the *acht-acht* or eight-eight, Americans called it the "eighty-eight," and its capabilities were greatly feared by Allied bomber crews. Whenever someone mentioned the 88mm gun to Harold Thompson in the years after the war, just hearing its name was enough to make him shudder.[14]

Just the sound of flak was enough to unnerve many bomber aircrews. One pilot recalled that when AAA shells exploded very close to the aircraft, "you did not hear the explosion as much as you heard the breaking of the steel shell itself, and this was a high-pitched 'skeerank, skeerank,' quickly followed by a dull 'kechoonk, kechoonk' as pieces of the flack went through your aircraft." Naturally, this would lead anyone to wonder what damage had been done to the aircraft. Many times, B-24 aircrews would look out to see holes opening up in the wings, which led them to call these "flak blossoms" because when flak shrapnel hit the wings, the B-24's aluminum skin would simply curl back "just like the petals of a flower."[15]

The German 88mm guns and most other AAA weapons were deployed as an organic part of the Luftwaffe. German AAA was called Flakartillerie. However, the common parlance for all AAA was "Flak," which was an abbreviation of "Flieger" or "Flugabwehrkanone," which meant "cannon for defense against aviation" in German. The typical 88mm battery consisted of four guns deployed in a square of approximately seventy yards. The battery would have a primary and alternate command post as well as either a Kommandogerät command device fire control computer or a portable Würzburg radar.[16]

When AAA was employed for home defense against bombers, the Germans divided Germany and the countries it occupied into air territorial areas called Luftgaue. In heavily defended target areas, German AAA, like the 88mm gun, was deployed on the outskirts of the area with concentrations of batteries on the lines of approach the Germans believed Allied bombers would travel as they readied for their bomb runs. The biggest strength of German air defense was its unity of command, which led to excellent coordination among air defense assets. These assets, which included fighters, AAA, warning services, and civil defense, were all placed under a single commander responsible for the air defense mission.[17]

AAA batteries were set up about six thousand yards apart for areas in the immediate vicinity of the targets. In the Fifteenth Air Force area of operations where the 451st flew, the Germans began increasing their AAA batteries in 1944 in a concentration of three AAA batteries of four guns, each called Grossbatterien. These batteries also used newer radars that were more resistant to Allied countermeasures. Vienna, Austria, a primary Fifteenth Air Force target, was considered the second most heavily defended city in the Third Reich, after only Berlin. Despite a heavier reliance on the use of chaff[18] to blind German radars, 44 percent of the Fifteenth Air Force bombers that were lost were victims of fire from German AAA.[19]

Because of the effectiveness of German AAA, units like the 451st began to employ the services of what they called a flak analysis officer during mission planning. This man was trained to calculate the areas where AAA fire was anticipated to be the worst. He used a chart, called a flak clock, that showed known enemy AAA gun positions protecting a specific target. He employed this data in a tool called the flak computer, which allowed the flak analyst to consider the maximum range of fire for each battery of guns, all possible headings for the bombing run, and the total time the bombers would spend in straight and level flight from the IP until a few seconds after bomb release. He next would compute the capabilities of each individual battery and for each thirty-degree section around the face of the flak clock. After this, he calculated the fire power potential for every gun and considered the course to and away from the target, assigning a priority for each potential heading. Once this analysis was complete, the flak analysis officer would provide his conclusions to the mission planners to determine the best approach to the target.[20] However, while this data was helpful, in the end, planners had to consider many other factors related to the bomb run, and often they found that some heavy concentrations of AAA simply could not be avoided.

While AAA would prove a daunting enemy defensive armament, what caused the most issues for American bomber tacticians and crews from late 1942 until mid-1944 were the fighter aircraft and crews of the Luftwaffe. German fighter air defense units were organized as Sturmgruppen (Storm Groups), with subordinate squadrons called Jagdgeschwader, or JGs. The primary aircraft flown by the German fighter pilots, who were called Jagdflieger, in these JGs were the Messerschmidt Bf 109 and the Focke Wulf Fw 190, each of which was manufactured in large numbers and several different models. The Bf 109G, first introduced in the Luftwaffe in 1942, provided the JGs with a "workmanlike" fighter with greater power and armament than earlier versions of the Bf 109. Its new 12-cylinder, liquid-cooled DB605A engine combined with a 20mm MG 151/20 engine-mounted cannon firing through the propeller and a pair of 7.92mm MG 17 cowl-mounted machine guns made it more than a match for Allied escort fighters and a terrible, highly effective weapon against American bombers.[21]

In 1944, as the fight against American bombers increased, the Luftwaffe added underwing-mounted 30mm cannons called the MK 108. One German Jagdflieger would later comment that the MK 108 "really was a terrible weapon" because it was capable of cutting off the wing of a heavy bomber. Feldwebel Oscar Boesch, of Sturmgruppen Jagdgeschwader 3 (JG 3), recalled, "We would break off the attack just before we were about to collide with our target. The devastating effect of our 30mm guns was such that we would often fly through a rain of fragments, some being complete sections of aircraft." However, this increase in firepower came at a cost in terms of weight, as the MK 108 weighed 165 pounds more than the original MG 152/20 cannons.

In general, the Jagdflieger who flew the Bf 109 liked the aircraft. One such man was Oberleutnant (equivalent to an American 1st lieutenant) Franz Stigler of JG 27. He would later say of the Bf 109, "I liked the 109F because it handled well at any altitude and was actually faster than the G. It also had a good rate of climb and a fast dive. We felt safer against the enemy. I didn't like having wing guns and avoided them, which made the Bf 109 much more maneuverable."

Meanwhile, the radial-engined Focke-Wulf Fw 190 proved to be a solid and dependable fighter that came to be known as the "Butcher Bird." It entered service with the Luftwaffe in September 1941 with the Fw 190A-1, followed by a succession of A-model variants. In May 1943, the Fw 190A-6 was fielded. It had two fuselage-mounted MG 17s and four MG 151/20 cannons, equipped with tracer ammunition that helped Luftwaffe pilots sharpen their aim when using the latter. However, the most numerous and feared Fw 190 fighter was the A-8 variant, with 1,334 aircraft produced. Powered by the 1,700hp BMW 801D-2 14-cylinder radial air-cooled engine, the Fw 190A-8 could reach a maximum speed of 450 mph at 15,000 feet and had a range of more than 650 miles at 25,000 feet, extending to over 900 miles when carrying an eighty-gallon drop tank.

One B-24 pilot later said he thought the Fw 190 "was built like a bank safe," given all its heavy armor. The Fw 190 tactic that some B-24 crews found most frightening was when a Butcher Bird would "fly head-on into the formation, just coming in straight at you, firing as they came." Then the Fw 190 pilot would pull back on his stick just enough to clear the bomber he was attacking before going through the rest of the formation. However, what was scariest about this tactic was that the B-24 crew knew that if their top turret or nose turret gunner could hit the fighter and kill its pilot, the attacking Fw 190 would probably collide with their bomber head-on.[22]

Another fighter employed by the Luftwaffe against American bombers like the B-24s from the 451st was the Messerschmidt Bf 110 *Zerstörer*. The Bf 110 was initially designed to be a long-range fighter that would escort German bombers into enemy airspace. It first flew in 1936 and was a favorite of Hermann Göring. While it could reach speeds of up to 316 mph in level flight, its poor maneuverability proved costly when it encountered Allied fighters. The Bf 110 was armed with either 20mm or 30mm cannon and aerial rockets. While the latter were not terribly accurate, when fired into bomber formations in large numbers they could be very deadly, as evidenced by the B-17s lost to rockets fired from Bf 110s during the Schweinfurt-Regensburg raids of August 17, 1943. However, because of their inability to succeed against faster and more maneuverable Allied fighters, most Bf 110s were converted into night fighters equipped with radar and used against aircraft from RAF Bomber Command.[23]

Another and less frequently used fighter was the Junkers JU 88. Like the Bf 110, the JU 88, which began its Luftwaffe career as a bomber, could not survive flying in the daytime if American bombers were escorted by fighters. Equipped with a 20mm cannon and aerial rockets, the JU 88 was primarily employed as a night fighter and was very successful in that role. However, on occasion, before long-range fighter escort was available to Fifteenth Air Force units, isolated groups of JU 88s would intercept American bombers.[24]

Despite the high casualties suffered by American bombers in 1943, the Luftwaffe's leadership was not satisfied with the performance of its fighters. On November 8, 1943, General Adolf Galland, commander of the Luftwaffe's fighter arm, issued the following orders to his unit commanders:

> German fighters have been unable to obtain decisive successes in the defense against American four-engine formations. Even the introduction of new weaponry has not appreciably changed the situation. The main reason for this is the failure of formation leaders to lead up whole formations for attack at the closest possible range. Göring has therefore ordered the establishment of a *Sturmstaffel*, whose task will be to break up Eighth Air Force formations by means of an all-out attack with more heavily armed fighters in close formation and at the closest range. Such attacks that are undertaken are to be pressed home to the very heart of the Allied formation whatever happens and without regard to losses until the formation is annihilated.[25]

Galland's orders resulted from analysis by one of his staff officers, who conducted a detailed study of gun camera film, combat reports, tactics, and weapons used in close-range attacks against Allied bomber formations. The analysis proposed adopting a "radical" tactical approach that would employ mass attacks against the rear of Allied bomber formations by tight formations of Fw 190s. The new tactic called for mass attacks because the analysis indicated that a single fighter attacking from the rear had virtually no chance of coming through an attack on a bomber formation's rear undamaged. However, if an entire Sturmgruppen made such an attack, the gunners in the American formation would be forced to spread their fire across the attacking force, weakening their defensive power. At the same time, while one group of fighters attacked the bombers, two other Sturmgruppen flying Bf 109s would climb to a higher altitude to attack any fighter escort the bombers might have.

One German Jagdflieger who made these attacks was Feldwebel Oscar Boesch of IV Sturmgruppen JG 3. He recalled that when he and his comrades made these rearward attacks, the bombers' gunners would fire while the Fw 190s were still out of range and waste am-

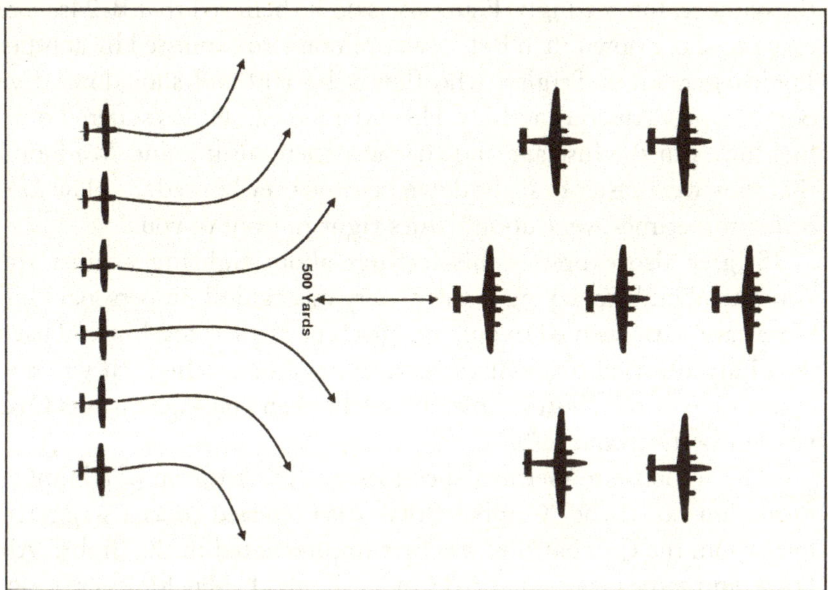

The Luftwaffe's mass attack tactic mandated by General Adolf Galland's orders. (*Author*)

munition. "It was obvious," he said, "they were just as scared as we were." Boesch also described what these attacks were like for men like him, saying, "Shaken by the slipstream of the B-17s and blinded by condensation trails, we were subjected to machine gunfire for minutes or seconds that seemed endless before being able to see the results of our attack. Despite the armor plating of our cockpits, we had good reason to dread the defensive fire of the bombers." Attacking line abreast, Boesch said their initial goal was to kill or disable the bomber's tail gunner. Once accomplished, they focused their fire on the intersection of the bomber's wing and fuselage. "You just kept at it," he said, "watching your hits flare and flare again. It all happened so quickly."

Another German, Leutnant Richard Franz of I *Sturmgruppen* JG 77, flew Bf 109s in attacks from slightly above the rear of the bomber formation. He and his comrades would dive down and open fire with 13mm and 30mm guns, trying like Boesch to knock out the tail gunner before firing his 30mm MK 108 at a range of about 160 feet from the bomber. Interestingly, Franz also said he believed that B-24s were easier to shoot down than B-17s, an opinion also expressed by another Jagdflieger, Franz Stigler, who flew a Bf 109 and shot down five bombers over Austria and Italy. He remembered, "B-24s suffered from fuel fumes in the fuselage and that was their weak point. We found that they were easier to shoot down because they burned. . . . The *Liberators* sometimes went up in flames right in front of you."

Stigler also expressed his feelings about fighting against the American bombers, saying it was a "very mechanical, impersonal kind of warfare" that seemed to only pit machine against machine. "That's why I always tried to count the parachutes," he recalled. "If you saw eight, nine or ten chutes come out safely, then you knew it was OK, you felt better about it."

The response to German successes was the creation of a bomber formation called the "Combat Box." Also referred to as a staggered formation, the Combat Box was first implemented in the Eighth Air Force, and some people credited Colonel Curtis LeMay for its creation. The idea behind the Combat Box was to fly in a formation designed to mass the bombers' defensive firepower and make it more difficult for German fighters to attack successfully. At the same time, the Combat Box had to be designed to ensure each bomber formation could effectively release its bombs on the target.[26]

Not surprisingly, the Combat Box saw various versions created to suit the needs of the different American operational environments. In the Fifteenth Air Force, of which the 451st was a part, some basic bombing tactics were defined. Still, the individual wings and groups were allowed to modify these to meet their specific needs. The basic formation was the three-aircraft Vee, called an element and the basis from which larger formations were developed. Two Vees of six aircraft would join to compose a Combat Box, and three Combat Boxes usually made up an attack unit, with two attack units coming from one group, like the 451st. Typically, there was fifty feet of vertical clearance between each element. Within a Vee, both wingmen flew level with the lead aircraft with a lateral spacing far enough to the side to ensure one-half airplane span clearance between the wingtips of the lead airplane and the wingmen. Longitudinally, wingmen flew far enough to the rear to ensure one-half airplane length of clearance between the tail of the lead airplane and the nose of the wingmen's aircraft.[27]

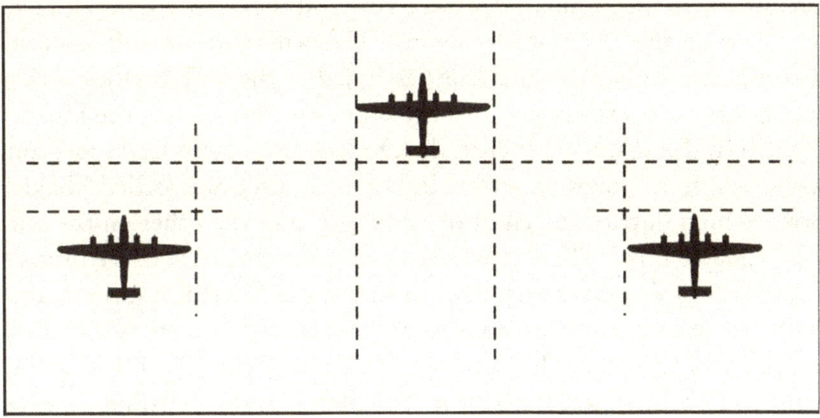

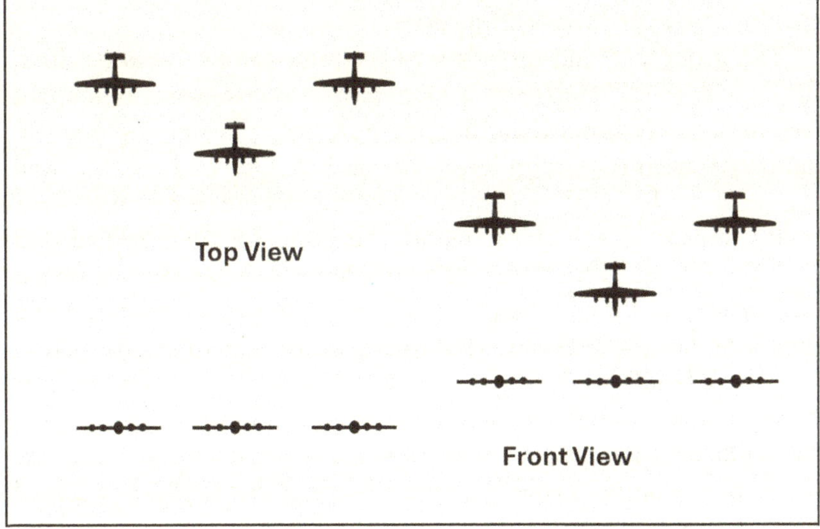

The basic Vee formation, top, which was the basis for all Combat Box formations. The six aircraft formation, bottom, consisting of two Vee formations. (*Author*)

Between December 1943 and July 1944, Fifteenth Air Force groups like the 451st flew in what was called a six-box formation consisting of forty aircraft, with the bomber group divided into two units of twenty B-24s each, one flying behind the other, and each unit consisting of three Vee-based boxes called squadrons. The squadron in the center of the first group was called "Able Box." It included the aircraft where the group leader was flying and the deputy group leader, who flew on the group leader's wing. The other four aircraft in Able Box were from the two squadrons assigned to the unit for the particular mission. These six bombers flew in two three-plane Vee formations in trail and at a lower altitude. On each side of this lead squadron were two more boxes of seven aircraft each. One was called "Baker Box," which flew to the right of Able Box, and the other on the left was "Charlie Box." These two boxes each consisted of two Vee formations with three planes each. But in Baker and Charlie, a seventh aircraft flew in each squadron box's center rear (sixth position) slot known as "Tail-end Charlie." This seventh aircraft was typically flown by the squadron's least experienced crew. The planes in the Tail-End Charlie position were very vulnerable to fighter attack. As a result, the position was also called the "coffin corner."[28]

The group's second unit flew in the same formation as the first. But its boxes were referred to as Dog, Easy, and Fox, and it flew about five hundred feet lower than the first unit. Each position in a box was numbered, with the group leader being Able One and the Tail-End Charlie of the leftmost rear squadron being called Fox Seven.[29]

By summer 1944, the Fifteenth Air Force had determined that these six aircraft, which were laterally wide and not very compact, were difficult to fly, and their bombing accuracy was not good enough. Therefore, headquarters decided to switch to a diamond formation made up of four boxes instead of six, with each flying in two elements of three planes, with the provision of adding a seventh aircraft to each box. As before, the trailing elements were stacked downward from the high group, leading to the Tail-End Charlie of the fourth box, called "Dog Ten." Experience proved that the four-box formation was easier to assemble and organize, provided a tight bombing pattern, and increased defensive firepower against fighters. However, while the diamond formation did increase bombing accuracy, it also led to increased losses to AAA fire.[30]

In an attempt to counter AAA in the target area, bombardiers were told to develop an evasive action plan to implement between the IP and the target. It was critical that the plan was made before takeoff and that every aircraft crew in the formation be thoroughly briefed. To be successful, the evasive action had to include changes in heading, altitude, or both. The changes in altitude were not to be made in a

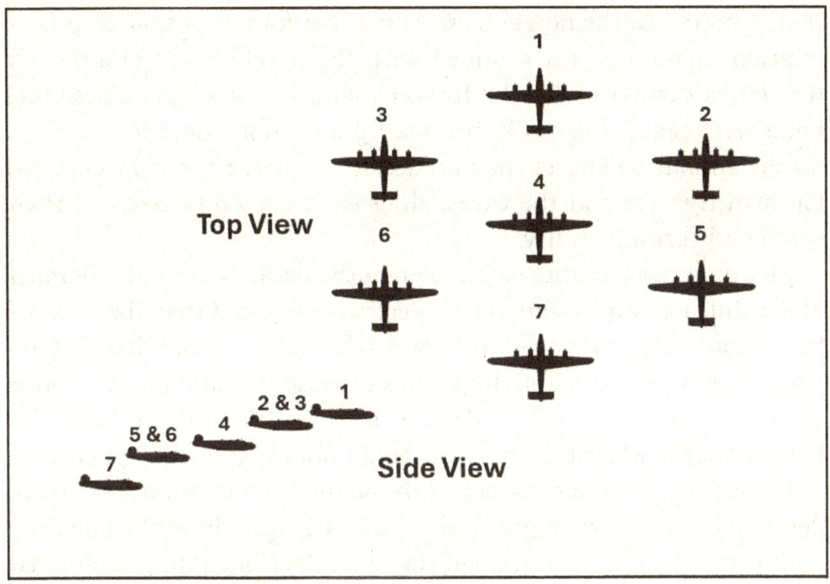

The 15th Air Force diamond formation. (*Author*)

constant glide because that would allow the German fire directors to accurately calculate the bombers' future position and still hit them. Therefore, the change in altitude had to vary the rate of descent, with descent rates between five hundred feet and two thousand feet per minute being the most effective. However, experience showed that while this approach worked in small formations, it was impractical for the large formations used on most missions. Major Charles Haltom, commander of the 726th Bomb Squadron, later noted that having flown as either the lead or deputy lead on many missions, he never saw evasive action used on a bomb run by the 451st Bomb Group. "It's hard enough flying formation when flying straight and level," he said, adding that it was "impossible if the ship you are flying wing-on is jerking around all over the sky." Therefore, most formations simply flew straight and level on the bomb run, especially if the AAA fire was very heavy.[31]

Without a doubt, the change that had the most impact on American bomber tactics and the success of the strategic bombing campaign was the advent of long-range fighter escort. Before early 1944, no Allied fighters had the range to escort bomber formations on deep penetration missions. That changed with the development of auxiliary fuel tanks carried under the fighter's wings or fuselage. These fuel tanks were called drop tanks because fighter pilots could toggle them off the aircraft whenever they needed to, such as when they engaged German fighters and the excess drag from the tanks reduced their speed and turning ability.

Early in the war, these tanks were unavailable because the Bomber Mafia did not want them. They were so convinced that the bomber formations they envisioned did not need a fighter escort that they resisted attempts to develop drop tanks because it would take resources away from the needs of the bomber force. So the official Army Air Force policy held that drop tanks should not be developed or encouraged. Luckily, however, advocates in the fighter community were not deterred by this shortsighted policy, and they quietly worked on drop tank technology in secret. Soon they had developed drop tanks that could carry 150 to 300 gallons for the Lockheed Aircraft P-38J *Lightning*. Once the losses on the Schweinfurt mission in October 1943 made it painfully clear that bombers needed a long-range fighter escort to survive, the drop tanks began to be manufactured and sent to the field for P-38s, North American Aircraft P-51D *Mustangs*, and Republic Aircraft P-47 *Thunderbolts*.[32]

Unfortunately for the Fifteenth Air Force, priority for long-range fighters went to the Eighth Air Force. It was not until the end of March 1944 that the Fifteenth Air Force received its first long-range fighters in the form of P-38Js. In April, the 31st Fighter Group and its P-51Ds arrived in the Fifteenth's theater. Shortly after that, the 325th Fighter Group transitioned from P-47s to P-51Ds, and the 52nd and 332nd Fighter Groups transferred from the Twelfth Air Force to the Fifteenth Air Force with their own P-51Ds. By the end of July 1944, the Fifteenth had the long-range fighter forces it needed to protect its bombers from German fighters.[33]

When the 31st Fighter Group received its first P-51Ds, it took some work to learn how to employ these new, high-performance aircraft as long-range escorts for bombers. No one in the Fifteenth Air Force had any experience, and they wisely decided to leave the development of escort tactics to the commander of the 31st, Colonel Sandy McCorkle. After working on several approaches, McCorkle and his men decided to employ a strategy where the fighters would fly considerably higher than the bomber formations, maintain squadron integrity as long as possible, and, when they had to engage with German fighters, always leave some part of the fighter force with the bombers. They also ruled that no one would pursue a German fighter to extremely low altitudes or out of the immediate battle area, and the fighters who engaged the Germans would regroup as quickly as possible.[34]

The fighter groups assigned to escort a bomber mission typically used forty-eight aircraft from three squadrons. Each squadron flew in a different position, with one high above the bombers while the other two were positioned on each flank of the bomber formation. The P-38s generally used a Vee formation, while the P-51s flew line abreast. Since both types of fighters flew at speeds much higher than the bombers, they constantly weaved around the bomber formations so they could reduce their speed. But this weaving came at a price in fuel consumption and, therefore, less operating range for the fighters. As a result, neither the P-51s nor the P-38s had the range to stay with a bomber formation for its entire mission. This problem was resolved by employing a relay approach wherein one group of fighters would take the bombers to the IP for the bomb run while a second group would meet the bombers as they exited the target area and try to get them safely home.[35]

As the fighters and bombers gained experience, they developed three types of escort profiles: direct support, area support, and a combination. At first, in spring 1944, direct escort was the only mission profile used by the Fifteenth Air Force's fighters. In this profile, the fighters remained close to the bombers to protect them. However, as spring turned to summer, the fighters began to employ the area support profile. This allowed the fighters to move ahead of the bombers to engage German fighters and clear the airspace ahead of enemy opposition. Finally, both profiles were combined on the deeper penetration bomber missions where the bombers attacked multiple targets. Here the fighter escort force flew direct support until the bombers began to split up to fly to their different targets. At that point, the fighters switched to area support and pressed ahead to take on the incoming German fighter assaults.[36]

Each mission the Fifteenth Air Force flew was based on long-range planning guidance from the Combined Chiefs of Staff provided to the United States Strategic Air Forces in Europe, or USSTAF. The USSTAF would then tell the Fifteenth Air Force Headquarters staff which specific target categories they were to bomb. Based on that list of categories, the Fifteenth Air Force staff selected specific targets using higher headquarters priorities, which changed constantly based on the dynamic war situation in Europe. The targets the Fifteenth Air Force selected were within seven hundred miles of the bomber bases in southern Italy, the bombers' maximum combat radius.[37] That meant the targets would be in northern Italy, southern Germany, southern France, or anywhere in Austria, Romania, Hungary, or Yugoslavia.

Specific targets were usually selected by the Fifteenth Air Force staff the day before a mission based on priorities and weather forecasts. The headquarters staff would also decide on the number of aircraft to be used, the direction of the attack, and the bomb types. The latter meant fragmentary, general purpose, armor piercing, semiarmor piercing, or incendiary, depending on the nature of the target. These details were sent down to the bomber and fighter wings, who coordinated mission details before sending orders to the bomber and fighter groups. The group-level staff would prepare final routing and a briefing for the crews, which was given on the morning of the mission. The night before the mission, the ground crews labored to prepare the aircraft and load the bombs on each plane.[38]

The crew briefing was usually held early in the morning. It was intended to give the aircrews all the information they needed to fly the mission, including routing, target identification, and anticipated opposition from German AAA and fighters. In the 451st, Colonel Eaton or the subsequent Group Commanders would announce the mission to the crews and explain the importance of the target.[39]

The Group Commander was followed by the Operations Officer, who outlined the planned route to and from the target, described which units would be involved, and indicated the types of formation to be flown. He provided the time schedule for every mission event (engine start, taxi, takeoff, assembly, IP arrival, time over target, and landing) and the rendezvous points with other bomber groups and the fighter escorts. Finally, he would cover the location of the IP; the axis, altitude, and airspeed for the bomb run; operational data on the target and its aiming point; bomb loading and fuzing data; required fuel and ammunition loads; any special tactics to be employed; the anticipated weather; and the communications plan.[40]

Following the Operations Officer, the Group Intelligence Officer took the stage to describe the target and provide information on any alternate targets or the "target of last resort" should weather prevent bombing the primary target. He then provided details on enemy defenses and tactics, including AAA batteries, fighter opposition, and camouflage, as well as information on any friendly forces that might be in the area. This was followed by reminders on escape and evasion techniques should anyone be forced to bail out over enemy territory. Finally, a time "hack" was given so everyone's watches were in sync, and any special briefings for navigators, bombardiers, or other crew members were announced and conducted.[41]

The special briefings for bombardiers were essential. In these sessions, bombardiers who would fly the mission were given detailed information about that portion of the mission from the IP to the target. Each bombardier received a target folder with all the needed information about the target area, and the senior bombardier from the group staff would present information on how to identify the target. This included prominent checkpoints on the ground that would help them identify the IP location and those along the route from the IP to the target. Finally, the bombardiers would be briefed on visual checkpoints in the immediate target area and the identification of the desired aimpoint on the target. Then the staff bombardier would go over any evasive action plan, if one were going to be used, before covering the plan for sighting and bomb release.

In some cases, the task of sighting the aimpoint and guiding the formation to bomb release was given to the bombardier on the lead aircraft. In those situations, the other bombardiers watched for the bombs to be released from the lead aircraft, which served as their signal to release their bombs. In other scenarios requiring greater precision, each bombardier would find the aimpoint through his bombsight and release his bombs individually.[42]

Once all the mission briefings were complete, the aircrews were driven to their aircrafts' parking spots. Each aircraft commander and his copilot reviewed the maintenance status of their plane with the crew chief. Then they and all the other crew members went through their required preflight checks. At the prescribed time, all aircraft would start engines and await clearance to taxi to the runway. The squadron formation leader would check with each plane in his formation using the radio before calling the tower for permission to begin taxiing. Once he was given permission, the formation leader would begin taxiing, followed in sequence by every aircraft based on its assigned number in the formation. Once the formation lead reached the runway, he pulled up at an angle near the end of the runway, as did all the other aircraft in the formation. At this point, each aircraft would run up its engines and prepare for takeoff.[43]

Usually, when the time prescribed for takeoff arrived, called H-Hour, the tower would shoot a flare into the air, indicating takeoff should begin. The formation leader taxied out onto the runway and began his takeoff roll. As soon as he began to move, the number two aircraft would pull into position on the runway and begin its takeoff as soon as the leader's wheels lifted from the runway, which usually was about thirty seconds. Each aircraft in the formation would follow similarly until everyone was airborne.

The leader flew the runway heading at 150 mph with a climb rate of three hundred to five hundred feet per minute for one minute plus thirty seconds for each aircraft in the formation. When the lead aircraft reached an altitude of one thousand feet, the lead aircraft commander would level off and maintain an airspeed of 150 mph. As soon as he had flown the time required for his formation, the lead aircraft commander would begin a shallow "half-needle-width" (about ten degrees of bank) 180° turn to the left. Ten seconds after the lead airplane started to turn, the second airplane began its turn, keeping the nose ahead of the leader, pulling into position from below and behind the leader's outside, or right, wing. Then, ten seconds after the second airplane started its turn, the third airplane began its turn, keeping the nose ahead of the leader, pulling into position on the leader's inside, or left, wing. This put the lead element of three aircraft in a Vee formation, and the second element would fly the same type of takeoff before assuming a position to the right of the lead element.[44]

The formation then flew to an altitude prescribed for the mission. The bombers would circle at a defined assembly position for thirty to sixty minutes until all aircraft from the group arrived and moved into formation. If other groups were to be part of the mission, the formation would group into combat waves, combat waves became combat wings, and those wings would move into a column formation. Each group formation might be six to seven miles long, and a complete bomber column could be 125 to 145 miles long.[45]

The bombers then flew in formation, rendezvousing with their fighter escort before flying into hostile territory. Usually, the first opposition to their mission came as attacks by German fighters. As the B-24s approached the IP, they began a climb to arrive at the final bombing altitude, usually twenty thousand to twenty-five thousand feet by the time they reached the IP. Once they reached the IP, the German fighters would stop their attacks, and the friendly fighter escort would depart for their home base. The IP typically was twenty-five to thirty-five miles from the target. Once the IP was reached, the wing formation broke into assigned attack units, flew the bomb run, and released their bombs.[46]

As bombers approached the target, AAA fire became the most intense, and it could be an agonizing time because the planes had to maintain formation and fly straight and level through the flak. Harold Thompson of the 727th Bomb Squadron said he came to fear the flak the most because, unlike fighter attacks, you could do nothing to defend yourself. As a result, he said he always imagined an 88mm shell coming right up through his seat. Therefore, instead of wearing the flak vest he was issued on his chest, he sat on it. Thompson also related that while he genuinely believed in what he and his comrades were doing in the skies over occupied Europe, every now and then, when the flak began to burst around his aircraft and spray it with shrapnel, he would think, "What in the hell am I doing here dropping bombs on people I don't know who are trying very hard to kill me."[47]

When all the wings from the Fifteenth Air Force attacked a single target, the bombs could fall on the target area for as long as forty-five minutes, creating what must have been a truly hellish and terrifying experience for those who were unfortunate enough to be on the ground around the target. After all bombs had been released, the attack units turned away from the target, re-formed into a column, and rendezvoused with the fighter escort assigned to meet them for the flight back to Italy. At this point, German fighter attacks would recommence until the enemy fighters had to return to base. Once the bomber column reached friendly territory, its fighter escort would head for home, and the bombers would split up into individual group formations for the return to their home bases.[48]

After the bombers landed, a truck took the aircrews to a building to be interrogated or "debriefed." The room used for these interrogations was filled with tables with a debriefing officer at each one. The aircrews would go to one of the tables where the debriefing officer asked questions and reviewed the mission events.[49] This usually included questions about when and where German fighter attacks occurred, how they were made, what types of German fighters they saw, and if the gunners damaged or shot any of them down. The crew members would tell the debriefing officer where they encountered AAA and try to characterize its intensity and accuracy. The bombardier would discuss his target identification and how accurate he believed his bombs had been.

One of the most essential items the debriefing officers tried to gather was information on any aircraft lost during the mission. The aircrews tried to say where an aircraft had been hit, how badly it seemed to be damaged, and if they saw any parachutes as the aircraft went down. This information would be compiled into a Missing Air Crew Report, or MACR, form. The MACR had been implemented by the Army Air Force in May 1943 "to record the salient facts of the last known circumstances regarding missing air crews." The MACR also provided a means of integrating current data with information obtained later from other sources to conclusively determine the fate of the missing personnel.[50] In many cases, German records related to missing aircrews were found after the war and added to the official MACR records maintained by the US National Archives and Records Administration.

Once debriefings were complete, the aircrews returned to their quarters, had a meal, or simply got drunk using the beer coupons they were given after each mission. Harold Thompson said he collected all his coupons until his crew completed their fiftieth and last mission. He used all the coupons he had been given to get beer for his men, and they had "one hell of a party."[51]

Meanwhile, the ground crews began to repair any damage caused to the group's aircraft by enemy flak and cannon fire from German fighters. This involved patching holes in the aluminum skin, replacing damaged engines, and repairing gun turrets and flight control cables. The work often went on throughout the night to prepare for the next mission, which might be the following day.

Harold Thompson recalled walking around his aircraft after one of his early missions, where it suffered significant damage. One engine had caught fire, one aileron and a rudder were shot to pieces, and the fuselage and wings were covered by holes from shrapnel. He thought there was no way the plane would be ready to fly the next day. However, when he went to the revetment the following morning, he discovered that a new engine had been installed and tested, the aileron and rudder repaired, all the shrapnel holes had been patched, and the aircraft was ready to fly. Since a difficult mission was planned for the day, he was unsure whether to be happy or sad that the ground crews had done such great work.[52]

B-24s of the 451st Bomb Group shortly after bomb release on the Regensburg-Prüfening Messerschmidt component factory, seen burning on the ground below. (*National Archives*)

Chapter Four

"Big Week"

Regensburg, February 25, 1944

The 451st Bomb Group's ground crews labored tirelessly through the night of February 24–25, 1944. Neither they nor the aircrews who would fly the mission planned for February 25 knew where the group's B-24s would be headed the next day. As the aircrews slept in their tents, all the ground crews knew was that "they would have to spend the night before every mission working their butts off." The engineering officers for the four bomber squadrons and their men filled each plane's fuel tanks to their limits. They performed all the required servicing and maintenance to ensure the forty aircraft from the 451st scheduled to fly the next morning were ready.[1]

The magnitude of the job and the responsibility given to the ground crews cannot be overstated. The job was immensely challenging and had to be completed on time. But it also had to be done carefully, given that the men were dealing with "tens of thousands of gallons of high-octane aircraft fuel." Moreover, the ground crews had to ensure they checked every servicing and maintenance item for each of the forty B-24s. This meant performing tasks such as checking and topping the oil tanks for each of the 160 engines in the attack force from the 451st.[2]

When the servicing was complete, the squadron armaments officers and their men began their work. Using heavy trucks and bomb trailers, they executed the "delicate" process of loading each aircraft's bomb bay with twelve five-hundred-pound general-purpose bombs. Each bomb carried a fuze that would be armed by the bombardiers once the aircraft were airborne. While the bombs were being loaded, other crews from the armaments section labored to thread thousands of rounds of .50-caliber ammunition into the gun turrets and waist guns.[3]

All the work was backbreaking, but each man knew his efforts' importance. It was often cold and damp during the late night hours, but no one stopped or paused. Instead, they worked uninterrupted until 4:30 AM, when the aircrews arrived one hour before the scheduled engine start time. Takeoff would be at 8:36 AM, but little did any of them know that those forty aircraft would be part of a bomber force from the Fifteenth Air Force that numbered almost 400 aircraft, with 176 of those, including all from the 451st, headed for the primary target, the Messerschmitt component plant at Regensburg-Prüfening.[4]

It was the last day of a six-day Allied bombing campaign against German aircraft manufacturing and assembly plants, which would be the most extensive bomber operation of the war. It was based on a plan called Argument, but everyone came to call it "Big Week."

The air echelon of the 451st arrived at its new base at Gioia del Colle on January 20, 1944, flying up from Teleghma, Algeria, in a single, sixty-plane formation.[5] The small town of Gioia Del Colle (Joy of the Hill) sat atop the Altopiano delle Murge, Italian for the Murge plateau, at an elevation of one thousand feet. Olive trees and a few small dairy farms dotted the area, but there was little else. The base was part of an initial array of somewhat primitive airfields established by the Fifteenth Air Force south of Foggia and Bari. The runways and taxiways were constructed using Marston Mat, and the men were housed mainly in tents. As more bases were built in southern Italy, this situation would not change much. The four officers from each plane's crew lived together in one tent, while the six enlisted men were housed separately. As was standard procedure, the tent city for the officers was in a different area from the enlisted personnel.[6]

Each tent was about twelve feet square, supported by a single, tall center pole. Wooden floors had been laid down inside the tent, and the tent door had a wood frame. Bedding consisted of standard-issue army cots and blankets; the cots were also the only place to sit. The army's engineers devised a unique heating system for each tent to combat the cold, wet Italian winter weather. They mounted a fifty-five-gallon fuel drum on a rack next to the tent with a rubber fuel line that led to a stove inside that was filled with a small mound of rocks. The tent's occupants adjusted a clamp at the end of the fuel line to carefully set up a steady drip of fuel onto the rocks. Once ignited, the fuel made a small fire in the stove, which heated the tent's interior. The problem was making sure the clamp on the fuel line did not loosen and send a surge of fuel into the stove, resulting in an "uncontrollable conflagration" that could be damaging or even fatal.[7]

So, unlike the men based in Britain with the Eighth Air Force, there would be no warm Quonset huts, showers equipped with running hot water, concrete runways to land on, or weekend passes to London. Instead, the men of the 451st would live in drafty tents with an uncertain heating system and get one helmet filled with hot water per day for shaving and washing.[8]

Gioia del Colle was a wet, muddy place when the aircraft arrived. As soon as the air echelon was in place, everyone began preparation for combat operations. The 451st was made part of the 47th Bomb Wing, which included three other bomb groups: the 376th, 440th, and 449th. On January 23, the group flew its first practice mission, and one week later, the 451st flew its first operational mission. That mission targeted the German radar station 5 miles from Fier, Albania, 140 miles east of Gioia del Colle. The mission was a classic "milk run," and there was no opposition from either German fighters or AAA. However, despite the group's aircraft making two bomb runs, the mission was a complete mess. The group's takeoff and assembly were slow and disorganized. The navigation across the Adriatic was good, but the bomb run was terrible, with not a single bomb hitting the target.[9]

Three days later, the 451st's B-24s attacked another radar station near Durrës, Albania, 125 miles across the Adriatic. The sortie was expected to be another milk run, but the crews encountered their first AAA this time. While the bombing was much improved, two men from the 727th were wounded by shrapnel from flak, the group's first combat casualties.[10]

After a mission to bomb the rail marshaling yards at Arezzo, Italy, on February 3, the 451st was tasked with bombing the rail marshaling yards and steel mill at Piombino on Italy's eastern coast. This time, the group experienced its first combat deaths when eight men were killed in a crash after takeoff, and a nose turret gunner in another plane was killed by shrapnel from an AAA burst over the target. This sortie was followed quickly by three missions against more Italian targets before heavy rain grounded the group during the middle of February.[11] However, the milk runs were over after these initial missions, as bigger things were in the offing.

Those bigger things were part of a plan called Argument. Argument had been drafted initially and modified by the Allies Combined Operational Planning Committee and called for a series of precision daylight bombing attacks by the Eighth and Fifteenth Air Forces, supported by nighttime area raids by the RAF Bomber Command, against high-priority targets in central and southern Germany. Those targets were principally facilities for the airframe and final assembly phase of single- and twin-engine aircraft production. The planners based Argument on the assumption that attacking aircraft manufacturing, especially that related to fighter aircraft production, would achieve damage to the German war effort more quickly than other types of targets. Ultimately, the targets selected for Argument were a combination of final assembly, antifriction bearings, and component parts manufacturing.[12]

Originally, Argument was supposed to begin in November 1943. But the late-fall and winter weather in the target areas would not allow the missions to be flown. By February 1944, however, the destruction of German fighter production had become an urgent need. As a result, Allied air commanders said they were willing to take higher risks to achieve Argument's objectives. On February 8, Lieutenant General Carl Spaatz, the USSTAF commander, ordered Argument to be completed by March 1, 1944. Luckily, by February 19, Allied weather forecasters believed the weather over central and southern Germany would improve and the six-day campaign could begin.[13]

The bombers from the Eighth Air Force began attacking the selected targets on February 20 in what everyone now called Big Week. Meanwhile, the Fifteenth Air Force assets continued supporting the Allied forces on the beachhead at Anzio, Italy. However, it was decided that while the Eighth Air Force would continue attacks on the aircraft factories at Schweinfurt, Gotha, Bernburg, Oschersleben, Aschersleben, and Halberstadt, the Fifteenth Air Force would begin attacks against the aircraft and component production facilities in Regensburg on February 22.[14]

Regensburg was in southern Germany, about sixty-five miles northeast of Munich. The city and its immediate vicinity had become one of the most strategically important parts of Adolf Hitler's Germany. Regensburg was home to factories producing everything from ball bearings and fighter and bomber aircraft to tanks, trucks, and artillery. Further, one of Europe's largest synthetic petroleum plants was near the city. In addition, given the scale of Regensburg's manufacturing operations, it became a central railway hub with one of Germany's largest rail marshaling yards. These facilities, in turn, resulted in the city being heavily defended by Luftwaffe fighters and AAA batteries. In the immediate area around the targets in Regensburg were three concentric rings of AAA batteries that included nearly six hundred guns, everything from the ubiquitous 88mm AAA gun to radar guided 110mm and 150mm guns. One pilot from the 724th Bomb Squadron later referred to Regensburg as "one of the most intense shooting galleries on earth."[15]

The 451st flew missions as a part of Big Week on February 22, 23, and 25. One of the major problems it encountered was that the Fifteenth Air Force had not received any drop tanks for its fighter groups to support long-range bomber escort (unlike the Eighth Air Force, which had already begun to receive drop tanks). So while there was an assigned fighter escort for each of the 451st's missions, they could not provide fighter cover that ranged into Austrian or German airspace, something the Luftwaffe would take full advantage of.

On February 22, the 451st was assigned to bomb the Messerschmitt factory at Obertraubling, which was about five miles southeast of the center of Regensburg. The group launched forty-one aircraft, but only thirty-eight could release their bombs on the target. Worse, when the group's bombers reached Regensburg, it was covered by dense overcast. Since the 451st had yet to receive any Pathfinder aircraft, it was forced to drop its bombs based on the estimated arrival time at the target, which caused little to no damage to the factory. The German AAA at the target was reported as being "intense" but inaccurate. However, as the formation passed Graz, Austria, and Munich, it was subjected to intense fire that was very accurate and damaged three aircraft.[16]

Further, after the 451st's bombers turned away from the bomb run, they were jumped by twenty to thirty German fighters, consisting of a mix of Bf 109s, Fw 190s, Bf 110s, and even a few JU 88s. These were the first enemy fighters the group had encountered thus far in the war. The German fighters failed to inflict any losses, but two of their own aircraft were confirmed as kills, with one probable and another reported as being damaged by the formation's gunners.[17]

The next day, February 23, the Fifteenth Air Force agreed to fly a mission with the Eighth Air Force against the Daimler-Puch aircraft component plant at Steyr, Austria, about ninety miles west of Vienna. In this instance, the target was too far from Britain's Eighth Air Force bases for their long-range fighters to escort them the entire distance to the target. So the missions for both sets of bombers were timed in the hope that the Germans would be forced to split up their fighter response between the Eighth and Fifteenth Air Force formations. While this worked out for the Eighth Air Force bombers, the Fifteenth Air Force was hit hard by the Luftwaffe. Of the eighty-seven B-17s from the Fifteenth that attacked Steyr, seventeen were lost to the German fighter force of Bf 109s and Fw 190s that intercepted them. Luckily, the 451st, which launched thirty-eight B-24s, lost only one aircraft to the enemy fighters, who attacked the formation about thirty miles northwest of Ljubljana, Yugoslavia.[18]

The 451st did not fly on February 24, but matters changed significantly on February 25. The 451st would be tasked to participate in the final mission of Big Week, a strike on the Messerschmitt component plant at Regensburg-Prüfening, a mission one man from the group characterized as "memorable."[19] This was planned to be a "full scale coordinated attack" by the Eighth and Fifteenth Air Force bombers. More than 300 B-17s and B-24s from the Fifteenth Air Force's 5th and 47th Bomb Wings would be part of the mission. The 5th Bomb Wing's B-17s from the 2nd and 301st Bomb Groups were to lead the Fifteenth Air Force strike on the Regensburg-Prüfening plant, with B-24s from their 97th and 99th Bomb Groups making attacks against storage facilities at Fiume in Yugoslavia and Klagenfurt airfield in Austria. The 47th Bomb Wing would come behind the 5th at some distance with 103 B-24s. The 450th Bomb Group would lead the 47th Bomb Wing's formation, with the 449th and 451st following. Meanwhile, the Fifteenth Air Force's 301st Bomb Wing would make a diversionary strike on the railyards and port installations at Fiume, Yugoslavia; the harbor at Zara, Yugoslavia; warehouses and sheds at Pola, Yugoslavia; rail lines at Zell-am-See, Austria; and the airfield at Graz-Thalerhof, Austria.[20]

This would be the first time the Eighth and Fifteenth Air Forces would attempt a closely coordinated attack on the same day against the same targets. The planners at USSTAF hoped this strategy would pay off by confusing the Luftwaffe's fighters and causing them to split up their forces and, thus, weaken the opposition. While the Eighth Air Force bombers would have a considerable fighter escort force to the targets and back, that was not the case for the Fifteenth Air Force bombers. While 85 P-38Js from the 306th Fighter Wing's 1st and 14th Fighter Groups would escort the bombers as far as possible, they could not go all the way to the target, which meant the bombers would be on their own to defend themselves against German fighters as they flew over northwestern Yugoslavia, Austria, and southern Germany.[21] As events would show, this had a dire impact on the 451st.

On the evening of February 24, the orders for the mission made their way down to Gioia del Colle from the Fifteenth Air Force and the 47th Bomb Wing. The group's operations, maintenance, and intelligence staff quickly began breaking down the mission requirements. The operations staff looked at the weapons, fuel, and routing requirements. The "frag order," as these orders were called, directed the 451st to undertake a "maximum effort," which meant the group was to get as many planes in the air as possible. After working with the maintenance staff, they figured they could assemble a strike force of forty aircraft.[22]

Meanwhile, the maintenance staff ordered the ground crews to work servicing, loading, and fueling the aircraft, and the intelligence staff analyzed the potential AAA and fighter threats. The takeoff time was set for 8:36 AM, and the time over target for the Regensburg-Prüfening factory was 1:39 PM. While aircrews would not know about the mission until early morning, the ground crews began their work immediately. They labored all night until a few hours before takeoff.[23]

The process of waking up the aircrews began at 2:30 AM, when orderlies assigned to this unpleasant duty began arriving at the tents for officers and enlisted members of the forty aircrews assigned for this mission. One of the officers' tents belonged to Lieutenant Roger McCollester's crew for the plane named *Mac's Flophouse*. McCollester was a twenty-one-year-old aircraft commander from Southport, Connecticut. He later wrote of his entrance into the Army Air Force, "It seemed as if one moment I was trying to make gas money so that I could borrow my father's car for a date, and the next, I was pushing the throttles forward on more than 5,000 horsepower and was enveloped in a daily 'game' of kill or be killed."[24]

The orderly, who was named Charlie, yelled to wake up McCollester, his copilot, Evert "Ev" Johnson, bombardier Olin "Hutch" Hutchinson, and navigator Bernard "Dibi" DiBattista, adding the news to his wake-up announcement that the mission was to be a maximum effort, breakfast would be served starting at 3:00 AM, and the mission briefing would start at 4:00 AM. McCollester replied, "Okay, thanks, but no thanks, Charlie," before adding, "Can't we just sack out for another hour or so," even though he almost certainly knew the answer. The orderly simply replied, "Come on, Mac; up and at 'em!"[25]

Over in one of the enlisted men's tents, Sergeant Atkinson and the men from *The Jolly Roger* were also sound asleep. To ward off the cold, Atkinson slept wearing his long underwear and wool socks while covered by not one but two wool blankets. Then, at 2:30 AM, their assigned orderly stuck his head in the tent and rudely shouted, "Up and at 'em, guys! Breakfast at 0300 and briefing at 0400. Get moving! This one's a maximum effort!" In reply, one of the gunners said, "Jesus, shit," as he turned on a lamp, illuminating the other men in the tent, all of whom sat sleepily on the edge of their cots while trying to get the cobwebs cleared from their heads. One of them commented that a maximum effort did not sound too good, to which Atkinson replied in his Mississippi drawl, "It ain't."[26]

As the officers and enlisted men for the mission began to wake up, everyone dressed as quickly as he could so he could make it to the mess tent in time to get in line, get his food, and eat in as leisurely a fashion as was possible under the circumstances. Each man went down the serving line with his metal mess kits in hand, holding them out so the mess orderlies could slop them full of the usual fare of powdered scrambled eggs, a slice of spam, and a hardtack biscuit before receiving a mug of hot coffee. While the mess tent was often filled with loud chatter and laughter, on mission days like this one, the room was mostly silent except for the clanging of mess kits. Everyone was deep in thought and still trying to wake up.[27]

As the men finished their breakfast, they headed for the briefing room, unaware of where this mission, which was only the tenth one flown by the 451st, would take them. Everyone milled about for a while before eventually finding a seat with the rest of his crew on the long wooden benches that filled the room. On the low stage at the front of the room was a board covered by a curtain. That board would tell them about the target for the day, and even though they knew a maximum effort likely meant a critical and probably well-defended target, many a man silently prayed that this would turn out to be another milk run.[28]

Once everyone was seated, the briefing officer stepped onto the stage and pulled aside the curtain as every crew member "involuntarily sucked in a breath and quietly muttered 'Oh, my God!'" The board was covered by a map with a long red string indicating the route of flight, which went from Gioia del Colle to an assembly point near Bari before crossing the Adriatic to reach the Yugoslav coast near Split and then stretching north-northeast across northwestern Yugoslavia just west of Zagreb into central Austria between Graz and Klagenfurt. From Austria, the red string extended into southern Germany, where it made a sharp westerly turn to the IP for the bomb run at the city of Rottenburg an der Laaber and then turned again to the north for the twenty-mile ingress to the target: the Regensburg-Prüfening factory.[29]

The importance of the target was clear. Together, the Regensburg-Prüfening and Regensburg-Obertraubling factories produced at least one-third of all German single-engine fighters and more than half of all Bf 109s. The 451st's target at Regensburg-Prüfening manufactured fuselages, wings, and component parts for single-engine aircraft, mainly Bf 109s, and produced, in the final assembly plant, approximately 280 aircraft per month. Furthermore, it produced almost all the component parts for Bf 109s and possibly subassemblies for the Bf 110 and Bf 210. The specific targets within the Regensburg-Prüfening factory complex included the final assembly shop in Building 7, the integrated final assembly and components erection facility in Building 20, the components erection shop for wings and fuselages in Building 16, and the machine shop in Building 12.[30]

After the bomb run, the red string turned right and back to the south along the same course as the inbound legs before arriving at Gioia del Colle again. The flight would take about eight hours but would almost certainly seem like an eternity.[31]

The briefing officer continued his presentation, using the same tone of voice as when he had covered less-daunting missions. Roger McCollester later commented, "Briefing officers must have been carefully selected for their ability to deliver bad news in exactly the same tone of voice as they used when delivering good news." The briefing officer calmly told them that the 451st could expect two hundred or more German fighters to intercept them, coming from Luftwaffe bases all over southern Germany and Austria. In what may have been an attempt to make the aircrews feel better, he also told them that two hundred P-38s and P-47s from ten fighter squadrons would escort them. However, all the aircrews knew that unlike their Eighth Air Force brethren, these fighters would have to break off their escort long before the bombers reached German airspace.[32]

After speaking about the importance of the target and the anticipated opposition, Colonel Eaton rose to speak. Even though he was ill and could not lead the mission as he would have liked, he apparently felt he needed to address his men before it began.[33] Eaton told them this was the mission they had trained for back at Fairmont and they should expect the enemy to throw everything it had at them. He reminded them about the importance of a tight formation, saying, "Only close formation flying will save you."[34] Of course, while it may

The route used by the 451st Bomb Group on the mission to Regensburg, February 25, 1944.

have been true that the best defense against German fighters when there was no friendly escort was a tight formation, that would not help the bombers counter the intense fire from the AAA rings surrounding Regensburg.

Once Eaton was finished speaking, the briefing officer rose once more to dismiss the men except for pilots, bombardiers, navigators, and radio operators, who needed to stay behind for the weather briefing. After most of the aircrew members had departed, the weather officer stood to tell them they could expect clear skies over the target and that while the weather conditions would likely deteriorate on the return leg, hopefully that would not stop them from landing back at Gioia del Colle. The radio operators were then given the specific codes for long-range high-frequency radio communications and the frequencies for plane-to-plane communications. For his part, as had become his personal practice, Sergeant Atkinson jotted down all the radio instructions on a piece of paper, which he tucked into his shirt pocket.[35]

With the briefing completed, all the aircrews walked to the supply tent, where they picked up their parachutes, which they clipped to their parachute harness, as well as their escape and evasion kits. The latter was intended to help them if they had to bail out over German-occupied territory. It contained an interesting variety of items, including nonmelting chocolate, chewing gum, halazone tablets for purifying water, and a map of the area they would be flying over that was printed on silk. The kit also contained forty-eight dollars in US gold seal currency and a curious item called a blood chit—a document printed on silk with a message written in several European languages. The message assured anyone reading it that if they provided the downed American with assistance, they could later redeem the chit for a guaranteed amount of money from the US government.[36]

Once they had their parachutes and escape and evasion kits, the waist gunners went to the ordinance tent to be issued the .50-caliber machine guns they needed to mount at their positions. Following this, everyone returned to his tent to get his flight bag containing his flight gear before trucks arrived outside to take them all to their aircraft on the flightline.[37]

Once they reached their aircraft, the men jumped out, put on their flight suits and gear, loaded their parachutes up into the bomb bay, and climbed aboard. After the waist gunners had mounted their machine guns in the fuselage windows, the entire crew gathered under the wing for final instructions from the aircraft commander. Once those had been covered, everyone reboarded the plane to go through the pretakeoff checklists for each crew position while the flight engineer, the plane's crew chief, and ground crew members began pulling the propellers through, a process whereby several men manually turned the propeller on each of the four engines. Radial engines like those used on bombers such as the B-17 and B-24 had a nasty tendency for oil to collect in the combustion area inside the engine cylinders that had been sitting upside down while the aircraft was idle. If the crews did not remedy this situation, a cylinder's piston might not move during engine start, damaging the engine. This was called a hydraulic lock. By manually rotating the propellers several times, the pooled oil would clear the cylinder's combustion area, and hydraulic lock could be avoided. The importance of this procedure is highlighted by the fact that the manual for the B-24 warned pilots that they must never attempt an engine start until the propellers had been pulled through.[38]

With the propeller pull-through complete, the flight engineer climbed aboard through the bomb bay, started the small generator that provided electrical power for engine start, closed the bomb bay's roll-up doors as well as the bulkhead door to the bomb bay, and took his place behind the aircraft commander and copilot for engine start. The crew chief stood by with a fire extinguisher as each engine was started, and all four engines were brought to life, one after another. Once the engine checks were complete and the taxi time had arrived, the aircraft began its taxi to get in line for takeoff.[39]

When the takeoff time arrived, the aircrews saw a flare fired from the control tower. The group began to take off, flying out in the prescribed formation order and merging the group before heading for the assembly point, where they would rendezvous with the formations from the 449th and 450th Bomb Groups. Once the entire combat wing was formed about nine miles west of Bari over Bitonto, Italy, the massive bomber formation began its journey to Regensburg by flying toward the Adriatic coast near Split.[40]

As the Fifteenth Air Force B-17s and B-24s made their way north across the Adriatic, German radar sites in Italy and Yugoslavia saw them approaching and began relaying information on the American bomber formations up the chain of command. After an hour of monitoring them, the Germans determined that this was another deep penetration mission, and they knew the American fighter escorts would depart as they moved into the area near Fiume on the Croatian coast. Between 10:00 and 10:15 AM, the Jagdfliegerführer, or fighter director for Austria, called JaFü Ostmark, began sending fighters to intercept the oncoming bomber force. The first to launch were Bf 109Gs from JG 27 and the nearby Verbändeführer Schule, the Luftwaffe's formation leaders' school, and JG 53. At 11:00 AM, Fw 190s from JG 108 and Bf 110s from Zerstörergeschwader 1 or ZG 1 took off to intercept the bombers. Before the day of the mission, JaFü Ostmark had also coordinated with JaFü Oberitalien, the fighter director for Upper Italy, for reinforcements, which he now called on. As a result, between 10:38 and 10:40 AM, JaFü Oberitalien scrambled Bf 109s from JG 53 and JG 77 from bases near Aviano and Udine in northern Italy.[41]

As the 451st's formation reached Fiume and its fighter escort departed, more than one hundred German fighters pounced on the three groups of B-24s. Aircrews from the 449th later said "the enemy pilots were experienced and aggressive, employing every tactic in the book."[42] As the Bf 109s slashed through the formation, they began to take a toll in terms of bombers damaged and destroyed.

Onboard the B-24 named *Hoppy*, Captain Lloyd Ryan of the 725th Bomb Squadron was flying as copilot when the first wave of enemy fighters swooped down. As he sat in the cockpit, Ryan saw one of the Bf 109s pass by to head south off their left wing. Within seconds, *Hoppy*'s flight engineer reported being hit in the leg, which caused him to abandon the top turret. The copilot took off two of the three pairs of gloves he was wearing to fend off the intense cold, unstrapped from his seat, and headed back to see if he could aid the wounded flight engineer. He could not do much to help, so he returned to the cockpit. When he sat in his seat, he saw that his windshield had been smashed by fire from the fighters, which also left the aircraft covered in bullet holes. The worst one must have come from an MK 108 cannon on one of the Bf 109s because it left a "jeep-size hole in the rudder." Once *Hoppy* landed after the mission, the wounded flight engineer was taken to a hospital. The aircraft was found to be so severely damaged it was beyond repair and had to be scrapped.[43]

The first 451st aircraft to go down was *Knock It Off* from the 724th, crashing about fourteen miles southeast of Ljubljana, Yugoslavia. Nine of the crew bailed out successfully, but all were captured by the Germans and became prisoners of war, or POWs. The tenth man, Sergeant Alfonso Duran, did not bail out even though he was physically able to do so. When interviewed about the events of that day, Sergeant Marvin Leibovitz, *Knock It Off*'s tail turret gunner, reported that as he prepared to bail out, he saw Duran sitting at the waist position escape hatch. Duran appeared uninjured but was apparently terrified at the prospect of jumping out of the plane. Leibovitz attempted to persuade Duran to bail out. When he could not, he tried to push Duran out of the aircraft. Duran steadfastly refused to go, and when there was little time left to make it out of the aircraft safely, Leibovitz had to abandon Duran. After the crew was processed by the German authorities, a German officer told them he had visited the crash site and that Duran's body was inside the wreckage.[44]

The German fighters continued their attacks unabated as the 451st's planes continued north toward Austria. Their next target in the formation was *Wee Willie* of the 725th, flown by Lieutenant Richard Kimmel. A group of ME 110s attacked the aircraft from around the three o'clock position, firing rockets as they closed in on *Wee Willie*. One of them struck the number four engine, which quickly caught fire. The fire spread rapidly along the wing as the aircraft turned right out of formation. Then, three Bf 109s attacked it aggressively, first shooting out the number two engine before knocking out both the waist guns and tail gun turret. The fire from the number three engine quickly spread down the wing and began to engulf the fuselage. Lieutenant Kimmel cried out over the intercom, "My God, the ship is on fire!" before ringing the bailout alarm.[45]

In the nose compartment, the navigator, Lieutenant James Boornazian, heard the bailout alarm and could see the ship was on fire. He opened the nose gear door hatch and bailed out at an altitude of about seventeen thousand feet. The bombardier, Lieutenant Harold Adams, saw Boornazian leave the aircraft and followed him out, although later had no memory of bailing out. He apparently lost consciousness because of lack of oxygen as he left the aircraft and did not regain consciousness until he reached ten thousand feet, where he found himself drifting down below his chute. Adams was injured upon landing but was immediately located by Yugoslav partisans who hid him in their covert medical station for the next six months before returning him to Allied forces in Italy.[46]

The other man in the nose compartment was the nose turret gunner, Sergeant Corbin McPherson. When the bailout alarm sounded, he was engaged in firing at a Bf 109 that was attacking from the eleven o'clock position and did not hear the alarm. He was able to hit the German fighter, which turned away trailing smoke. As McPherson fired, he turned the turret as far as it would go in azimuth, and when the turret stopped turning, he looked back to see the nose compartment empty and the nose gear door hatch open. McPherson realized the navigator and bombardier had bailed out, and he quickly began to exit the turret. As he did so, a 20mm cannon shell came through the front of the turret and exploded, wounding him in the leg. Despite that wound, he crawled back to get his parachute and could see that the bomb bay was on fire. McPherson turned around, snapped on his parachute, and bailed out through the nose gear door hatch. As he descended in his parachute, he saw another parachute above him, which belonged to Lieutenant George Strickner, but saw no other parachutes below him. McPherson landed in the woods near Ljubljana and evaded capture for two days before being rescued by Yugoslav partisans.[47]

The partisans took McPherson on a march through the countryside for the next four days until they reached the village of Cerkno, about twenty-five miles west-northwest of Ljubljana. There he was reunited with Lieutenant Boornazian, who had also met up with partisans led by an officer from the British Special Operations Executive, Captain Eric Davies. Davies and his men had also found *Wee Wille*'s tail turret gunner, Sergeant James McCauley, and brought him to Cerkno. Unfortunately, McCauley had been hit in the groin by a 20mm cannon shell during the attack by the Bf 109s and was in serious condition. Despite the medical assistance provided by the partisans, McCauley died a few days later in Boornazian's arms and was buried in the village cemetery.[48]

The plane's copilot, Lieutenant George Strickner, arrived in Cerkno two days later with another partisan patrol. He had bailed out through the flight deck's overhead hatch and said Lieutenant Kimmel was right behind him as he bailed out. Strickner also saw Sergeant Edward Kostrzewa, the flight engineer and top turret gunner, who was lying on the flight deck, apparently wounded and unable to climb up to the hatch. The copilot related that he did not know what happened to Kimmel, but he never saw him bail out.[49]

As for the other crew members, the survivors believed that the right waist gunner, Sergeant Gene Kore, and ball turret gunner, Sergeant Lloyd Cook, were either wounded and could not bail out or were killed during the fighter attacks. As the three survivors waited in Cerkno, the only other member of the crew unaccounted for was Sergeant Harold Baxley, the left waist gunner. However, another group of partisans soon arrived in the village carrying word of Baxley's fate. Apparently he had managed to bail out before the aircraft crashed, but his parachute caught fire, and he fell to his death. The Yugoslav fighters had found the waist gunner's body and buried it after recovering his dog tags, which they gave to Lieutenant Boornazian.[50]

The partisans took Boornazian, Strickner, and McPherson on a journey toward the Albanian border that lasted more than sixty days. Once there, the partisans escorted them to a secret airfield where they were picked up by an Allied aircraft and flown to Bari.[51] However, there was one remaining mystery. In July 1944, Mrs. Lulu Cook, mother of Sergeant Cook, the ball turret gunner, received a letter purportedly written by her son on March 2, 1944. The letter said he was a POW, but Mrs. Cook stated that the handwriting was definitely not her son's. Following that incident, no word was ever received from the Germans on his status through the International Red Cross.[52]

After *Wee Willie* went down, the *Peacemaker* was attacked by fifteen Bf 109s, fell out of formation, and crashed about seven miles south of the Austrian border with Yugoslavia. Sergeant Israel Willig, a tail turret gunner in another aircraft flying ahead of *Peacemaker*, reported seeing the aircraft receive numerous hits in the fuselage before it quickly lost altitude and passed out of sight. Willig said no fire was seen, and he could not determine if the plane was out of control. Eventually, it was learned that two crew members were killed in the crash, and eight others bailed out, five of them being captured. At the same time, three successfully evaded capture and were returned to duty.[53]

As the 451st continued into southern Austria, the fighter attacks continued. Another B-24, *The Citadel*, flown by Lieutenant Nicholas Zender, was lost, crashing near Zederhaus, Austria, which was about 50 miles northwest of Klagenfurt, Austria, and 140 miles from the target at Regensburg. Flying in *Hoppy*, Lloyd Ryan was on *The Citadel*'s right wing and saw a Bf 109 attack the aircraft head-on. Cannon shells from the German fighter set the number three engine on fire, which then spread to the entire right wing. Eventually, the wing burned off and fell away from the aircraft. At that point, the plane fell into an uncontrollable spin, and the fuselage caught fire. Two eyewitnesses, Sergeants Benneville Rhoads and Henry Dieter, saw only four parachutes open, but it was later learned that five members of the crew were captured by the Germans and became POWs. However, the German fighter that caused *The Citadel*'s demise was hit by machine-gun fire from *Hoppy*'s nose turret gunner as it made its head-on attack against *The Citadel* and went down.[54]

As the 451st planes approached the IP, German fighters claimed another victim. This time it was *Hard to Get* from the 726th. A rocket from an enemy fighter knocked out the number one engine, and cannon fire caused the number three engine to begin smoking. This cannon fire also killed the left waist gunner, Sergeant Ernest McNeese. The aircraft fell out of formation about fifteen miles southeast of the target, turned to the right, and descended from twenty-two thousand feet to thirteen thousand feet as the bombardier released the bombs to lighten the aircraft. After turning away, German fighters saw the damaged B-24 leaving the formation and flying alone. Three Bf 109s pursued it, renewing their attacks. A "running fight" ensued as the aircraft commander, Lieutenant Richard Coleman, flew his wounded plane toward northern Italy. Once *Hard to Get* reached the Alps, the German fighters broke off their pursuit, but as soon as the plane cleared the mountains and flew into Italy, more German fighters arrived and attacked the B-24. These new attacks scored hits on the fuel tanks, forcing Coleman to order his crew to bail out about ten miles north of Udine.[55]

When the bailout alarm rang, the navigator, Lieutenant George Dewey, was already prepared to bail out, but he noticed that the nose turret gunner, Sergeant John Mahoney, had not heard the alarm. The aircraft had now caught fire, and the flames began spreading. So Dewey went to tell Mahoney to bail out. As the navigator helped Mahoney get out of the turret, there was an explosion, and *Hard to Get* became "a mass of flames." As the two men got the nose gear door hatch open, Dewey noticed that the bombardier, Lieutenant John Car-

Locations of 451st Bomb Group aircraft lost during the Regensburg mission.

dinal, had been knocked unconscious by the explosion and was lying on the deck of the nose section. At first, he could not revive Cardinal as the spreading flames began to burn both men. Dewey shook Cardinal, checked the bombardier's parachute, took him to the open hatch, and threw him out of the burning plane. As Cardinal fell, the blast of cold air apparently revived him because he opened his parachute and landed safely. While suffering from burns, Dewey and Mahoney followed Cardinal out of the hatch and safely made it to the ground.[56]

Dewey landed near Mahoney and the ball turret gunner, Sergeant John Chamberlain, who had bailed out using the camera hatch door in the rear of the waist section. The three men immediately started east toward the Yugoslav border, hoping to link up with Tito's partisan fighters. After about two hours, they were making slow progress because of their wounds. Shortly after that, a squad of German soldiers who had apparently been pursuing them surrounded the group and took them prisoner. The Germans marched them to a nearby airfield for interrogation. That night, the Germans moved all three men to a hospital in Udine for treatment. In the hospital, they were reunited with Coleman and Cardinal, who were also being treated for burns.[57]

Meanwhile, radio operator Sergeant Elsie Blankenship, flight engineer/top turret gunner Sergeant Paul Mouton, and tail turret gunner Sergeant Jack Hale not only bailed out and landed safely, but also managed to evade the German and Italian soldiers searching for them, made contact with Yugoslav partisans, and eventually returned to duty. The only man unaccounted for was the copilot, Captain Monroe Quillen. While most of the crew believed he had been killed in the crash of the aircraft, Lieutenant Dewey said that he later saw Quillen in Nuremberg. Unfortunately, no further status on the copilot was reported.[58]

The final casualty for the 451st was *Double Trouble* from the 725th. As best as can be determined, AAA hit *Double Trouble* en route to the target, but the aircraft continued on the bomb run, crashing on the return flight about twenty miles southwest of Ljubljana. Copilot Lieutenant Frank Gerrity, navigator Lieutenant James Cottrell, bombardier Lieutenant George Evans, flight engineer/top turret gunner Sergeant Harold Koslow, and nose turret gunner Sergeant Don Abernathy became POWs. However, pilot Lieutenant Edwin Pries, ball turret gunner Sergeant Steve Varga, right waist gunner Sergeant Joseph McCord, and tail turret gunner Sergeant Thaddeus Tokarski were listed initially as missing in action. Eventually, their status was changed to killed in action.[59]

Around 1:24 PM, the 451st formation reached the IP at Rottenburg an der Laaber, and the bombers turned toward the Regensburg-Prüfening factory on a heading of 010°. As the formation made that turn, the enemy fighters pulled away lest they get hit by their own AAA fire, which now began in earnest. As the bombers made their way north through rings of AAA batteries, the flak became very intense. "The sound of our engines was deafening," Lieutenant Roger McCollester recalled, "but in spite of that, we could hear the 88mm shells through our headsets. The shells left puffs of gray smoke in the sky, and as the intensity of the barrage increased, our sphincters got tighter grips on our parachute cushions; anyone who says they weren't scared to death in these situations is a liar!" McCollester recalled that, as he turned his aircraft into the bomb run, "Flak burst all around us, but we had to concentrate on flying formation." Worrying about the flak or even looking at the gray-to-black bursts of smoke from their explosions was pointless since they "were helpless to do anything about them," as bursts sprayed the fuselage with deadly shrapnel.[60]

The weather was clear as the B-24s made their bomb run, and the bombardiers had no problem locating the target aiming point in the center of the factory complex. This was something of a surprise because the 451st was supposed to be the third group to attack the target. As a result, everyone expected a great deal of smoke to cover the target area. Still, Major Haltom, flying as the group lead, said the target could be seen clearly as soon as the formation reached the IP. They arrived over the target at 1:29 PM, and all the remaining aircraft released their bombs. The bomb run had seemed like "a couple of eternities" to Roger McCollester. He said that when his bombardier called "Bombs away!" over the intercom, "Sweeter words were never heard." The bombs struck the factory with great accuracy, leaving the plant in flames. Later analysis revealed that "scarcely a building escaped damage, many being utterly destroyed."[61]

As soon as the bombs were released, the formation began a sharp turn to the right, followed by evasive action that included a series of random turns and changes in altitude. Once the bombers had passed the final ring of AAA batteries, they resumed a normal flight path and remained at twenty-four thousand feet. Having survived the flak near the target, everyone's worries returned to the prospect of more attacks by German fighters. It would be forty-five minutes before their friendly fighter escort would rendezvous with the bombers over the Adriatic, leaving plenty of time for the Luftwaffe to intercept the B-24s again. However, the Germans, who had lost thirteen fighters destroyed and seven damaged by defensive fire from the 451st's gunners, apparently had enough, and there were no more enemy fighter attacks.[62]

The weather began to worsen during the return flight, as had been predicted. Once the formation passed the Austrian-Yugoslav border, it began to gradually descend, reaching ten thousand feet by the time it arrived at the Adriatic coast. At that point, a group of P-38Js arrived to escort the planes home. Lloyd Ryan wrote in his diary, "Everyone breathed a sigh of relief. There was never a more welcome sight." For his part, Roger McCollester made a quick head count over the intercom to make sure everyone on the crew had come through unscathed. No one had been injured, and learning that, he said, "Inside, I felt a silent prayer of thanks float upward. And my butt finally let go of the parachute."[63]

When the bombers were about two hours from Gioia del Colle, Major Haltom received a radio message saying a heavy rainstorm had hit the base and, as a result, Gioia del Colle "had been almost washed away."[64] Therefore, all the 451st bombers were directed to land at Foggia. Once his navigator had calculated a new heading, Haltom led the formation down through the overcast for the final leg of the mission. The clouds were so thick the formation had descended to almost five hundred feet before breaking out of the overcast. The landing at Foggia was uneventful, but since they had landed at a different field from their own, there were no postmission debriefings.

Once the aircraft were safely on the ground, Haltom received an urgent message ordering him, his navigator, and his bombardier to immediately board a truck that would take them back to Gioia del Colle because they were needed for a special briefing at 47th Wing Headquarters the next morning. The truck quickly arrived, but they did not return to the main base until early in the morning of February 26. Haltom cleaned up, changed from his flight suit to his uniform, and quickly stopped to see Colonel Eaton before heading to the briefing at wing headquarters. Eaton was still confined to bed, and Haltom gave him a short critique of the mission. Then he and his navigator and bombardier went to wing headquarters, where the new wing commander, General Hugo Rush, was being welcomed. The meeting was also held so Lieutenant Colonel Gideon from the 450th Bomb Group could receive the Distinguished Service Medal for leading the bombers on the Regensburg mission.

After the award ceremony, General Rush asked Major Haltom to brief those in attendance about his impressions of the mission. Haltom told the group that it was clear no bombs had hit the target until the

451st arrived. This "seemed to indicate that we were the first element over the target." This meant that the bombs from other groups, which included Lieutenant Colonel Gideon's, had either missed the target or, worse, that those groups had bombed the wrong target. While later photo reconnaissance proved that the 451st was the first to bomb the target, those in the briefing were surprised to hear this news. As soon as Haltom had finished, one of the generals asked him to repeat the statement about the bombing of the target. He replied with the same story, which was then confirmed by his navigator and bombardier.

The meeting concluded, and as Haltom and his fellow crew members were walking down the hall outside, Gideon chased Haltom down, whirled him around, and with his face red in fury screamed, "What the hell are you trying to do to me?" At that, Haltom asked in confusion, "What do you mean?" Apparently, Gideon was furious that Haltom had told everyone at 47th Wing Headquarters that Gideon's group had missed the target and did so only minutes after Gideon had been awarded a medal for leading the mission. The major replied he had honestly told them what he had seen. Gideon was livid, and Haltom thought the man might "have a stroke right on the spot." Both men left the building and went back to their respective home bases. While Haltom expected there would be some repercussions from the incident, he never heard another word about it.

One possible explanation for the absence of any earlier bombing when the 451st formation made its bomb run could be related to problems the 449th Bomb Group experienced during its assembly at Bitonto. When the 449th arrived at the rendezvous point, it could not find the aircraft from the 450th or 451st and started the mission independently. However, five minutes after departing the rendezvous point, their group lead saw a large formation of B-24s approaching from the right at the same altitude on a collision course. This may have been the 450th's aircraft. To avoid a potentially disastrous midair accident, the 449th's formation made a 360 degree turn to its left, allowing the other formation to cross its planned flight route. However, as the 449th came out of the full-circle turn, one of its squadrons lost contact with the others from the group and decided to go on with the B-24s that had almost collided with them. This confusion and the turn to avoid it may have caused both the 450th and 449th to fall behind the 451st and attack the target later than planned.[65]

As for the final results of the February 25 mission on the Regensburg-Prüfening plant, the American plan that called for a coordinated attack to weaken the German fighter force's ability to react effectively did pay off but only for the Eighth Air Force bombers. Unfortunately for the 451st and the other Fifteenth Air Force units, the German air defense commanders focused their attacks on the relatively larger forces of the Fifteenth. As a result, of the 111 bombers from the Eighth and Fifteenth Air Forces that hit the target, fourteen B-17s and nineteen B-24s were lost, six of which were from the 451st. This equaled a relatively high loss rate of 30 percent.[66]

However, the American bombers inflicted considerable damage despite this, and the Regensburg plant could not return to full production levels for four months. The final assembly shop in Building 2 and the main workshop in Building 4 were destroyed or severely damaged by several direct hits and near misses. Further, the final assembly shop was gutted, and blast damage to both buildings was extensive. The workshops in Buildings 6, 8, 12, and 14 were destroyed or severely damaged by numerous direct hits or near misses.[67] Even German radio broadcasts said the Regensburg-Prüfening Factory attacks had destroyed 50 percent of their productive ability.[68]

The 451st was awarded its first Distinguished Unit Citation, dated April 23, 1944, for its performance in the bombing and destruction of the Messerschmidt Regensburg-Prüfening Factory. The citation stated, "The loyalty and devotion to duty of the personnel of the organization was demonstrated on 25 February 1944 when it was called upon for maximum effort to aid in the destruction of one of the major targets in southern Germany" by "delivering over Germany 30 tons of high explosives, being one of the three bombardment groups credited by higher authority for the destruction of the aircraft factory."[69]

Colonel Robert E. L. Eaton, first commander of the 451st Bomb Group. He would complete fifty combat missions with the 451st, remain on active duty after the war, and retire as a major general. (*National Archives*)

Captain James Beane, first commander of the 724th Bomb Squadron. He was flying on *Gashouse* as co-pilot when it was shot down during the April 5, 1944, mission to Ploesti. He became a prisoner in a Romanian POW camp and was liberated in late August 1944.. (*National Archives*)

Technical Sergeant James C. Atkinson, Radio Operator on *The Jolly Roger*. The plane was shot down during the raid on Ploesti, but Atkinson survived and was taken prisoner. (*Courtesy William Atkinson*)

Lieutenant Harold Thompson, pilot and aircraft commander in the 727th Bomb Squadron from July-November 1944. (*Author*)

The Vultee BT-13 Valiant, the basic trainer flown by most American pilots during World War II. (*National Archives*)

B-24 Liberator bombers move down the assembly line at Ford's Willow Run plant. More than 8,500 of these aircraft were built at this factory before war's end. (*National Archives*)

An overhead shot of the 451st bomber, *Burma Bound*, showing the front gun turret, the astrodome, the pilot and co-pilot's cockpit, and the top turret gun position. Note the engine at top has been feathered, while the one at bottom has been hit by the enemy and is trailing smoke. (*National Archives*)

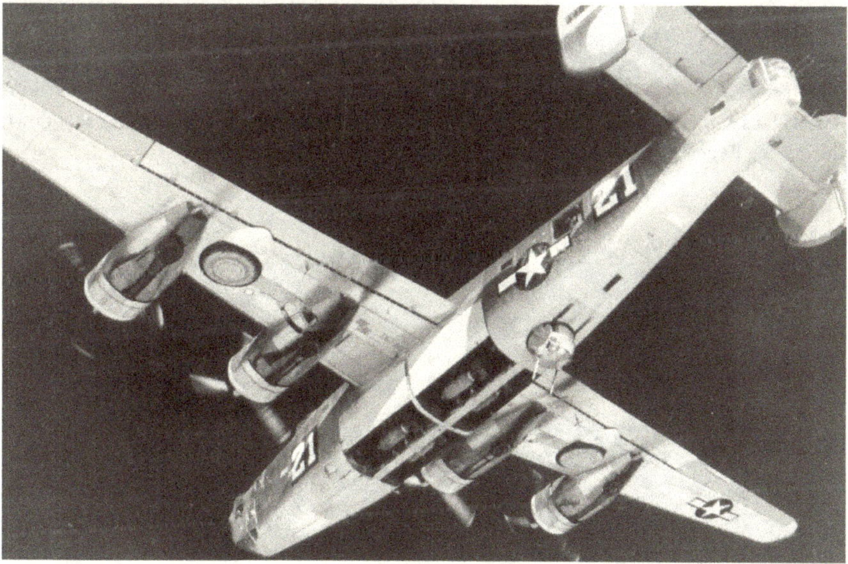

The underside of a 451st B-24 shows the aircraft's two bomb bays with their unique rollup doors, as well as the ball turret gun and tail gun turret positions. Note the landing gear folded up into the wings. (*National Archives*)

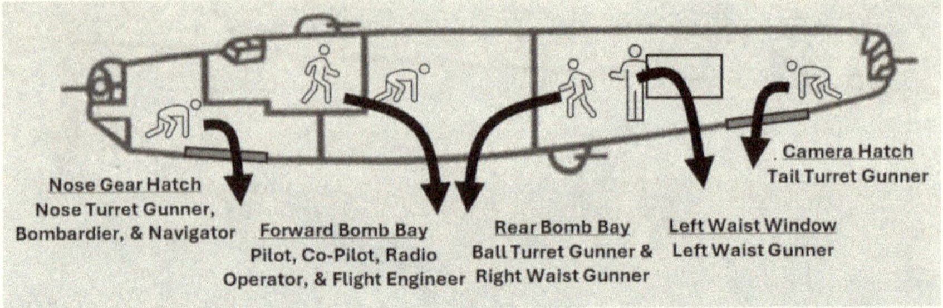

The designated bailout positions for each B-24 crewmember. While these positions were designated in the aircraft manuals, circumstances often dictated that crewmembers use whatever exit was closest at the moment the bailout order was given. (*National Archives*)

The 451st's *Hard to Get*, showing a clear view of the nose gun turret. *Hard to Get* was shot down during the Regensburg mission. (*Courtesy B-24 Best Web*)

Cockpit of the B-24 with its seventy-one controls, levers, switches, and instruments. The pilot sat at left, the co-pilot at right. (*B-24* Liberator *Army Air Force Pilot Training Manual*)

Waist gunner positions aboard a B-24. The positions were staggered so that the gunners would not interfere with each other. During a mission at high altitude, gunners wore oxygen masks, head gear, and electrically warmed flight suits for warmth and protection. (*National Archives*)

The top gun turret on a B-24, located behind the cockpit. This gun position was operated by the flight engineer during combat. (*National Archives*)

The console for the AN/APS-15 radar system. The radar could detect major features on the ground (e.g., large buildings, rivers, bridges) allowing the operator to guide the aircraft to the target. (*National Archives*)

A battery of German 8.8-cm Flak 18 antiaircraft artillery. With no defense against it, the "88" was among the most feared enemy weapons by bomber crews. (*Bundeswehr Archive*)

The Messerschmitt Bf 109F. This versatile German fighter aircraft featured two synchronized machine guns above the engine and a devastating 20mm cannon firing through the propeller hub. (*Bundeswehr Archive*)

The Focke-Wolf Fw 190, nicknamed *Würger*, "Butcher Bird," by Luftwaffe pilots. Models that fought Allied bombers featured a formidable armament of two synchronized machine guns above the engine and four 20mm cannon in the wingroots and outerwings. (*Imperial War Museum*)

The Messerschmitt Bf 110 *Zerstörer*, "Destroyer." This two-man fighter aircraft was effective against Allied bomber formations until the advent of longer-range fighter aircraft escorts. (*Bundeswehr Archive*)

The P-38J Lightning, known as *Der Gabelschwanz Teufel*, fork-tailed devil, by the Germans, featured a battery of .50 caliber machine guns in the nose and was the first American fighter aircraft able to accompany Allied bombers deep into Germany. (*National Archives*)

A P-51D Mustang equipped with two wing-mounted 108-gallon auxiliary or "drop" tanks. The tanks enabled the aircraft to escort bombers on long-range missions. Before engaging the enemy, the tanks would be jettisoned. The Mustang is considered the best American fighter aircraft of the war. (*National Archives*)

451st bomber crews attend the pre-mission briefing at Gioia de Colle before the February 8, 1944, mission to the Piombino marshaling yards and steel mill. (*National Archives*)

451st aircrews attend a post-mission debriefing at Castelluccio. (*National Archives*)

Mac's Flophouse, the aircraft flown by Lieutenant Roger McCollester and his crew on the Regensburg raid. They successfully bombed the target and returned to base unscathed. (*Courtesy B-24 Best Web*)

The Citadel, the aircraft flown by Lieutenant Nicholas Zender and his crew. They were lost during the Regensburg raid. (*Courtesy B-24 Best Web*)

Double Trouble, the B-24 flown by Lieutenant Edwin Pries and his crew, crashed in Yugoslavia with the loss of five crew members during Regensburg raid. (*Courtesy B-24 Best Web*)

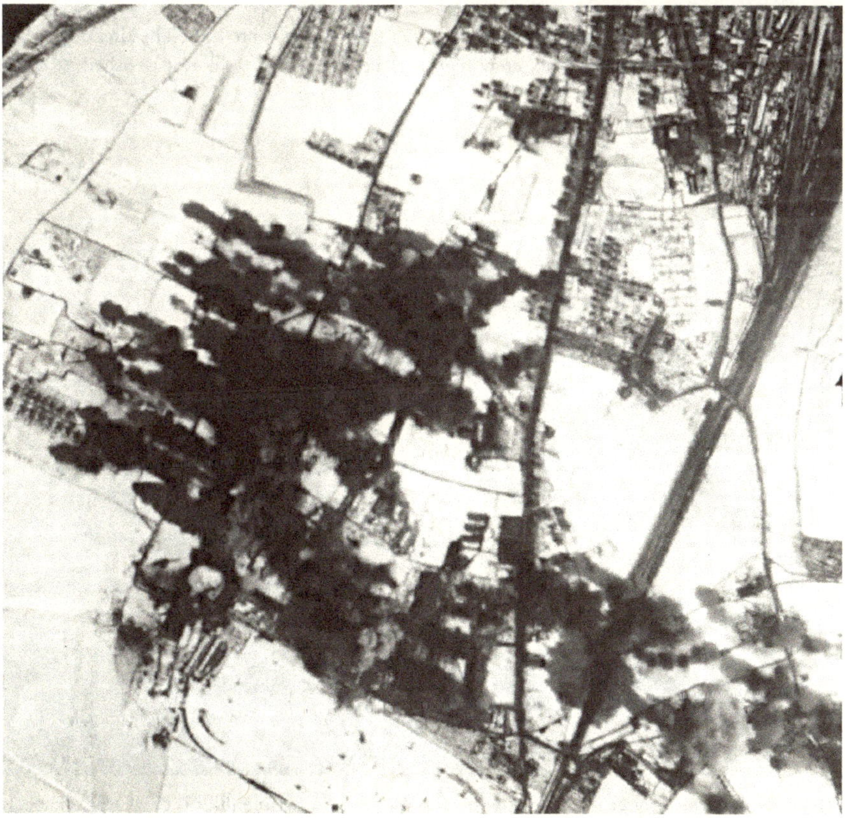

Post-strike reconnaissance photo showing the damage done to the Regensburg-Prüfening factory. (*National Archives*)

The Jolly Roger with her original crew that flew her from Nebraska to Italy. The aircraft was shot down during the Ploesti raid; six crew members became POWs, the rest perished. (*Courtesy William Atkinson*)

Cravin Raven, the aircraft flown by Lieutenant Winfred McAlister and his crew, was one of the victims of JG 51's vicious attacks during the Ploesti mission. Five crew members were captured and became prisoners; the rest were killed. (*Courtesy B-24 Best Web*)

Gashouse, the plane flown by Captain Robert Stone and his crew, would go down following the bomb run at Ploesti. The entire crew was able to evacuate the aircraft safely. (*Courtesy B-24 Best Web*)

The damage done to the Ploesti refineries following the raids that started on April 5, 1944. (*National Archives*)

Lieutenant Robert Anderson's *Weesie* was the only plane lost by the 727th Bomb Squadron at Markersdorf. Five of the crew were able to bail out from the stricken aircraft and became POWs; the others were killed. (*Courtesy B-24 Best Web*)

A burning German fighter aircraft falls to earth. As the war progressed, German fighter opposition faced increased allied fighter escort and better bomber tactics. (*National Archives*)

Thunder Mug flown by Captain George Tudor during the raid on Markersdorf. The plane returned with more than 150 holes from enemy gunfire, but none of the crew was injured. (*Courtesy B-24 Best Web*)

The Markersdorf aircraft factory before the bombing mission of August 23, 1944. Compare this with the photograph on page 151. (*National Archives*)

B-24s of the 451st Bomb Group return home to Castelluccio. Seeing their home airfield close by after a mission provided a profound sense of relief to the aircrews. (*National Archives*)

Chapter Five

The Oil Campaign Renewed

Ploesti, April 5, 1944

The Jagdflieger of the Luftwaffe's JG 51 likely could not believe their eyes. After taking off in their Bf 109s from the new base near Niš, Yugoslavia, on the afternoon of April 5, 1944, the Jagdfliegerführer for JaFü Balkan had vectored them toward a formation of American bombers. As they approached the lumbering American planes from above and to the bombers' rear, instead of the massive column of enemy aircraft they anticipated, they saw a small group of only four B-24s below—an easy target.

JG 51 was a highly experienced fighter *gruppe*, having been in combat since the war's earliest days. They had fought the fighters of the RAF in the Battle of France and the Battle of Britain in 1940 before moving to combat Soviet pilots along the Eastern Front. However, in March 1944, as Romanian oil refineries, such as the largest at Ploesti, came within range of bombers from the new American Fifteenth Air Force, they were transferred to the airfield at Niš. From there, they could oppose any Fifteenth Air Force formation heading from their bases in southern Italy toward targets in Romania, particularly those headed for the oil complexes at Ploesti.[1]

The Bf 109s and a group of Romanian IAR 80 fighters quickly organized themselves for the attack, with the Romanian pilots set to make the initial assault. The first of the IAR 80s dived from the bombers' nine o'clock position, sweeping into the formation and firing its guns before being hit and shot down by one of the bomber's nose turret gunners. Meanwhile, the JG51's Bf 109s broke to their left. They climbed about one thousand feet above the bomber formation, placing the afternoon sun at their back, complicating the enemy gunners' task. Once they were ready, the Bf 109s dived down from the B-24s' seven to eight o'clock position.[2]

The bombers' gunners opened fire as the swiftly approaching German fighters reached a range of about five hundred yards. But their efforts to defend their planes accomplished little. The German fighters opened fire with their 7.92mm machine guns and 20mm cannon with devastating effects. Across the bomber formation, engines and wings quickly caught fire, and the bullets smashed into and through the B-24s' thin aluminum skin. In one bomber, machine gun bullets from a Bf 109 entered the cockpit, shattering the instrument panel. At the same time, another had one of its rudders blown away. It did not take long before all four bombers were on fire and began to fall from the sky. Parachutes soon appeared as desperate American aircrews abandoned their planes, and seconds later, three of the four B-24s exploded, leaving nothing but large jagged pieces spiraling to the earth in flames.[3]

Following the mission to Regensburg on February 25, the aircraft of the 451st remained scattered because the runways at Gioia del Colle were still so muddy and waterlogged that they were unusable. However, within a few days, the Fifteenth Air Force had determined the base would not be available for some time. So Fifteenth Air Force decided to split the 451st into two operating units and relocate them. One unit, consisting of the 724th and 726th Bomb Squadrons, was sent to San Pancrazio, fifteen miles southwest of Brindisi. The other two squadrons went to Manduria, which was about ten miles west of San Pancrazio. Colonel Eaton was to command the portions of the 451st based at San Pancrazio, which was to be called the advanced unit, while Linan Blackmon, now a lieutenant colonel and the Deputy Group Commander, would be in charge of those elements at Manduria, which was to be known as the rear unit. The move was to start on March 3 and required the aircraft to fly to the new bases, but it also meant that all personal baggage, ground equipment, and support personnel would have to move from Gioia del Colle to San Pancrazio or Manduria by truck. The latter was particularly grueling, and much of the 451st was on the road shuttling between Gioia del Colle and the two new bases for the better part of ten days.[4]

Corporal Karl Eichhorn of the 724th and the squadron's other personnel began their move to San Pancrazio on March 2, and it was not a smooth process. On March 5, Eichhorn's armaments ground crews were told they would move the following day. They spent the entire day packing, taking down their tents, and dismantling the heating stoves. However, they were soon told the move was delayed, which meant everyone had to be crammed into the three tents that had yet to be broken down and packed. On March 7, those remaining tents were taken down, and their previous occupants left by truck. That meant that Eichhorn and the others had to spend that night sleeping in the open with only a shelter half to cover them, as all the blankets had already been shipped out. "It was," he remembered, "a bitter cold and miserable night."[5]

Finally, on the afternoon of March 8, Eichhorn and his fellows from the armament section loaded onto a truck for the ride to San Pancrazio. The roads were very muddy, and it took over three hours to make the seventy-five-mile trip to San Pancrazio via Taranto. The trucks pulled up in the early evening, and, thankfully, Eichhorn and his group discovered the other ground crews from the squadron had already set up their tents. They unloaded and moved in, but there was nowhere to sleep since there was no time to reassemble their bunk beds. So, being the enterprising young men they were, he and the others went on a scavenger hunt. They collected scrap wood and roof tiles from nearby bombed-out buildings, placed them on the tent floor, and used them as makeshift beds. While they were uncomfortable, the wood and tiles did keep them off the muddy ground.[6]

With the group's aircraft in place, operations resumed, and new missions were flown. Between March 7 and April 4, 1944, the 451st flew thirteen missions to targets, including the submarine pens at Toulon, France, and Vienna and Klagenfurt in Austria. These resulted in losing three aircraft, two to enemy action and the third to a crash on takeoff.[7]

While this was going on, significant shifts were again being made in Allied bomber campaign plans that were influenced by the disastrous August 1, 1943, raid by B-24s on the Ploesti oil fields in Romania. Known as Operation Tidal Wave, the raid was made by 164 B-24s from five bomb groups flying from bases in Libya. The plan was extraordinarily complex, involving a low-level bombing attack on seven of Ploesti's ten oil refineries. Timing and accurate navigation during the bomb runs were critical, and mistakes related to both led to crucial errors.[8]

Moreover, the Germans and Romanians mounted a fierce defense of the oil complex, and fifty-five B-24s were shot down, crashed, or impounded after being forced to land in neutral Turkey. In the end, out of the 1,765 aircrew members who flew the mission, 310 were killed, and 186 were either captured by German and Romanian forces or interned in Turkey. Moreover, while the attack reduced Ploesti's potential production by 40 percent, diligent repair and reconstruction efforts and shifts in production to undamaged refineries by the Germans and Romanians returned production to preattack levels within eight months.[9] It was clear that Ploesti's production capabilities and those of the other refineries around the Third Reich would not be severely reduced by single bombing missions.

Oil production was as crucial to the German war effort as it was to the Allies. The initial efforts to refine oil occurred in Scotland almost ninety years before World War II, and the first successful commercial oil refinery began operations just a few miles north of Ploesti at Campina, Romania, in 1857. In the late 1930s, Germany imported about 70 percent of its liquid fuel from other nations, making it vulnerable once the war began. Despite German efforts to increase domestic oil production, finding sources it could control and protect was vital. When it brought Hungary and Romania into the war as allies, it gained access to refineries near Lake Balaton in Hungary and those around Ploesti. The latter became particularly important because they would account for almost 30 percent of the German military's oil supply.[10]

The results of Operation Tidal Wave showed that a concerted bombing campaign that involved multiple missions against each oil facility would have to be planned and executed. In March 1944, planners working for Lieutenant General Carl A. Spaatz estimated that fifty-four refineries were responsible for producing 90 percent of Germany's oil supplies. Of these, twenty-seven refining complexes at Ploesti, Silesia, and the Ruhr were seen as especially important. Spaatz believed that destroying all twenty-seven facilities would reduce the German military's diesel fuel and gasoline supply by 50 percent. Furthermore, if all fifty-four refineries were destroyed, German oil production might fall to zero by September 1944. Therefore, he advocated a new bombing campaign focused on German oil production.[11]

However, Spaatz's idea ran into strong opposition from Allied headquarters, where all efforts were focused on supporting the invasion of Europe, which was planned for summer 1944. General Dwight Eisenhower, Supreme Allied Commander Europe, leaned toward a bombing campaign supported by the British that would seek to destroy the railway system of Western Europe, which would cripple German efforts to support its forces opposing the coming Allied landings in France. However, Spaatz persisted in trying to convince the Combined Chiefs of the importance of his proposed oil bombing campaign. On March 17, Lieutenant General Henry "Hap" Arnold told Spaatz that the Combined Chiefs, while not approving his larger-scale plans for an oil bombing campaign, had no objections to undertaking raids by the Fifteenth Air Force against Ploesti. As a caveat, however, Arnold recommended that it might be politically wise to target rail facilities at the refineries in Ploesti, thereby appearing to support the campaign on rail transportation. Of course, Arnold knew that given the limitations on precise bombing, many bombs were sure to hit the oil refineries next door to those rail facilities. As one bombardier would say after studying part of the target folders for Ploesti's rail yards and noting the proximity to the oil refineries, "It was obvious that no one would be upset if the whole damned place [the oil refineries] went up!"[12]

This all gave birth to a campaign against Ploesti that would start on April 5, 1944, be followed by two more raids in April, and continue into summer 1944. The staff at the Fifteenth Air Force faced the difficult task of planning missions against a large, complex set of ten refineries that were heavily defended. The Germans knew the vital significance of their oil supplies as well as the Allies did, and they also knew Ploesti's importance in their overall oil production capability. Therefore, they positioned 150 fighters from the Luftwaffe and Romanian Air Force to defend Ploesti along with 140 heavy-caliber AAA guns, including 88mm, 105mm, and 120mm weapons. In evaluating Ploesti as a target, one group of Army Air Force experts said, "Damaging oil refineries successfully by aerial bombardment is one of the most difficult missions assigned to a strategic air force. Where a target such as Ploesti is so heavily defended that it requires a large proportion of blind or obscured bombing from high altitude, this difficulty is accentuated."[13]

The latter issue on visibility emphasized the potential problems posed by the weather in southern Europe. The route from southern Italy across the Adriatic first passed through western Yugoslavia, considered the "rainiest spot in Europe." Furthermore, around Ploesti, clouds were known to rise as high as twenty thousand feet, and from April through August, each month typically saw only twelve to fifteen days without complete overcast. This meant that trying to bomb Ploesti repeatedly using visual techniques via the Norden bombsight would be an issue.[14]

The plan laid out by the Fifteenth Air Force for the April 5, 1944, mission called for the 98th Bomb Group to lead the bomber column, followed by the 449th, 376th, and 450th, with the 451st flying as the last group in the 47th Bomb Wing's formation. There would also be a fighter escort of P-38s. Still, given the Fifteenth Air Force's continuing shortage of long-range fighter capability, the fighters could only go as far as eastern Yugoslavia. The 451st would launch thirty-four aircraft from their two bases, consisting of eight planes each from the 724th and 725th and nine planes each from the 726th and 727th. The 725th would lead the 451st's first attack wave, followed by the 724th. Next would come the 726th in the second attack wave, with

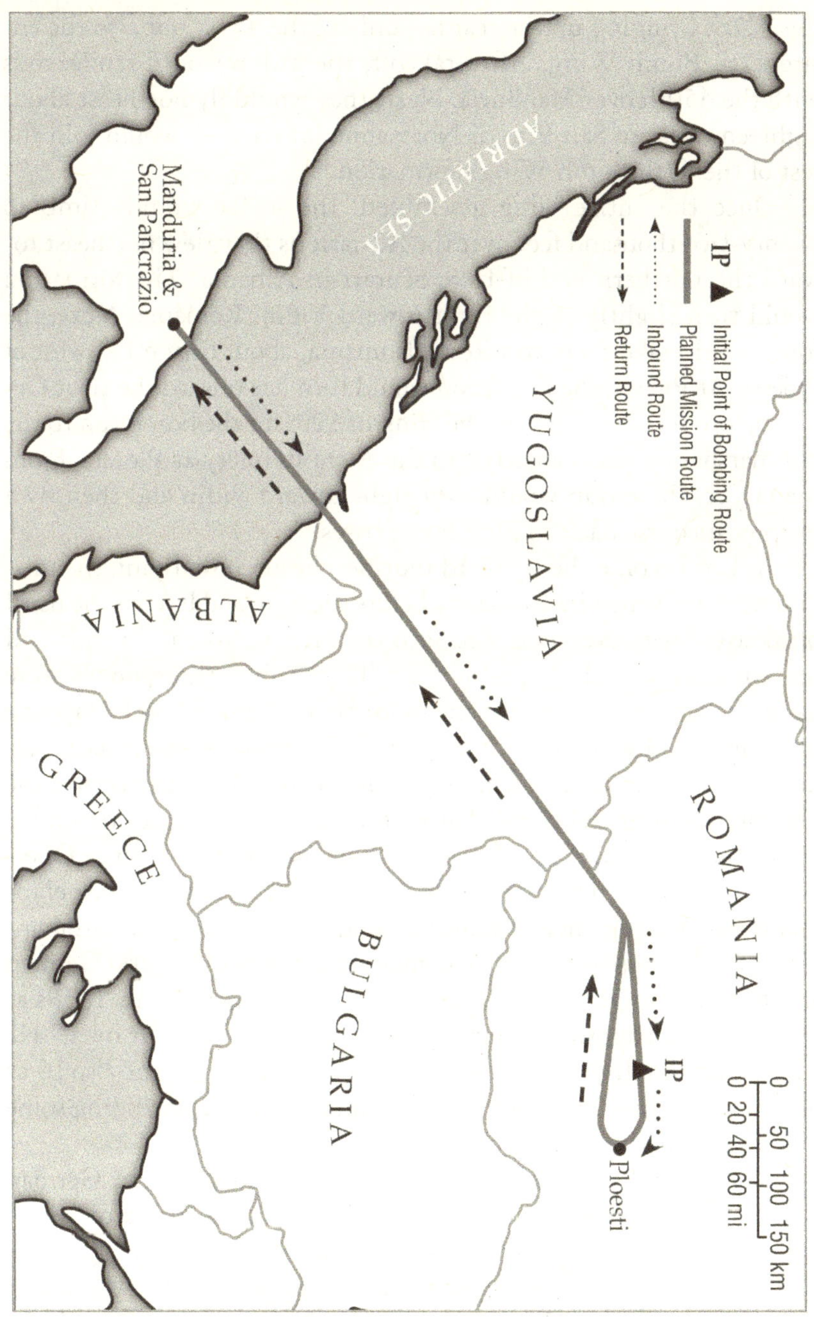

The route used by the 451st Bomb Group on the mission to Ploesti, April 5, 1944.

the 727th bringing up the rear not only of the 451st but also the entire 47th Bomb Wing. After takeoff, the group would rendezvous with the 450th over Manduria. Next, they would fly northeast about eighteen miles to San Vito di Normanni, where they would join the rest of the 47th Bomb Wing's formation.[15]

Once the entire wing assembled, the 451st would climb to twenty-two thousand feet over the Adriatic as they flew northeast toward the northern end of Lake Scutari in Albania. The formation would turn slightly to the right toward Vidin, Romania. Next, the route would take them to Pitesti, Romania, about fifty miles west of Ploesti. At Pitesti, the formation would turn left toward the IP at Ocnita before turning right to a heading of 120° for the bomb run to the rail marshaling yards adjacent to the Astra Refinery at Ploesti. From the target, the group would turn right toward Vidin and then fly a reciprocal course back to their home bases.[16]

As had become the standard routine, the aircrews flying the mission were awakened by an orderly before dressing and having the usual breakfast. Then, everyone filed into the briefing room. As usual, all the aircrews secretly hoped for a milk run, but those hopes were dashed when the curtain over the route map was pulled back. Tapping the map with his pointer for an unneeded emphasis, the briefing officer said, "That's right, men, Ploesti, Romania." When he turned the presentation over to Colonel Eaton, the group commander reminded them that this would be the first mission against Ploesti since Operation Tidal Wave. Then he said the Germans had spent the last eight months increasing their defenses around the oil complex. Eaton approached the map and said, "You may expect as many as 200 German and Romanian fighters in the area. You will be escorted by P-38s as far as eastern Yugoslavia, but after that, you'll be on your own." He added that intelligence information indicated there might also be as many as three hundred AAA pieces around the target, including some hidden under haystacks in nearby fields.[17]

The Group Commander emphasized the threat posed by German fighters. First, he noted that the pilots in the area were among the Luftwaffe's best, and they could be expected to be especially aggressive in defending a target so crucial to the German war effort. Worst of all, however, was that the 451st would be the last group to attack the target. The colonel noted that the 451st would "be the most vulner-

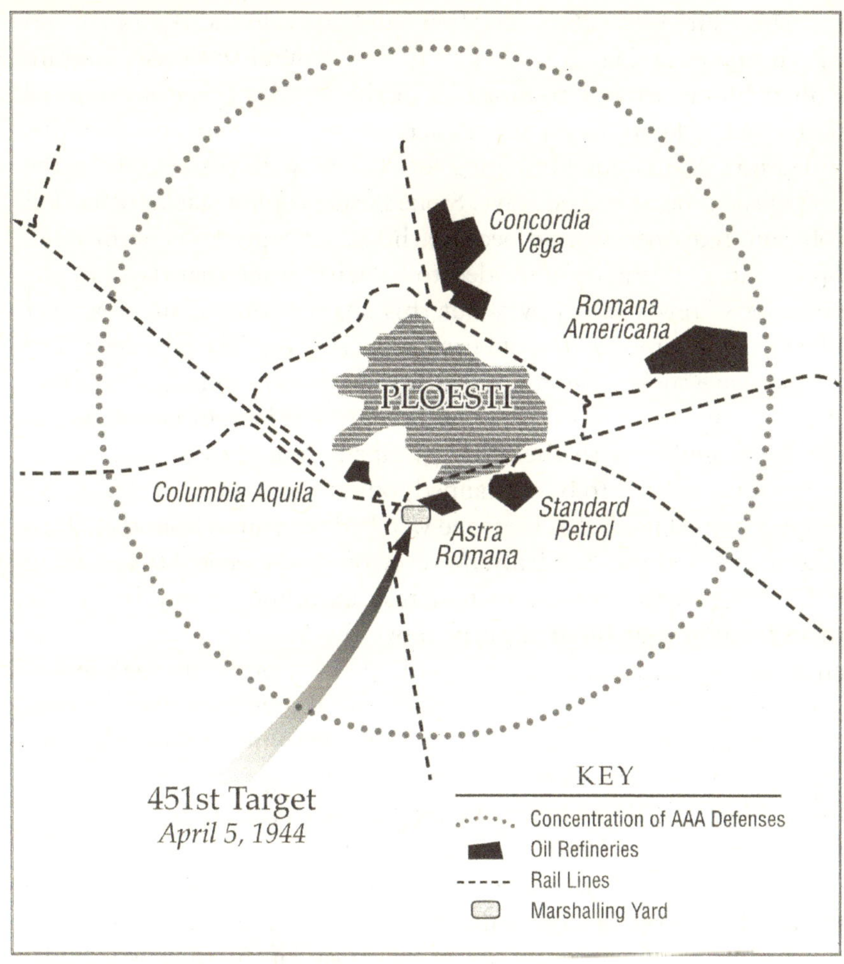

The Ploesti target area, April 5, 1944.

able to fighter attack." He emphasized the need for flying a tight formation, and for gunners to conserve their ammunition on the way into the target so there would be enough remaining to defend their aircraft on the return trip. With that, Eaton concluded his remarks, and the weather officer gave his forecast, which called for cloud decks at ten thousand and twelve thousand feet over Italy but clearing skies over the Adriatic and partial cloud cover at the target.[18]

The 724th and 726th aircraft at San Pancrazio and the 725th and 727th planes at Manduria began to taxi around 9:45 AM. Captain Robert Stone, aircraft commander of the 724th's *Gashouse*, recalled that their takeoff from San Pancrazio was normal and that his squadron's "ships quickly joined formation" with his aircraft in the lead of the group's second wave. Stone's usual copilot, Lieutenant Paul Johnson, remained behind because the 724th Squadron commander, Major James Beane, had decided to fly with Stone that day. No one on Stone's crew was happy about this change because no crew ever liked to have someone new onboard, especially on the flight deck. The second wave tucked themselves in behind Stone's and slightly above them. They rendezvoused with the aircraft from Manduria and headed for the assembly with the other groups at San Vito di Normanni. Everything seemed to be as planned, but it was not.[19]

All seemed normal as everyone watched the planes from the 725th take off at Manduria. Suddenly, however, one B-24 seemed to be having difficulty getting airborne. Its nose rose above the runway, but as the main landing gear lifted slightly above the Marston Mat, the entire aircraft shook and wobbled before falling down hard onto the runway. The fuselage immediately broke apart, and the entire aircraft became engulfed in flames. Some parts of the aircraft tumbled down the runway, and the burning tires from the main landing gear kept going before rolling into the grass on the infield. With the aircrews from the planes waiting to take off looking on in abject horror, emergency vehicles raced toward the burning wreckage, hoping to extinguish the fire and find survivors, but only one man lived through the inferno.[20]

Besides the terrible loss of life, the crash on the runway complicated matters for the 725th and 727th bombers waiting to take off. At first, some of the remaining aircrews thought the group might cancel their squadron's participation in the mission. But they soon learned that they would take off and proceed as planned once the wreckage on the runway was cleared. However, there was no way they could continue "as planned" because they fell farther behind the rest of the 451st as each minute passed. Finally, takeoffs resumed, but they were an hour late departing Manduria. Aboard *The Jolly Roger*, this was painfully apparent. Lieutenant Thomas Fallon, the plane's copilot, turned to the aircraft commander, Lieutenant Lewis Williams, and said, "Goddamn! We'll be so far behind the other groups that we'll never catch up!" Williams replied, "Yeah. Not a place we want to be. Dead last in a bomber stream."[21] The reason for Williams's concern was apparent: German fighters preferred to attack from the rear of a formation, and if they were the last aircraft in the wing's column, his plane and the others from the 727th would be the most vulnerable.

The rest of the group also experienced difficulties. When the 724th and 726th aircraft reached San Vito di Normanni, where they were to rendezvous with the 450th Bomb Group, the planes from the 450th were nowhere in sight. Apparently, the 450th had continued toward Ploesti without completing the assembly. Moreover, the 450th was now leading the attack because another bomb wing, the 304th, had aborted the mission. The 304th and its four bomb groups were supposed to lead the Fifteenth Air Force formations to Ploesti, but dense cloud cover prevented them from assembling all their groups, so they turned back.[22]

Meanwhile, the planes from the 451st pressed on alone, with the 450th apparently somewhere ahead of them. During the climb to their cruise altitude, they encountered the dense layers of clouds predicted by the weather officer, which covered the Adriatic and continued into Yugoslavia. The poor visibility resulted in the second wave from the 724th losing visual contact with the rest of the 451st's planes and becoming separated. They never regained contact with the first wave. Lieutenant Roger Johnston, the navigator on *Gashouse*, later said, "I do not know for sure to this day whether our wave may have even passed up and gone ahead of the intended first wave, but we were on our own."[23]

Well ahead of the 727th's formation, the 724th continued their climb to altitude over the Adriatic. As they reached the Yugoslav coast and cleared some of the cloud decks, Robert Stone and the crew on the *Gashouse* could see aircraft from other bomb groups nearby. Ahead, another cloud deck formed over the mountains just east of Lake Scutari. Flying into them might cause his squadron's formation to scatter again, so Stone advanced his throttles and began a slow climb to put them above the clouds. The first wave from the 724th was still nowhere in sight, but Stone elected to continue toward the target.[24]

While the bombers from the 451st were making their way into Yugoslav airspace, the German defenses began to react. The radar sites along the Albanian and Yugoslav coasts monitored the long stream of bombers, feeding data to the Jagdfliegerführer for JaFü Balkan. When the bomber stream did not turn north at the coast, it was clear they were headed inland. Given the size of the formations, it was obviously a significant attack on a high-priority target. That could mean they were headed for Ploesti. German and Romanian fighters were scrambled, and the Jagdfliegerführer began to organize his forces.

One fighter *gruppe* scrambled was JG 51, commanded by Major Karl Rammelt and based at Nisch airfield near Niš, Yugoslavia. After fighting in France and on the Eastern Front, JG 51 was transferred back to Germany and trained to counter heavy bombers in the defense of the Reich mission.[25] This meant that the 451st would be attacked by a highly experienced and skilled set of pilots specifically trained to attack bomber formations.

As the leading elements of the bomber stream approached the IP at Ocnita, a small group of enemy fighters were seen in the distance, flying parallel to the bombers. These fighters watched the bombers for a while before making some preliminary, weak passes. But soon after that, about fifteen more fighters arrived, all Romanian, and the actual attacks began. The Romanian fighters quickly climbed above and ahead of the bombers before commencing fierce head-on attacks from the twelve o'clock position. The B-24 gunners opened fire, and the fighters swept past them and then dove to safety below the bombers, where they were out of range of the B-24s' guns. Then they began a wide, arcing turn to the right, placing themselves above and parallel to the left side of the bomber formation. They next made high-side firing passes, sweeping through the formation again as the B-24 gunners blasted away at them.[26] However, once the formation reached the IP, the fighters pulled away so the batteries of AAA could do their deadly work.

As Robert Stone flew the *Gashouse* through the attacking fighters toward the IP, his navigator, Roger Johnston, reported the cloud coverage was clearing ahead of them, so they would have little trouble locating the target. At the same time, Sergeant William Berry, the aircraft's tail turret gunner, said he could see a group far behind them receiving a heavy attack.[27] Most likely this was the formation from the 727th.

As the planes from the 727th had climbed through those dense cloud decks over the Adriatic, their formation with the 725th became scattered.[28] When they cleared the overcast, the aircraft from the 727th found themselves far behind those from the 725th. The first box of aircraft from the 727th, led by Lieutenant John Cavanaugh, was above and ahead of the second box, led by Lieutenant William Stenning, who was flying *St. Peter's Ferry*. Two other B-24s who had lost their own group joined the formation behind the second box, further beefing up the formation. However, despite their presence, the situation caused by their late takeoff had seemingly worsened. The squadron's formation was severely behind the rest of the group, becoming more vulnerable to attack by the minute.

Aboard *The Jolly Roger*, Lieutenant Williams was becoming increasingly concerned about their situation. So he got on the radio and called Lieutenant Cavanaugh, telling him they needed to speed up the formation to "catch up with the rest of the Group." Cavanaugh replied tersely, "Hold position. Maintain radio silence." Hearing that, Williams turned to glance at his copilot and said, "Bill, we're sitting ducks out here."

As *The Jolly Roger* and the other 727th aircraft reached twenty-two thousand feet, Williams turned and nodded to Sergeant Atkinson, his radio operator, who was standing just behind the flight deck. This signaled Atkinson to help the flight engineer up into the top gun turret. Atkinson turned to Sergeant Charles Isherwood and pointed toward the turret with his thumb. The crew's usual flight engineer was sick, and Isherwood had been assigned to replace him for this mission. Atkinson knelt down, allowing Isherwood to step onto his knee and hoist himself into the turret. At that point, it was time for the bombs to be fuzed. Lieutenant Kenneth Preston, the bombardier, crawled up the tunnel from the nose, and Atkinson opened the bomb bay bulkhead door for him. Atkinson led the way onto the bomb bay catwalk so he could reach his waist gun position as Preston followed him into the bomb bay and began pulling the pins from the fuze for each bomb.

Once Atkinson reached the waist section, he helped the ball turret gunner, Sergeant William Wiley, into the cramped space of the ball turret. When Wiley was seated, Atkinson gave him a pat on the head, which caused Wiley to look up at him and nod. Atkinson closed the top hatch on the ball turret and lowered it into the slipstream below the aircraft. With that task complete, Atkinson turned to Sergeant Joe Yurtanas, who calmly gave Atkinson a nod and began to crawl back to the tail gun turret. With all the gunners now in position, Atkinson took his waist gun in hand, cocked it to charge the gun, and began to scan the skies for the enemy fighters they all expected to soon appear.

As the 727th's planes reached the coast, Sergeant Yurtanas called from the tail on the intercom to tell Lieutenant Williams that the two B-24s that had joined the formation were now turning around and going home. "There's no one behind us except *Cravin Raven*," he added. Williams acknowledged the call from his tail turret gunner and told him, "Keep a sharp eye out." But as he looked ahead, the pilot of *The Jolly Roger* could see that they were not catching up with the rest of the group's formation and were actually falling farther behind. Once again, he called Lieutenant Cavanaugh on the radio, begging him to "pour on the coals," but Cavanaugh again refused to do so. At this point, the four aircraft in the second, lower box consisted of *St. Peter's Ferry*, *The Jolly Roger*, *Super Moose*, and *Cravin Raven*, and they "could not have been in a worse situation." However, as bad as their situation might have been, it was about to become catastrophic.

As the 727th's formation passed Niš and made a slight turn to a heading of 050°, Yurtanas called out over the intercom that he could see a Bf 110 north of them flying in parallel with the bombers. Upon hearing this, Lieutenant Fallon said, "He's radioing our position to his unit, that sonofabitch." The copilot was probably correct because a group of Romanian Bf 109s and IAR 80s appeared shortly afterward. They divided into two groups and began circling the lower box while remaining just out of range of the B-24s' guns. Suddenly, several IAR 80s turned into the 727th's formation and attacked, diving down from the nine o'clock position.

The top turret, ball turret, and left waist gunners opened fire as the fighters closed in and flew through the formation. On *The Jolly Roger,* Lieutenant Williams looked over his left shoulder to see one IAR 80 sweeping in over their left wing with his guns blazing. The Romanian pilot avoided fire from the two turrets and waist gunner, but as he pulled away in front of *The Jolly Roger*, Sergeant Edwin Moore, the nose turret gunner, swung his turret to the left, placing the fighter in his sights. He fired several bursts, scoring a direct hit on the IAR 80, which began to pour smoke badly, causing the Romanian pilot to throw back his canopy, stand in his seat, and then bail out of his stricken plane.

No sooner had the Romanian fighters made their attack than the Bf 109s from JG 51 arrived. Looking back from his tail gun turret, Sergeant Yurtanas saw Major Rammelt's fighters appear. Somehow remaining calm, he announced over the intercom, "We've got a dozen or more 109s coming at us from 6 o'clock. Some low and some high." Unknown to Yurtanas and the other American gunners, Rammelt was leading the high flight. He and his pilots began to close on the four B-24s, and when they were within one thousand yards of the bombers, they turned to the left and climbed until they were about one thousand feet above them. This maneuver placed the early afternoon sun behind the German fighters, making it harder for the B-24 gunners to accurately get the enemy planes in their sights. Once this maneuver was complete, Rammelt and his men lowered the noses of their aircraft, pushed their throttles forward, and began to dive on the B-24s from the seven to eight o'clock position, opening fire with their machine guns and cannons from a range of about five hundred yards. The results were devastating.

Aboard *The Jolly Roger*, the bullets and cannon shells ripped through the aircraft's thin aluminum skin. They smashed into the top gun turret and the ball turret. The tail turret and waist gunners felt a "sickening thud" below them as one of the deadly enemy rounds hit the ball turret. Sergeant Wiley screamed over the intercom, "I'm hit!" Meanwhile, Sergeant Isherwood watched the tracer rounds whizzing toward *The Jolly Roger* and felt a "jolt" when they struck the turret. Then he smelled the odor of plastic melting and saw two gaping holes only inches from his head in the top of the turret's Plexiglas dome.

At the same time, more enemy fire hit the left wing, ripping massive holes in its surface and causing the number two engine to catch fire, while cannon fire ripped off the plane's right rudder. In the cockpit, Lieutenant Williams struggled to maintain control of the aircraft and feather the burning engine when bullets smashed his instrument panel and part of the windshield. The holes in the windshield caused the slipstream to blast into the cockpit, pelting Williams and Fallon with broken glass from the instrument panel. Williams glanced out his window and saw *St. Peter's Ferry* become engulfed in flames and careen out of formation. When he looked over his right shoulder through the small window in the bomb bay bulkhead door, Williams could see the bomb bay was on fire. Williams slammed the throttles forward and the three remaining good engines roared loudly as their manifold pressures exceeded fifty inches of mercury, well above the allowable limits for the engines. Williams knew *The Jolly Roger* was "mortally wounded," and he was desperately trying to keep his plane in the air so his men had a chance to bail out.

Back in the waist section, Atkinson and the other waist gunner, Sergeant Chester Zablinski, started to open the ball turret hatch to help Sergeant Wiley. Suddenly, Atkinson's flight suit caught fire, and the heat in the waist section became terribly intense. Atkinson and Zablinski realized they had to bail out and leave their wounded comrade behind. Both men immediately dived through the waist windows. Atkinson did not even pause to clip on his parachute completely, tucking it "under his arms like a football" before diving out the window as his "headphones, throat microphone, and oxygen mask" tore loose.

As the waist gunners bailed out to save themselves from the increasing flames in their section, Lieutenant Williams got on the intercom and told everyone to bail out. He pushed the bailout alarm bell switch, which sent one long sustained ring echoing through the aircraft.

Hearing the alarm bell ring down in the nose section, Lieutenant Preston grabbed the doors to the nose gun turret, opened them, reached in, and pulled Sergeant Moore out of the turret with one firm motion. Preston and Moore grabbed their parachutes and snapped them into their harnesses. At the same time, Lieutenant Roy Johnson looked up from the navigator's table to see enemy tracer rounds zooming past the astrodome. Peering out the dome, he saw the left rudder fall away along with a section of the left wing just outboard of the aileron. At that moment, *The Jolly Roger* began a sharp roll to the left, telling Lieutenant Williams that he was rapidly losing control of the aircraft.

Looking down past his feet and the rudder pedals, Williams could see Johnson crawling through the tunnel from the nose section to retrieve his parachute, which he always hung on the tunnel's bulkhead door. Next to Williams, Lieutenant Fallon stood up in his copilot's seat so he could snap on his own parachute. With his parachute in place, Fallon stepped back onto his seat and threw the overhead hatch open. That hatch was not intended for bailout, but apparently, Fallon wanted to use the closest available opening to leave the aircraft. Fallon managed to pull himself up and out the hatch, but his feet got caught in the door's opening as the blast from the slipstream pinned him against the top of the plane's fuselage. Seeing his copilot's predicament, Williams stood up, grabbed Fallon's feet, and pulled them free, allowing Fallon to fall away from the aircraft.

While Fallon tried to bail out, Sergeant Isherwood climbed down from the top gun turret, moving aft toward the bomb bay. He grabbed the bomb jettison handle and opened the bomb bay doors, releasing the bombs and providing him with an avenue of escape. He snapped on his parachute, stepped onto the catwalk, and rolled down out the bomb bay doors.

By this time, the entire waist section was engulfed in flames, blocking the path from the tunnel to the tail gun turret where Sergeant Yurtanas was snapping on his parachute. When he reached the tunnel opening, he could see that he had to find a way through fifteen feet of "searing heat" to reach the camera hatch door, which was in the rear part of the fuselage compartment. He gritted his teeth and crawled as fast as possible to the hatch door, pulled it open, and pitched himself down away from the burning plane.

Since Lieutenant Williams could not know if everyone had bailed out, he continued his fight in the cockpit to keep *The Jolly Roger* under control. Finally, he decided he had done all he could to provide his crew with a stable platform for exiting the aircraft. The moment had come for him to also bail out. He switched on the autopilot, which seldom worked as it should, hoping it could keep the aircraft level enough for him to make his way to the bomb bay for bailout. He went through the radio operator's compartment and the bomb bay bulkhead door and jumped down onto the catwalk. But just as he started to bail out, *The Jolly Roger* rolled over, pinning him inside the bomb bay.

As Williams was trying to fight his way out of the bomb bay, Johnson emerged from the tunnel to the nose section to find the flight deck empty, with blasts from the frigid slipstream filling the cockpit. Looking behind him, he could see Lieutenant Preston and Sergeant Moore trying to open the nose gear doors. They were jammed shut, so the two men began stomping on them, trying to free the doors and get them open. Finally, the doors popped open, and the two men rolled out of the aircraft. Suddenly, the aircraft began yet another uncommanded roll, which threw Johnson toward the open overhead hatch where Fallon had bailed out. The desperate navigator climbed through the hatch, clutching his parachute. But he was thrown out onto the fuselage before he could don his chute. He rolled onto the left wing, where the rotating prop from the damaged number two engine spun just a few feet from his face. He continued to slide down the wing as he snapped on his parachute before rolling off the wing and into the air.

Meanwhile, as the three remaining engines continued to roar at full throttle, Lieutenant Williams managed to crawl back to the flight deck, where he grabbed the yoke and manhandled *The Jolly Roger* upright once more. But when the pilot returned to the bomb bay, the aircraft rolled over again. He crawled back to the cockpit once more, got the aircraft level, and returned to the bomb bay. There he quickly rolled out of the open bomb bay doors, but this time, his flight suit snagged on an object in the bomb bay. As the aircraft continued to roll, Williams found himself sliding into and out of the bomb bay as the slipstream slammed him back and forth. Finally, his flight suit pants tore away from the object holding him, and he found himself rolling down the bottom of the fuselage toward the ball gun turret. He slammed into the turret, and luckily, the gun barrels were pointing away on the opposite side of the turret. Had Williams hit them, he might very well have been impaled. Now he fell away from the aircraft, pulling on the parachute ripcord and watching the canopy open above him. As he drifted down in his parachute, he saw *The Jolly Roger* falling away beneath him before exploding in a massive fireball, breaking into three pieces, and careening down toward the Romanian countryside.

As Sergeant Atkinson fell through "a hurricane of wind rushing past him," he groped desperately over the parachute, searching for the metal clips that snapped onto D-rings on the front of his harness. The wind burned his eyes as he used his left hand to maintain a "death grip" on the parachute's carrying handle. With the ground approaching faster than he realized, Atkinson felt the clip in his hand, grabbed it tightly, and snapped it onto the harness D-ring. There was no time to find the other clip, so he pulled the ripcord, opening the parachute. The sudden snap resulting from the upward force of the streaming parachute opening injured Atkinson's left shoulder, and he felt a "sudden, severe pain" there. Then, when the canopy opened, its force snapped his head back violently, causing "immediate pain in his neck."

Once the parachute had opened and he was drifting down, Atkinson noticed how tranquil the skies around him were. After the roar of the plane's engines and the loud chattering of its machine guns, it must have seemed almost serene. But the ground was coming up toward his feet extremely fast now. Before he was ready, he struck the ground with a "sudden jolting force" as his knees came up right below his chin and he rolled over onto his back.[29]

While Atkinson was struggling, Sergeant Isherwood jumped out from the bomb bay and pulled his own ripcord. As his canopy opened, he could see *The Jolly Roger* falling as the fire spread from the bomb bay through the fuselage and all the way to the tail, turning the aircraft into a ball of flames. Isherwood saw another parachute nearby and pulled on the shrouds so he could drift closer toward it. When he neared it, he saw its occupant was Lieutenant Fallon, who had escaped once Lieutenant Williams freed his feet from the cockpit's overhead hatch. After he was out the hatch, Fallon bounced along the top of the fuselage, hitting one of the plane's antennas before rolling away between the tail's two vertical stabilizers. Isherwood shouted to the lieutenant, asking the copilot if he could control his parachute to adjust the descent direction. But Fallon responded that he could not do so. Isherwood replied, shouting, "I'll see you on the ground! Good luck!"

Meanwhile, the pilot, Lieutenant Williams, having finally escaped the aircraft, found himself drifting down in a fall that would take nearly twenty minutes. His face and hair burned, and he struggled with the parachute's canvas container, which was tangled in the shrouds and kept hitting him in the face. When he felt his singed hair, he thought his brains might be oozing out of his skull. Just then, he saw a B-24's rudder coming near him, "swishing by in a side-to-side fashion like a leaf falling from a tree limb" before narrowly missing him. After falling through a cloud deck, he could see the surrounding countryside, a village, and fire and smoke where *The Jolly Roger* had crashed nearby.

Most of the crew of *The Jolly Roger* who bailed out were quickly captured and taken into custody by either the Germans or local Romanian officials. The plane's flight engineer, Sergeant John Mytych, was found near the aircraft's wreckage by five people from the local village. He was severely injured, so the Romanians gathered him up and started toward the hospital in Călinești, but Mytych died en route. The same group of Romanians also found Sergeant Zablinski's lifeless body about one hundred yards from the crash site. Lieutenant Edward Robert, bombadier on *The Jolly Roger*, was found with a severe chest wound. The Romanians took him to a hospital in Pitesti, but he died the following day. The remaining six crew members became POWs.[30]

With *The Jolly Roger* in its final death throes, similar scenes played out aboard the squadron low formation's lead aircraft, *St. Peter's Ferry*. The enemy fighters pressed their attack on Lieutenant Stenning's plane, first shooting out the tail gun turret and the ball gun turret. Stenning was determined to make it to the target, and he called out over the interphone, "We'll make it to the target yet. Get ready for the bomb run." However, just like *The Jolly Roger*, the aircraft began to burn within minutes. Stenning had no choice but to turn his wounded plane out of the formation as the flames increased in intensity. When *St. Peter's Ferry* neared Pitesti, he ordered the crew to bail out and sounded the bailout alarm.[31]

Back in the waist section, Sergeant Robert Graham climbed out of the ball turret as soon as the left waist gunner, Sergeant Donald Bieman, opened the hatch. When he climbed up into the fuselage, Graham saw Sergeant Arthur Burge, the right waist gunner, lying near his position in a pool of blood. He had been hit by shrapnel from a rocket fired by a German fighter and told the other gunners to "hit the silk" before falling to the deck, apparently dead. Bieman and the tail turret gunner, James Bennett, gestured to Graham, telling him to bail out.[32]

Bennett moved to the camera hatch door, opened it, and rolled out. Bieman, who had been wounded in the stomach by shrapnel from another German rocket, followed Bennett through the hatch, not realizing that the same shrapnel that had hit him had also torn through his parachute. While Bieman's parachute opened, several of the canopy panels had been shot through, causing the young gunner to fall to his death. His body was found by the Romanians near the town of Târgoviște.[33]

As Bennett and Bieman bailed out, Graham finished strapping on his parachute and prepared to bail out. However, as he passed by Sergeant Burge, he saw him move slightly. Realizing Burge was not dead after all, Graham bent down and shook him. Burge regained consciousness, and while the burning aircraft continued falling, Graham helped clip the parachute to the waist gunner's harness. Graham then went with Burge as he crawled toward the open camera hatch, assisted him in rolling out the opening, and then bailed out himself. Both men were captured, and while Graham became a POW and was liberated by Soviet forces in September 1944, Burge died of gangrene in a Bucharest hospital in July 1944.[34]

Meanwhile, in *St. Peter's Ferry*'s nose compartment, the navigator, Lieutenant Peter Marioles, told Lieutenant Robert Blaschke, the bombardier, to bail out. Blaschke opened the nose gear door hatch and said, "Pete, see you back in Italy!" He dropped down through the open gear door with Marioles and the radio operator, Sergeant Aaron Koenigseker, behind him. They all made it to the ground safely before being captured, although Blaschke hurt his back when he hit the ground.[35]

On the flight deck, Lieutenant Stenning continued to fight desperately to keep the aircraft under control as it continued its fiery descent. Even as it fell, German fighters continued to pursue their mortally wounded prey. Stenning ordered his copilot, Lieutenant William Robbins, to bail out. Robbins unstrapped from his seat and crawled through the tunnel into the nose section to bail out through the front gear doors. Meanwhile, Sergeant Wylie Carroll, the flight engineer, stood behind Stenning. Carroll helped Stenning into his parachute while the pilot fought the flight controls and bravely tried to keep flying the aircraft as long as possible. Carroll then donned his parachute and headed back toward the bomb bay to bail out. But when he reached the bulkhead, he discovered the bomb bay doors were jammed closed. As he tried to free them, the aircraft's structure buckled at the bulkhead, pinning him inside. Before he could extricate himself, the *St. Peter's Ferry* was forced to surrender to the flames consuming it and exploded in a ball of fire, killing both Carroll and Stenning. Romanian soldiers found their bodies in the wreckage of the plane a few miles outside the village of Moreni, and they were buried with full military honors.[36]

Lieutenant Claremont Brownell's *Super Moose* also took savage hits from the attacking Bf 109s. Many of the control cables seemed to have been shot away, and "Brownie," as he was called by his crew, immediately began to struggle with the flight controls along with his copilot, Lieutenant Dale Smith. Brownell ordered the crew to bail out. The aircraft began to burn, falling out of what was left of the formation between Slatina and Pitesti. Brownell and Smith knew they had to do all they could to keep the aircraft straight and level and stop it from rolling over until everyone could bail out.[37]

In the tail of the aircraft, the tail turret gunner, Sergeant Harold Wahl, had seen the attack by Rammelt's fighters begin and called out a warning over the intercom that Bf 109s were coming in from six o'-clock. Seconds after the attack began, however, Wahl's turret received a direct hit by 20mm cannon shells. The waist gunners saw a "bright flash" in the tail, followed by a dense cloud of smoke. When the smoke cleared, nothing remained there except wreckage, and "it seemed that one could walk right out of the tail of the ship." The tail gun turret had been completely blown off the aircraft, and Sergeant Wahl with it.[38]

As Rammelt's planes ripped *Super Moose* with machine-gun and cannon fire, one of their shells hit the top gun turret where the flight engineer, Sergeant Walard Harding, was trying to fend off the attacking enemy fighters. But the German shell hit Harding in the upper right arm, severely wounding him and making the arm unusable. He fell from the turret to the deck and called out for help. Lieutenant Smith immediately unstrapped from his copilot's seat and went to assist Harding. He could see there was no way Harding could put on his parachute, so Smith grabbed it and clipped it to the flight engineer's harness. But somehow, Smith had the presence of mind to realize that with Harding's right arm hanging limply by his side, there was no way he would be able to pull the rip cord with his right hand. So Smith unsnapped the parachute and reattached it upside down, allowing Harding to open his chute with his left hand.[39]

The bombardier, Lieutenant Samuel Cadwallader, had already opened the bomb bay doors, jettisoned the bombs, headed to the bomb bay, and attempted to put out a fire that had started there without success before bailing out through the open doors below. So Smith pulled Harding to his feet and guided him back to the bomb bay's

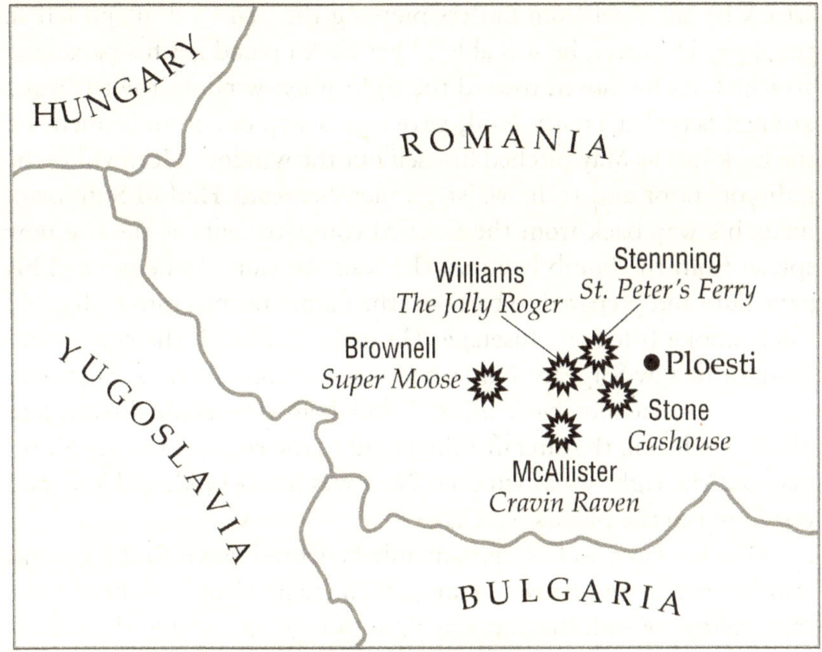

Locations of 451st Bomb Group aircraft lost during the Ploesti mission.

catwalk. As they stepped down onto the catwalk, Smith pushed Harding out through the open doors, and the flight engineer fell safely away from the aircraft. At that moment, Smith could have found his own parachute and followed Harding to safety, but he did not do so. Instead, he returned to the cockpit, strapped himself into his seat, and helped Brownell fight for control of the aircraft.[40]

In the nose section, the navigator, Lieutenant Robert Berg, could see the flames consuming the aft part of the aircraft and knew the ship "was beyond saving." As soon as the bailout command was given, he and the nose turret gunner, Sergeant Keith Westphal, donned their parachutes and moved to the nose gear door hatch to kick it open. As the icy wind from the slipstream filled the nose and blew Berg's charts around the compartment, Berg slid down through the opening, followed seconds later by Westphal.[41]

In the waist section, Sergeant Alan May had climbed out of his ball turret and begun clipping on his own parachute. He was suddenly struck by shrapnel from bullets piercing the plane's skin and fell to the deck. However, he was able to get back up and get his parachute attached. As he moved toward the right waist window, the left waist gunner, Sergeant Henry Noll, gave him a slap of encouragement on the back just as May pitched himself out the window. Meanwhile, the radio operator and right waist gunner, Sergeant Harold Shireman, made his way back from the forward compartments as the fire now spread from the bomb bay into the waist section. As he donned his parachute and prepared to bail out, the flames burned him badly, and thick smoke filled the fuselage. He looked through the smoke and thought he saw Sergeant Noll's body on the floor. As far as Shireman knew, Noll had not been injured, but before he could investigate Noll's condition, the aircraft rolled hard to the right, throwing Shireman out the right waist window. Noll was left behind, and his body was found in the plane's wreckage[42]

Minutes later, as five crew members drifted down to the ground in their parachutes, Brownell and Smith tried valiantly to keep *Super Moose* under control. But this was all in vain. Minutes later, the aircraft exploded, killing them both. Their bodies were found by the Romanians in the wreckage of the aircraft about fifteen miles south of Pitesti.[43]

The final aircraft from the 727th's low flight was *Cravin Raven*, flown by Lieutenant Winfred McAllister. The plane was hit by everything the Germans had to fire at them—rockets, machine-gun bullets, and 20mm cannon shells—and was last seen descending rapidly. While the aircraft fell out of formation after the first attack, the intercom was shot out during a second pass by Rammelt's fighters, and the aircraft caught fire in the center of the fuselage. Two of the crew members, Sergeant John Oprisko, the ball turret gunner, and Sergeant John Wood, the right waist gunner, were hit by enemy fire. Oprisko managed to bail out but died of his wounds a few days later. Wood was hit by a 20mm cannon shell that blew off his head.[44]

Lieutenants Jack Sergent, navigator, and Alphonso Szymanek, bombardier, both bailed out, most likely through the nose gear door hatch, were captured, and became POWs. Sergeants Charles Bistline (flight engineer), John Massa (left waist gunner), and Milton Wexler (tail turret gunner) all bailed out successfully and were captured. The plane's copilot, Lieutenant William Story, also managed to bail out,

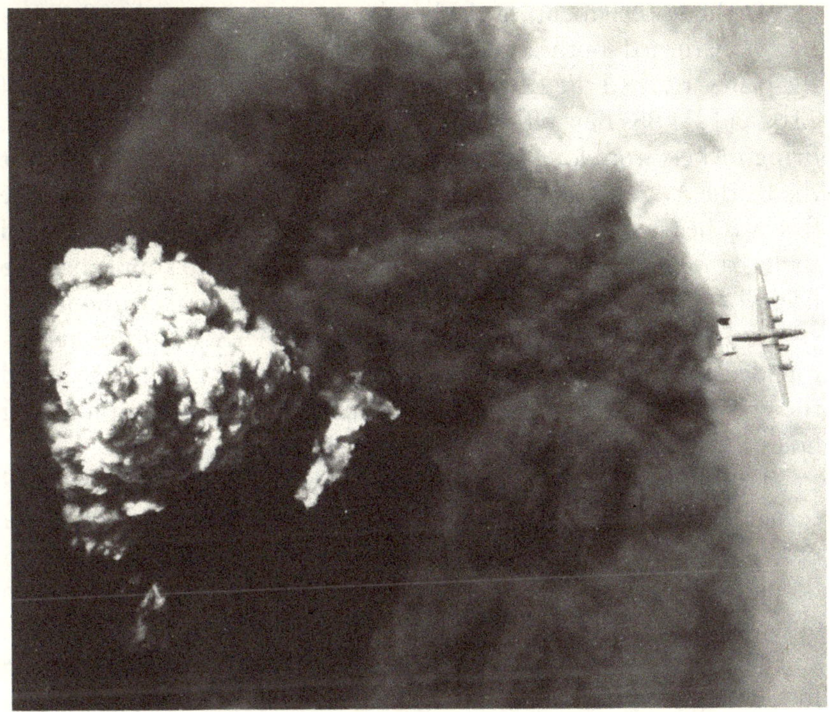

A B-24 of the 451st Bomb Group flies past the explosions and fires from the Astra Romana refining complex. (*National Archives*)

but his parachute never opened, either because it failed or because he had been rendered unconscious during his exit from the aircraft.[45]

Meanwhile, Sergeant Joe Schermerhorn, the plane's radio operator, must have become trapped onboard, as his body was found near the wreckage with his parachute unopened. Like Lieutenants Stenning and Brownell, the pilot, Lieutenant McAllister, remained at the aircraft's controls until it was too late, and the aircraft exploded in midair. His body was recovered from the wreckage and buried with full military honors in the village of Bogați, Romania.

While it took multiple passes and several minutes for Rammelt's men to finish off the 727th's low flight, all the planes were severely damaged during the first pass by JG 51s fighters. Within just three minutes, the entire formation of four B-24s had been sent reeling toward the ground.[46]

As the lead elements of the bomber stream reached the IP at Ocnita, they turned southeast, heading toward the target at Ploesti. Once the planes reached the IP, the fighters pulled back, although some Bf 110s and JU 88s flew off to the side and out of range of the bombers, firing rockets from long range. With no fighters near the bombers at the IP, the AAA batteries around Ploesti opened fire. As expected, the flak was heavy and varied from aimed fire, where the batteries fired shells based on the estimated track of the bombers, to simple barrage fire, where the Germans fired at the bomber formations without precisely aiming. However, no matter how the AAA was fired, it surrounded the formations in a dense pattern of gray-black bursts, and the crews could hear shrapnel "banging, clattering, and punching holes through the thin skin of the B-24."[47]

The planes from the 451st arrived at the IP at about 2:40 PM and turned toward the target. The morning clouds had cleared, and the target immediately appeared about twenty-five miles ahead. Even though the Germans had ignited smoke pots around the complex to obscure it from sight, the surface winds dispersed much of the smoke, and the bombardiers had no difficulty finding their aimpoint in the marshaling yards. One bomber after another released its loads, and in the words of one crew member, "We really clobbered them that day. Flames shot high in the air, and we could see secondary explosions in the refinery and loading areas."[48]

With numerous fires clearly visible throughout the refinery and rail complex, clouds of smoke that were "visible for miles" rose into the afternoon sky. In the second of the 451st squadron waves, Captain Stone turned the *Gashouse* toward the target, switched on the autopilot, and handed control of the aircraft to his bombardier, Lieutenant Russell Crans. As Crans guided the aircraft to the release point, Stone could hear shrapnel striking the *Gashouse*. Down in the nose section, Crans opened the bomb bay doors, located the aiming point with his bombsight, and released the load, calling out "Bombs away!" over the intercom. He turned and looked up at Johnston, and the two men nodded at one another in approval.[49]

With the bombs released on the target, Captain Stone took control of the aircraft and started the right turn away from the target. However, almost as soon as he had the yoke back in his hands, he "heard and felt an explosion in the aircraft," which Johnston later said sounded like a "thud" on the left wing. On the flight deck, Stone looked over his left shoulder and saw that a AAA shell had hit the left wing and exploded just outboard of the number one engine. The effects of the explosion were immediately apparent. Stone said, "A rather large hole was in the wing, parts of a fuel tank was flapping in the wind, the left aileron cable was either jammed, or severed, and the #1 engine was dead."[50]

The *Gashouse* began to labor, swerving to the right in a "slow, gradual descent." As Stone struggled to regain control, the copilot, Major Beane, ordered the crew to bail out, saying over the intercom, "Get the hell out of here, boys, and make it quick!" Stone was able to get the aircraft into a more stable state by reducing power to engines three and four on the right wing while increasing power to the number two engine on the left. Stone managed to turn the aircraft west, but the *Gashouse* continued to lose altitude rapidly.[51]

As Johnston and Crans heard the command to bail out, followed by the bailout alarm ringing, the two men pulled the emergency handle on the nose gear doors and opened the hatch. Johnston bent over to make his jump out the hatch when Crans "booted" him "in the butt," and the navigator fell through the open hatch, still wearing his oxygen mask with his oxygen hose trailing behind him until it broke off from its connector. Crans followed him out the nose gear hatch, but neither man knew that the nose turret gunner, Sergeant Bennie Hayman, had never heard the command to bail out because his interphone was out.[52]

Hayman was firing at a German fighter coming in from twelve o'clock when he turned around to see Johnston and Crans bailing out. He immediately climbed out of the turret but could not find his parachute. After madly looking about, Hayman saw it had slid about three feet from where he had stowed it. The nose turret gunner quickly snapped it into his harness, moved to the nose gear door hatch, and jumped out feet first.[53]

When Sergeant John Steurer, the flight engineer, heard the order to bail out, he was manning the top gun turret. After donning his chute, he saw that the bomb bay doors were open and walked across the catwalk to the rear of the aircraft to check on the two waist gunners, Sergeants Patrick Marnell and Robert Yeaton; the ball turret gunner, Sergeant Eugene Cuff; and the tail turret gunner, Sergeant William

Berry. When he saw that no one was wounded and everyone had already bailed out, he turned back to the bomb bay and safely left the aircraft.[54]

Captain Stone and Major Beane were still flying the aircraft as a new set of Bf 109s began attacking the wounded plane. By this time, attacking bombers that had been damaged and fallen out of formation had become a standard Luftwaffe tactic, which they called *Herrausschutz*. This was often highly effective in assuring the destruction of the bomber. Still, in this case, it was even more effective because all the gunners aboard *Gashouse* had bailed out. The fighter attacks set the right wing on fire, and their bullets penetrated the cockpit, slamming into the back of Stone's seat. A 20mm cannon shell also came through the left side of the cockpit, exploding below Stone's seat and wounding him in the left leg and knee.[55]

With the right wing ablaze, Stone realized further attempts to keep the *Gashouse* flying were hopeless. Major Beane made a quick intercom check to see if anyone else was still onboard and then got up to visually check the nose and waist sections. Once he told Stone everyone was gone, the two men donned their parachutes, went to the bomb bay, and bailed out. When they were out of the aircraft, the *Gashouse* rolled over and dived toward the ground before crashing and exploding in a valley below.[56]

The remaining aircraft from the 451st made the return trip without incident. All the German fighter attacks ceased about fifteen minutes after the B-24s turned away from the target. As the formation started back over Yugoslavia, their P-38 fighter escort finally arrived, although clearly too late and too far from the target to do any good.

The 451st lost five aircraft, with four more damaged, not including the plane that crashed during takeoff. In addition, the postmission Daily Operations Report listed nine aircrew killed in action, with seventeen more missing in action. While the 451st's losses had been severe, the damage to the Ploesti target was significant. In total, Fifteenth Air Force bombers had dropped 588 tons of bombs, with most missing the marshaling yards. However, those bombs that missed the marshaling yards had hit the Astra Romana refining complex, and its "production capacity had been significantly compromised." Furthermore, the 451st's gunners downed eighteen enemy fighters, scoring eleven more as probable kills.[57]

On July 12, 1944, the 451st received its second Distinguished Unit Citation for the mission to Ploesti. In September, when General Nathan Twining, commander of the Fifteenth Air Force, formally presented the citations for the Regensburg and Ploesti missions, he said, "The 451st went through two of the hardest aerial battles in the Mediterranean theater to earn the battle streamers and accomplished both of them with a maximum of success, much to the enemy's loss."[58]

A German fighter plane, right, pulls away after successfully attacking *Extra Joker*, left, which is going down in flames. (*National Archives*)

Chapter Six

Overwhelming Opposition

Markersdorf, August 23, 1944

On August 23, 1944, Captain George Tudor, a twenty-six-year-old pilot from Nebraska,[1] was assigned to the lead position for the 725th Bomb Squadron, which was to fly at the rear of the 451st's group formation in an attack on the Markersdorf Airdrome west of Vienna where German Bf 109 aircraft awaited final assembly. His squadron formation was supposed to have included seven aircraft from the 725th. However, two aircraft aborted the mission on the ground, and another was forced to return to Castelluccio while over the Adriatic because of problems with its engine superchargers. This left his element of the 451st's formation with only four aircraft. Further, Tudor and his crew were not flying their usual aircraft, a B-24H they had christened as the *Extra Joker*.[2]

That name had been given to the plane when Tudor and his crew made their initial overseas deployment and stopped in Marrakech, Morocco. While the crew chief was performing his preflight checks before the aircraft and crew departed Marrakech for Tunis, Tunisia, he found a playing card lying on the ground beneath the plane, and that card was the extra joker. After takeoff, the crew chief went forward to the cockpit, told Tudor about finding the card, and suggested *Extra Joker* as the name for the plane. Everyone agreed that was a good name, and later, "Extra Joker" was painted onto the aircraft's nose.

However, the bombing requirements for Tudor's crew on the Markersdorf mission made the *Extra Joker* a liability. This was because the plane was equipped with a Sperry bombsight. Tudor's bombardier, Lieutenant Bob Donovan, said the Sperry bombsight had an inadequate trail or rate setting capability for dropping the 120-pound fragmentation bombs they would be carrying on this day's mission. As one man later put it, because of their relatively low weight, these fragmentation bombs tended to fly in every direction when released and looked like a "picket fence." Since Tudor's aircraft was to lead the squadron, Donovan needed to make his release as accurately as possible, and a Norden bombsight would be required. As it happened, a new aircraft named *Thunder Mug* was parked next to the *Extra Joker*, and it had a Norden bombsight installed. So after Tudor met with the new aircraft's pilot, Lieutenant Kenneth Whiting, the two aircraft commanders agreed to swap planes for the mission, with Whiting to fly on Tudor's right wing as deputy lead in the *Extra Joker*.[3]

Several hours later, as the 451st's planes approached the IP for the target, they flew over a cloud deck from which German Bf 109s had been climbing to quickly attack the formation before darting back down through the clouds. Unfortunately, the 451st's fighter escort of P-51s broke with tactical protocol and dived down through the clouds in pursuit of the German fighters, leaving the formation unprotected. With the American fighter escorts gone, another group of German fighters unleashed their main attack on the B-24s.[4]

In waves of ten to fifteen aircraft, Fw 190s, the Luftwaffe's vaunted "Butcher Bird," dived down on the bombers, firing their deadly 20mm cannons long before they came within range of the B-24s' .50-caliber machine guns. As the 451st's lead aircraft called frantically for help from the American fighter escorts, the Fw 190s swept through the formation before breaking off to the left or right, positioning themselves for another attack. From his place at the rear of the group's formation, Tudor could see one bomber after another seriously damaged and falling out of formation. The sky ahead seemed filled with men bailing out and opening their parachutes in desperate attempts to escape their burning bombers. George Tudor later wrote that "watching the bodies eject from the planes ahead" was one of his most vivid recollections from the war.[5]

But it was not just the aircraft ahead of him that were being brutally attacked by the waves of German fighters. When Tudor's crew turned to their right, they looked on in horror as the *Extra Joker* was savagely assaulted by the Fw 190s. It quickly caught fire as 20mm cannon shells repeatedly smashed into the fuselage. Tudor's right waist gunner, Sergeant Lindley Miller, could clearly see the *Extra Joker* out his waist window. Later, he said it was "really a horrible and terrifying sight to see her get it." As the flames grew and began to consume the entire aircraft, the *Extra Joker* flew along for a while "like a roman candle." Its fuselage was covered in holes from the cannon shells, which likely meant there was catastrophic damage inside to equipment, like the control cables, as well as the crew members. No one would ever know with certainty what damage was done because, within minutes, the *Extra Joker* fell from the formation in flames. Even though it was clearly too damaged to stay in the air, German fighters continued to pursue the *Extra Joker* while it fell in its death throes, slamming more deadly cannon fire into the bomber. It did not take long for the aircraft to go into a tight spin with nothing left of the plane but a "mass of flames."[6]

No one saw any parachutes emerge from the conflagration, and all ten men were presumed dead. They were not alone, however, as many more aircraft and men would be lost over Markersdorf that day.

On April 6, 1944, the day following the first Ploesti mission, the 451st started moving to what would be its final base for the remainder of the war: Castelluccio. The airfield was about three miles northeast of the village of Castelluccio di Sauri and almost ten miles south of Foggia, where the Fifteenth Air Force had its headquarters. The base had been built by the Army Corps of Engineers as part of a complex of Fifteenth Air Force airfields established within twenty-five miles of Foggia. It included one Marston Mat five-thousand-foot-long runway oriented roughly northwest to southeast with a cleared area for gear-up crash landings on either side. There were also taxiways leading from dispersed parking places in revetments, which were also constructed using Marston Mat.[7]

The group moved via truck and aircraft and completed its initial deployment in three days. The new base was on a high, flat plateau prone to dust storms when the weather was dry. The only building on the airfield was a large villa that once was the home for the Italian admiral who owned the land, which was immediately claimed by Colonel Eaton for his group headquarters. However, some outlying barns were scattered across the base, and one of them became the briefing room. Another was used for training sessions, while an old chicken coop became a barber and tailor shop. But the four squadron staffs were not to be denied facilities that were at least a little better than tents and immediately began building houses made of limestone blocks. While the field was still somewhat crude, and most of the officers and men continued to live in tents, it was a vast improvement. Karl Eichhorn of the 726th later said, "It was a beautiful sight to behold after our experiences at Gioia and San Pancrazio!"[8]

Each squadron had its own designated area. The 726th was near the northwest end of the runway, while the 725th was just east of the 726th's area. The 724th was based at the other end of the runway near the group headquarters, and the 727th found itself on the far side of the runway near its center. Some men quickly discovered a small stream that flowed around the 726th's part of the plateau and used it to take a bath in its "ice-cold water," only the second bath many of them had had since leaving the United States four months before.[9]

Within a few days, all the group's men had set up their tents, stoves, bunks, and larger tents near the flightline to support the ground crews. Things were also improved by the presence of many former soldiers from the Italian army. These men were hired by the Army Air Force, and some worked in the kitchens while others labored to construct the stone block buildings on the base. Many of them turned out to be good masons. By early summer, they had constructed an officers' club and several buildings that served as workshops for the ground crews. During this period, the 451st was reassigned from the 47th Bomb Wing to the new 49th Bomb Wing. The new organization was an outgrowth of what was originally a training wing based in the United States. Between February and April 1944, the 49th Bomb Wing moved to Italy and was assigned the 451st, 461st, and 484th Bomb Groups.[10]

On April 12, the 451st flew its first mission from Castelluccio and its first mission under the 49th Bomb Wing. Missions continued throughout spring and summer 1944, and the group flew eight more missions to Ploesti from May to mid-August before the oil fields were captured by the advancing Red Army on August 30. Further, it flew missions on August 14 and 15 to support Operation Dragoon, the name given to the Allied invasion of southern France. During May through July, an increasing number of missions were flown against targets in and around Vienna. The area was home to oil refineries, critical rail infrastructure, and aircraft manufacturing facilities like the Messerschmidt factory at Weiner Neustadt.[11]

During spring and summer 1944, Weiner Neustadt had been subjected to especially heavy bombing. In fact, the bombing of Weiner Neustadt and the sites of other aircraft manufacturing plants forced the Germans to begin dispersing their manufacturing and assembly efforts. For the plant at Weiner Neustadt, this involved moving operations to Bad Vöslau, about eighteen miles southwest of Vienna, and Zwöllfaxing, around eight miles southeast of Vienna. The third dispersal location was the Markersdorf Airdrome, twenty-one miles west-northwest of the Austrian capital. Because the airfield had two large hangars, one of which was almost fifteen thousand square feet, and a large parking apron, the Germans decided to move the final assembly of Bf 109s from Weiner Neustadt to Markersdorf. The hangars provided space for workers to assemble the aircraft component structures into a finished aircraft. Once each aircraft was assembled, it was moved outdoors onto the parking apron before being flown to an operational unit. As a result of these actions, the Markersdorf Airdrome became a target for the Fifteenth Air Force.[12]

The airfield at Markersdorf was built in 1938, shortly after the Anschluss incorporating Austria into Nazi Germany. The ceremonial first spade of earth for construction of the airdrome was dug by none other than Hermann Göring, the German government's minister for air and head of the Luftwaffe. The base had a grass field for takeoffs and landings, concrete taxiways and parking, and brick barracks capable of housing 2,500 men. The airdrome had been used as a training base for most of the war. However, once aircraft assembly moved there from Weiner Neustadt, Allied intelligence did not take long to discover its new role. It was bombed for the first time on July 8, 1944, which was followed by another attack on July 26. These raids damaged the hangars and destroyed as many as thirty aircraft but did not stop the assembly operations.[13]

On August 22, 1944, the 451st received orders from the Fifteenth Air Force via the 49th Bomb Wing to participate in a mission against the Markersdorf Airdrome the following day. The plan called for all three bomb groups from the 49th to make the attack with the 484th in the lead, followed by the 451st and then the 461st. The planes from the 49th would be the first over the target, with four more bomb groups from the 55th Bomb Wing coming in after them. The 451st was to put twenty-eight B-24s into the air, seven from each squadron. All the 451st's aircraft would carry 120-pound fragmentation bombs, which were to be targeted in the area where completed Bf 109s were parked. At the same time, the planes from the 55th that followed would drop 500-pound general-purpose bombs on the assembly hangars.[14]

Engine start was scheduled for 7:30 AM, with taxi at 7:40 and takeoff at 7:50. The route for the mission called for the 451st to rendezvous with the 484th southeast of Castelluccio over Bovino at an altitude of six thousand feet, and the 461st would join as the trailing group. From there, the wing formation would turn north and climb to a base altitude of twelve thousand feet by the time it reached a position called the "Key Point," which was midway across the Adriatic. The wing would turn to the northeast, cross the Yugoslav coast, and continue until it reached Ormoz, Yugoslavia, climbing to an altitude of nineteen thousand to twenty thousand feet. The formation would turn north toward Friedberg, Austria, before turning northwest to the IP for the bomb run at Hohenberg, Austria. From the IP, the bomb run was to be made on a heading of 345° for twenty miles to the target. After the bomb release, the group would turn to the left to rally before heading southeast back into Yugoslavia, with the next leg going southwest back over the Adriatic before landing at Castelluccio.[15]

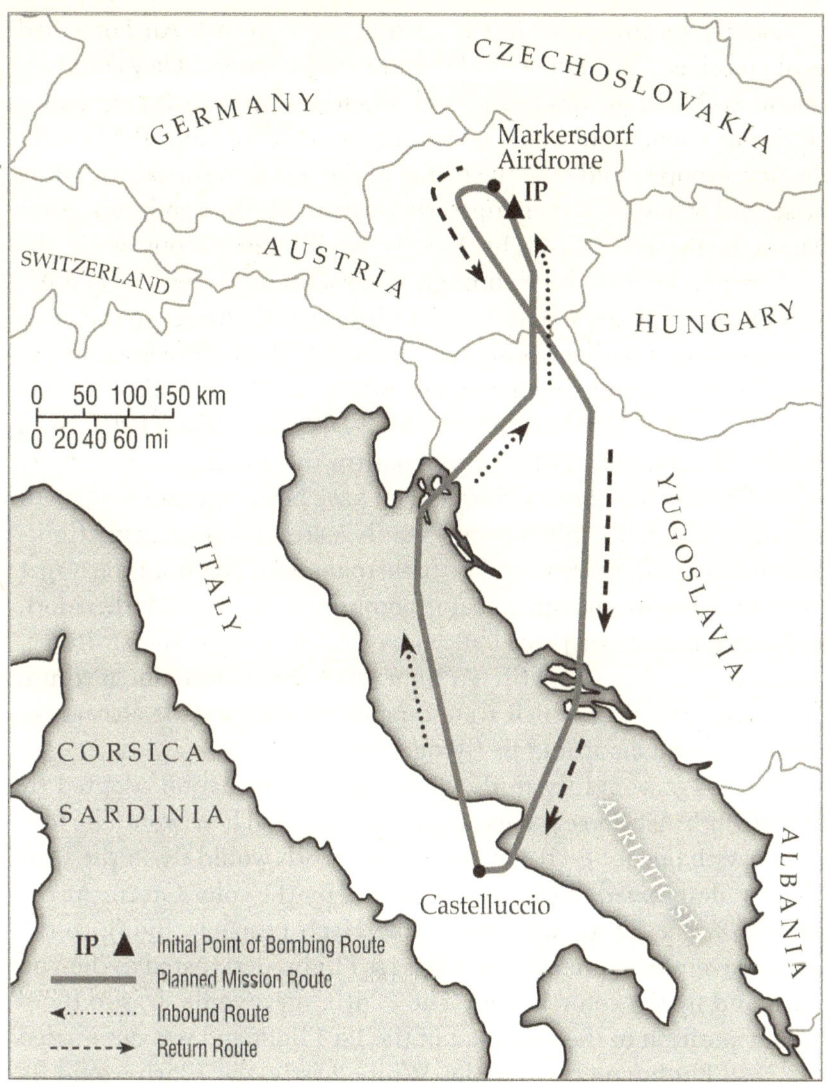

The route used by the 451st Bomb Group on the mission to Markersdorf, August 23, 1944.

Luckily, by this point in the air war, the Fifteenth Air Force had finally received long-range P-51D and P-38J fighters. They could escort the B-24s to the target and back when equipped with drop tanks. For this mission, there would be two groups of forty-eight P-51s each. The first group would take the planes of the 451st to the target, while the second would pick them up as they turned off the bomb run. After that, a flight of forty-eight P-38Js would rendezvous with the bombers to take them back through Yugoslavia until they reached Allied-controlled airspace. However, the Intelligence Annex to the wing operations order had one ominous statement: "Fighter defense of VIENNA area will probably not exceed 60-70. . . . There is also the possibility of an additional 35-40 ME 109s and FW 190s from MUNICH. Operations of 22 Aug confirm the indications that more enemy fighters have been airborne than have been encountered by our formations on earlier missions to VIENNA area." While enemy fighters were expected, there would be little to no AAA fire from the target this time. Despite the other major bombing attacks on Markersdorf, the Germans had not placed any heavy AAA guns at the airdrome. The only guns there were fifteen light AAA pieces and nine medium AAA pieces, none of which were capable of reaching the altitude at which the bombers would be flying.[16]

The 451st would fly in the new diamond formation adopted by the Fifteenth Air Force earlier in summer 1944. There would be four flights, with one for each squadron. The 726th would fly in the Lead position, designated as the 1st Flight and by the color Green. At the same time, the 727th would take the High position, flying to the right, above, and slightly behind the 1st Flight, designated as the 2nd Flight and by the color Yellow. The 724th, meanwhile, was to fly in the Low position to the lower left of the 1st Flight and was designated as the 3rd Flight and by the color White. Lastly, the 725th would fly in the Tail position in the center rear of the group's formation, designated as the 4th Flight and by the color Red.[17]

The lead aircraft for the group would come from the 726th, flying in the number one position in the 1st Flight. As was the case whenever the group commander chose to fly in the group's lead aircraft, Colonel Eaton flew as copilot on the lead plane with the squadron commander serving as pilot and aircraft commander, which in this case was Major Tom Walkey. Eaton could have flown as the pilot, but he believed that

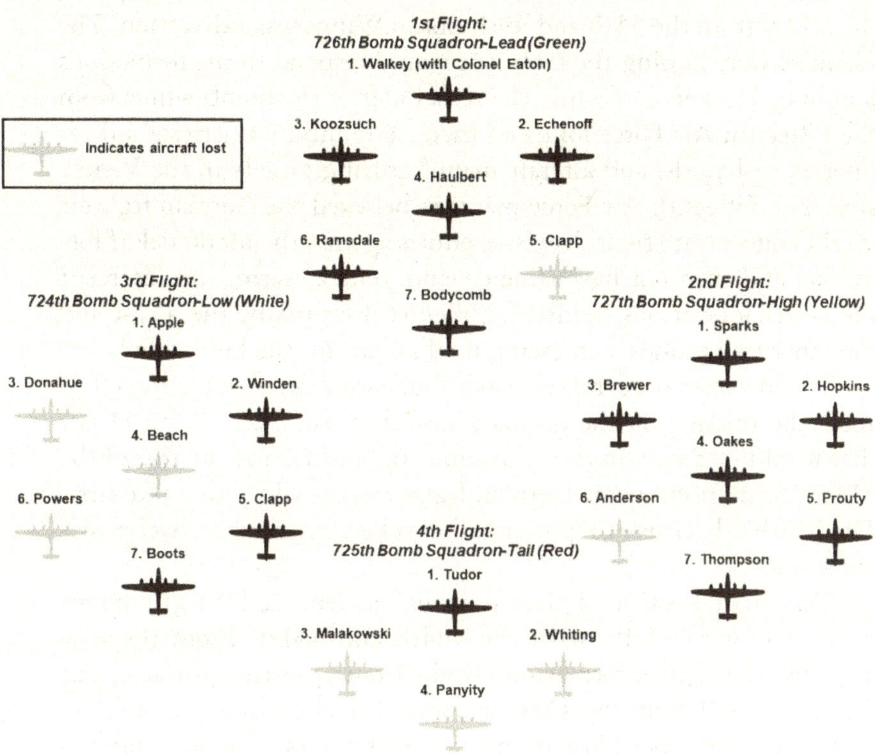

The 451st Bomb Group formation on August 23, 1944. (*Author*)

experience indicated one pilot could not properly fly the aircraft and simultaneously exercise command of the group. Further, the lead aircraft also had the Group Navigator, Lieutenant Ralph Byers, and Group Bombardier, Lieutenant Frederick Hughes (known casually as "Honest" Hughes), flying in their respective positions.[18]

The mission began as did every other one, with ground crews working diligently to prepare all twenty-eight aircraft assigned to the mission. This task was more challenging in this case because the group had flown on a mission to Vienna the preceding day. As the ground crews continued their work, the aircrews were awakened early for breakfast and the mission briefing. While the details of the planned attack were covered in the briefing, the aircrews were not told that the mission to the Markersdorf Airdrome by their bomb group and the others from the 55th and 49th Bomb Wings was a diversion. The planners were hoping the Germans would respond to the formations bombing Markersdorf while the remainder of the bomb wings from the Fifteenth Air Force followed them to bomb more-critical oil refineries, rail yards, and aircraft manufacturing targets in the Vienna area. The Fifteenth Air Force planners believed the German fighters might concentrate their defensive efforts against the Markersdorf formation and then not have time to land, refuel, rearm, and intercept the larger formations headed for Vienna. Essentially, the 451st and the other two groups were being used as bait for the Luftwaffe.[19]

Engine start occurred on time, but two aircraft were forced to abort the mission on the ground, both from the 725th's 4th Flight that would be flying in the vulnerable Tail position at the rear of the 451st's formation, where German fighters were likely to strike first. The 725th's defensive firepower had now been reduced by twelve machine guns.[20]

Taxi and takeoff took place without incident, and the group rendezvoused successfully with the 484th and 461st. From the rendezvous, the wing's formation climbed out over the Adriatic, but another aircraft from the 451st was forced to abort due to a problem with one of its superchargers and returned to Castelluccio. Unfortunately, the aircraft was also from the 725th, which meant the planes flying in the Tail position had just lost the defensive firepower from six more machine guns.[21]

As expected, German radar picked up the approaching bomber stream as it approached the Yugoslav coast and began forwarding tracking information. In this case, as soon as the 484th aircraft turned to the north at Ormoz, the Jagdfliegerführer at JaFü Ostmark began alerting his fighter assets and scrambling them into the air. One of the fighter units dispatched to intercept the bombers was IV. (Sturm)/JG 3, a highly experienced fighter *gruppe* led by Hauptman Wilhelm Moritz. They took off in Fw 190s from Schongau Airfield, Germany, about thirty-five miles southwest of Munich, at 10:10 AM. This meant the statement in the Intelligence Annex about enemy fighters coming from the Munich area for the mission was correct. While Schongau was 214 miles west-southwest of Markersdorf, it was still well within the combat radius for the heavily armed Fw 190s.[22]

Unknown to the 451st's aircrews, these fighters had their own diversionary plan waiting for the Americans.

As the 49th Bomb Wing turned northeast at Ormoz, they were joined by the P-51s assigned to escort them to the target. The friendly fighters took their usual position high above and to either side of the bombers from where they could pounce on any approaching German fighters, and the bombers crossed into Austria. As they went farther into Austria, a deck of heavy cumulus clouds began to build up, rising to seventeen thousand feet, a mere two thousand feet below the bomber formations, which were now headed north before turning northeast toward the IP. At the same time, other cumulus clouds began to build in towering formations on either side of the bombers' flight path, reaching as high as twenty-three thousand feet.[23] This type of cloud can often grow into formations that produce violent thunderstorms, which could be dangerous for any aircraft that flew nearby or through them. While these clouds did not build into thunderstorms, the cumulus clouds below and on either side of the 451st planes hid a more urgent danger: German fighters.

As the 451st's bombers approached the mountains about twelve miles south of the IP, they remained close behind the planes from the 484th. However, the 461st's formation allowed a cloud deck to come between them and the rear of the 451st. Flying through these dense clouds, they momentarily became lost. When they emerged from the clouds, there was a large gap between them and the rear of the 451st's formation, a gap the German fighters were about to exploit. Seeing the trailing end of the 451st's planes exposed, the Germans elected to leave the 484th's formation alone and concentrate on the 451st in a series of three attacks.[24]

Usually, German fighters employed tactics designed to allow them to attack straggling bombers that had been damaged by flak. However, in this case, knowing there was no AAA at Markersdorf that could hit the bombers, they decided to make aggressive attacks designed to break up the 451st's formation before it reached the target. The first attack came about 12:10 PM. Bf 109s that had hidden themselves in the cloud deck just below the bombers suddenly accelerated and climbed directly out of the clouds, opening fire on the 451st B-24s as they closed in from five to seven o'clock. The gunners onboard the bombers called out the threat and opened fire as the Bf 109s quickly dived back into the cloud cover and "went down to the deck."[25]

At this point, it would have been standard tactics for a few P-51s escorting the formation to pursue the Germans as they dived through the clouds toward the ground. However, on this occasion, the entire escort group of forty-eight P-51s dived down and through the clouds, chasing the Bf 109s. These first attacks were a clever diversionary tactic by the Germans and worked flawlessly. With all the P-51s making an aggressive, headlong pursuit of the enemy aircraft, the 451st's bombers were left to defend themselves against a German force estimated to include as many as fifty Fw 190s.[26]

Seeing the P-51s depart, the Fw 190s dived down through the clouds, coming in from the bombers' rear quadrant. The first wave of enemy fighters had six to ten aircraft, and five more waves came in behind them. Each wave seemed to pick its own box of one B-24 squadron flight and blast away at them with their 20mm cannons, seeming to concentrate their fire on the area between the ball turret and the tail turret. When each wave reached a point about three hundred yards away from the bomber box, they would split up into two groups, break off to the right and left, reform, and make another attack from three or nine o'clock in waves of three to five Fw 190s each, targeting any bombers that seemed to have been damaged by the first wave.[27]

The next phase of the fighter attacks was the "main brunt," lasting about five minutes as the 451st's formation approached the IP. The aerial assault by the German fighters continued throughout the bomb run, focusing on damaged B-24s. In these assaults, the Fw 190s attacked singly from three o'clock to nine o'clock low, climbing up through the bomber formation in the costliest enemy attacks for the group's bombers.[28]

During the initial German fighter attacks, Colonel Eaton made "frantic efforts" to contact the fighter escort and get them to return to defend the bombers, but to no avail. Several of the Fw 190s concentrated their attacks on the 725th's 4th Flight flying in the Tail position. Their 20mm cannons wreaked havoc first on the *Extra Joker*, flying behind and to the right of the squadron's lead aircraft, flown by George Tudor. As the enemy cannon shells slammed into the *Extra Joker*'s fuselage, the plane suddenly caught fire midship and under-

Extra Joker in flames as German 20mm cannon shells strike its fuselage. (*National Archives*)

neath the left wing. The fire consumed the entire aircraft within minutes as the *Extra Joker* fell from formation in a ball of flame. Even though the bomber was mortally damaged, the Fw 190s followed it down as it went into a spin. The crew of Tudor's plane watched in vain for any men bailing out as the *Extra Joker* finally fell from view before crashing about six miles northwest of the IP.[29]

Two other aircraft in the 725th's flight suffered a similar fate. One of those was the aircraft flown by Lieutenant Glenn Panyity, whose plane occupied the "tail-end Charlie" position at the rear of both the 725th's and the group formation. From his right waist position in Tudor's aircraft, Sergeant Lindley Miller saw the enemy's 20mm fire "cut him [Panyity's aircraft] in half at the ball turret."[30] Corporal Wilbur Williams, who was Panyity's tail turret gunner, later reported that he believed Panyity was killed in the attack because there was no bailout signal given from the cockpit. Williams also said that the nose turret gunner, Corporal Charles Maurath, was killed instantly by a 20mm shell that made a direct hit on the nose turret. With the aircraft obviously in serious trouble, Williams bailed out along with navigator Lieutenant John Hoyt, bombardier Lieutenant Grover Blevins, radio operator Corporal Ephraim Rump, left waist gunner Private Emanuel Baier, and ball turret gunner Sergeant Jack Glance. They all left the aircraft at the right time as the entire tail section came off, followed by the wings. At that point, the plane went into a spin, crashing about a mile southeast of Naßwald, Austria, where the Germans found the bodies of Lieutenant Panyity along with those of copilot Lieutenant John Carroll and flight engineer Sergeant William Hurst. German reports indicated all three bodies, as well as that of Corporal Maurath, were buried at the crash site, which was in a dense forest. The men who bailed out were all captured by the Germans near Naßwald. The two officers were sent to Stalag Luft III near Żagań, Poland, and the enlisted men went to Stalag Luft IV near Tychowo, Poland.[31]

The other aircraft in the 725th formation fatally hit by the German fighters was *Seldom Available*, flown by Lieutenant Willis Malakowski in the number three position to the left rear of Tudor's *Thunder Mug*. The Fw 190s knocked out the number three engine, which Malakowski and his copilot, Lieutenant John Murray, successfully feathered. In the attacks, the tail turret gunner, Corporal Robert Suvada, was wounded in the right arm but continued to operate his guns. Malakowski advanced the throttles on his three good engines and remained with the formation as his gunners battled the continuing enemy fighter attacks. *Seldom Available* made it to the bomb run and the turn off the target, but eyewitnesses say the aircraft began to struggle after that and lose altitude.[32]

When the aircraft was about fifty miles southwest of the target near Bruck an der Mur, Austria, it became clear the plane was no longer flyable. Malakowski ordered the crew to bail out. Sergeant Clyde Phillips, the flight engineer and top turret gunner, went to the aircraft's rear to ensure everyone had heard the bailout order. Phillips returned to the open bomb bay, where he, Malakowski, and Murray bailed out. Ball turret gunner Corporal Carroll Wyman, right waist gunner Corporal Samuel Morehead, left waist gunner Corporal Louis Anthony, and Suvada bailed out through the open camera hatch while nose turret gunner Corporal William Busby, navigator Lieutenant Howard Brown, and bombardier Lieutenant Robert Rhillinger made their way out of the aircraft via the nose gear door hatch. All ten crew members landed near Bruck an der Mur and were taken into custody by the Germans and Austrian civil police. As with the crew from Panyity's plane, the officers were sent to Stalag Luft III while the enlisted men became POWs at Stalag Luft IV.[33] With the loss of *Seldom Available*, George Tudor's plane was the only one in the group formation from the 725th that made it home to Castelluccio.

But the 725th's flight was not the only one suffering losses. In the 727th's 2nd Flight flying in the High position, Lieutenant Robert Anderson's plane, *Weesie*, was positioned in the number six slot in the left rear of the formation just in front and to the left of Lieutenant Harold Thompson's plane, *Our Gal*. *Weesie* was hit by fire from the Fw 190s, which caused two engines to become engulfed in flames. Anderson was forced out of formation about five miles south of the IP, which only caused the German fighters to concentrate their efforts on bringing the wounded B-24 down. Soon, however, the two engines were the least of Anderson's worries when a large fire broke out in the bomb bay. It was clear the crew had to bail out. Anderson, copilot Lieutenant Carl McConnell, navigator Lieutenant Charles Foley, nose turret gunner Corporal William Miller, and flight engineer and top turret gunner Sergeant George Gilbert were able to bail out. The four other crew members apparently did not do so. The bodies of Sergeant Bronson Grubbs and Corporal Julian Ford, who were last seen at their respective positions in the ball turret and tail turret, were never recovered. However, the two waist gunners, Corporal Joseph Karpinski and Sergeant Charles Hermann, were onboard when the aircraft exploded and crashed north of the town of Neuberg an der Mürz. After Sergeant Gilbert was captured by local authorities, a civilian police officer showed him the severely burned dog tags of both men. The police officer told Gilbert that their bodies had been found in the plane's wreckage on a nearby mountainside. Anderson, McConnell, and Foley were also captured near Neuberg an der Mürz, handed over to the Luftwaffe, and sent to Stalag Luft III. Gilbert and Miller initially went to a Dulag-Luft POW transfer camp before being sent to a POW camp in Bucharest, Romania.[34]

While *Weesie* would be the only aircraft lost by the 727th that day, the 724th was not so lucky. Flying on the left of the formation in the Low position meant the aircraft from the 724th were the most susceptible to the Fw 190s that had decided to fly down into the cumulus deck below the formation and use it as cover from which they would suddenly burst, attacking the 724th's planes from below.

Harold Thompson, who was flying in the 727th's flight, later recalled seeing the German fighters dart out of the cloud deck just two thousand feet below the 724th's flight, repeatedly firing on the B-24s before diving back into the safety of the clouds.[35]

One of the first aircraft the Germans attacked from the 724th Flight was *Hard to Get*, under Lieutenant James Powers's command.[36] As the formation turned toward the IP, the tail turret gunner, Corporal Franklin Atwood, called out that Fw 190s were attacking from six o'clock and began firing his guns immediately. The radio operator and left waist gunner, Corporal Daniel Suzyn, said that seconds later, 20mm cannon shells began "popping off along the entire length of the plane." One of the first of those shells hit Atwood "squarely in the chest and knocked him out of the tail turret," killing him instantly. Another of the 20mm shells hitting *Hard to Get* smashed into the fuselage near the camera hatch, setting the waist section on fire.

Eyewitnesses in nearby aircraft reported that the left wing was severely damaged by the German fighters' cannons and quickly caught fire. In seconds, the wing and fuselage were enveloped in flames, and the aircraft was seen to tip over on its right wing before rapidly losing altitude. In the waist section, Corporal Suzyn groped in the growing flames for his parachute and began fastening it to his harness while Sergeant Charles Anderson, the right waist gunner, bailed out his waist window, followed by the ball turret gunner, Corporal Alfonso Garde, and the squadron photographer, Sergeant Dwight Moss, who had been wounded by 20mm shell fragments. At that point, Moss apparently lost consciousness. He was likely thrown clear through the waist window because when he regained his senses, Moss was floating down in his parachute with no idea how or when he pulled the ripcord. Suzyn's face and head were burned, and his clothes were smoldering from his close call with the flames in the burning waist section.

Meanwhile, the flight engineer and top turret gunner, Sergeant David Beck, headed for the bomb bay, which he had opened before jettisoning the bomb load. He fastened on his parachute and prepared to bail out but saw the navigator, Lieutenant Ray Chisholm, coming toward him from the nose section. Chisholm had been gravely wounded in the leg by a 20mm shell and needed Beck's assistance to get to the bomb bay for bailout. Beck and Chisholm had made it to the catwalk just before the aircraft went into a spin, which threw Beck clear of the *Hard to Get*. However, Chisholm could not get out and was probably trapped in the aircraft by the spin along with Lieutenant Powers, copilot Lieutenant Merle Vanderhorst, bombardier Lieutenant Sydney Samet, and nose turret gunner Corporal Leonard Wager.

Everyone who bailed out of *Hard to Get* was quickly captured by the Germans, and all went to POW camps except for Moss, who first went to a German military hospital for treatment of his wounds. From all indications, Beck was the last man to leave the aircraft. The day after his capture, the Germans showed him the dog tags for Powers, Vanderhorst, Chisholm, Wagner, and Atwood, which they recovered from the aircraft wreckage near Sankt Pölte, Austria.

In the center of the 724th's flight was the aircraft piloted by Lieutenant Robert Beach.[37] While this should have been the safest position in the squadron's formation, it was not. Around 12:20 PM, about five minutes after the German attacks commenced, Sergeant Joseph Maurer, the tail turret gunner in Lieutenant Gerald Apple's plane, which was flying in the lead position for the squadron directly ahead of Beach's ship, saw eight Fw 190s burst out of the cloud formation at 10 o'clock to attack Beach's plane. Other eyewitnesses saw the hail of 20mm cannon shells from these eight Butcher Birds set fire to the elevators on the horizontal stabilizer, the tail turret, and engines number three and four on the right wing. Beach immediately lost all pitch control of the aircraft because of the loss of the elevators and feathered the two burning starboard engines. However, the flames had spread to the right wing's fuel tanks by the time he got the engines shut down. Realizing the situation was hopeless, he got on the intercom and ordered everyone to bail out before ringing the bailout alarm bell.

In the nose section, Lieutenant Robert Jensen, the bombardier, and Sergeant Michael Callahan, the nose turret gunner, were quickly able to release the hatch to the nose gear doors and bail out. At the same time, Lieutenant Herbert Klossner, the navigator, crawled through the tunnel from the nose section and headed to the bomb bay for bailout. When Klossner got to the bomb bay, Lieutenant Philip Pratt, the copilot, was already there. Pratt was the first to jump from the bomb bay, followed by Klossner, who saw Pratt's chute open, and Sergeant Benjamin Ransom, the flight engineer and top turret gunner. Meanwhile, waist gunners Sergeants Kenneth Brust and Donald

Kennedy, ball turret gunner Sergeant James Cooper, and tail turret gunner Corporal George White all bailed out successfully from the camera hatch door.

Beach, Ransom, Cooper, and Klossner were captured by enemy authorities the following day near Mariazell, Austria, while Brust and White were taken near Annaberg. Nothing was initially known about Pratt and Callahan. All those captured were taken first to Annaberg and held by civilian police until they were sent on to a Dulag Luft for processing.[38] Beach later reported that while he was in jail at Annaberg, the town Burgermeister (mayor) told him that he considered Americans to be "gangsters" who "should be dealt with as such." From this apparent hostility, Beach became concerned that his two missing crew members, Pratt and Callahan, might have been killed by local civilians. At the same time, the local police asked Klossner if he knew Pratt or Callahan. Klossner, not wanting to give any information to the enemy, answered that he did not know either man, so the police dropped the matter.

German reports found after the war revealed that Lieutenant Beach may have been right about Pratt and Callahan's fate. While the only thing these reports said about Callahan was that he was dead and had been buried in a cemetery in Frein an der Mürz, Austria, the report about Pratt was far more suspicious. In the report, the Germans documented that Pratt's body had been found near the road between Frein an der Mürz and Mürzsteg with bullet wounds to the "left thigh, upper arm, and back of the head." The latter sounds very much like someone had executed Pratt. Pratt was also buried in a cemetery in Frein an der Mürz.

The circumstances of Pratt's and Callahan's deaths were finally revealed during a military commission convened in Salzburg, Austria, from July 16–24, 1947.[39] After his capture, Lieutenant Pratt was taken to the Aumann Inn in Frein an der Mürz, where the authorities interrogated him. After he had been questioned, Pratt was turned over to two SS men, Untersturmführer (Second Lieutenant) Fritz Thaler and Oberscharführer (Sergeant) Walter Irmer, who were ordered to take Pratt to the police station in Mürzsteg. The two SS men loaded Pratt into their Fiat automobile and headed south down the road to Mürzsteg. However, as they neared a waterfall called Totes Weib about a mile from Frein an der Mürz, the car's radiator cracked, and they had to stop along the road to make repairs. During this repair stop, Thaler told the tribunal that Pratt got out of the car and attempted to escape. Thaler claimed he fired three or four shots at Pratt, who fell dead by the roadside.

However, a young woman who was riding her bicycle down the road at the time told the tribunal a different story. She testified that she observed Pratt standing by the car with his hands tied behind his back. He then walked a few feet away and was looking up at the wall of rock next to the road when she heard a shot ring out. Pratt collapsed and the two SS men moved him to the side of the road before returning to the car. As far as she could tell, Pratt seemed to still be alive. But about ten minutes later, the two SS men picked Pratt up and moved him to the rear seat of the car. It was then that the young woman heard a second shot.

After this testimony, Thaler admitted under cross-examination that Pratt had not tried to escape and that he had shot him deliberately. Since Pratt's postmortem examination showed he had been shot in the left thigh, upper arm, and back of the head, it seemed clear that while the initial wounds to the thigh and arm were caused by Thaler's first shots, the shot to the back of the head occurred once Pratt was back in the car, which meant this was an unsanctioned execution.

After delivering Pratt's body to the police in Mürzsteg, Thaler and Irmer returned to Frein an der Mürz where Oberscharführer Walter Bockhorni told Thaler that another American airman had been captured and Thaler was being ordered to also take him to Mürzsteg. This airman was Sergeant Callahan. After placing Callahan in their car, Thaler and Irmer started for Mürzsteg but soon realized it was now too late at night to get him there. After a brief discussion, they decided to take their American prisoner to an old paper factory about a mile from Frein an der Mürz for the night. Once there, they got Callahan out of the car, and Thaler took him inside the machine hall. Irmer was following behind when he heard shots in the machine hall. When he entered, he saw Callahan lying on the floor, dead. Thaler again claimed the American had tried to escape. However, like that of Lieutenant Pratt, Callahan's autopsy showed he had been shot in the back of the head at close range.

The tribunal thought Pratt's and Callahan's deaths had consistent and suspicious aspects. First, Pratt was shot in the middle of a mountainous valley with sheer cliffs surrounding it while his hands were tied behind his back. There was likely no way he could have successfully escaped. However, even if either Pratt or Callahan were trying to escape, Thaler could have shouted a warning to halt, fired warning shots, or simply chased them and placed them back into custody. Finally, the fact that both men had been shot in the back of the head at close range convinced the tribunal that Thaler had, indeed, murdered both prisoners. Therefore, the tribunal found Thaler guilty of the charges and sentenced him to twenty-five years imprisonment beginning July 24, 1947.

The other mystery related to the loss of Lieutenant Beach's aircraft surrounds the squadron photographer who was onboard for this mission, Corporal George White. Sergeant Ransom saw White with Beach on the ground when they were captured, and some of the enlisted men saw him alive as a POW as late as January 1945. However, he was never repatriated, and there was no German record of his fate. One theory offered by those who were also prisoners at Stalag Luft IV is that White may have died during the infamous forced march from Poland to Germany in winter 1945, if not from sickness in the brutally cold weather then from being shot by the German guards.[40]

The other aircraft from the 724th flight was *Fertile Myrtle*, under Lieutenant Cornelius Donoghue's command, flying in the number three slot just to the rear and left of Lieutenant Apple's aircraft.[41] One eyewitness in Apple's plane, left waist gunner Sergeant Lorenzo Bloom, saw *Fertile Myrtle* attacked by a wave of eight Fw 190s around 12:19 PM. All eight enemy fighters attacked from six o'clock, and their initial cannon fire caused the number three engine to immediately catch fire along with part of the right wing. The aircraft then turned off to the left, leaving the formation and descending while appearing to still be under control.

In the nose turret, gunner Sergeant Stanley Black heard the bailout alarm bell ringing. Glancing to his right, he saw the right wing was on fire. About that time, the navigator, Lieutenant James Bitzinger, began pounding on the back of the turret, yelling for Black to get out. The gunner left the turret, put on his parachute, opened the nose gear door hatch, and bailed out with Bitzinger and the bombardier, Lieutenant Clarence Roettger, right behind him.[42]

Fertile Myrtle falls out of formation after being severely hit by enemy cannon fire. (*National Archives*)

Fertile Myrtle was last seen near Ober-Grafendorf, Austria. However, the crew bailed out about twenty miles southwest of Ober-Grafendorf near Annaberg. While the entire crew was believed to have bailed out, the final status of four of them was never clearly determined. In addition to the men in the nose section, copilot Lieutenant George Hogan, ball turret gunner Sergeant Carl Lottman, left waist gunner Sergeant Wayne Johnson, tail turret gunner Sergeant Claude Baker, flight engineer and top turret gunner Sergeant Raymond Ranville, and radio operator and left waist gunner Corporal Alfonso Diaz were captured near Annaberg. Baker had been wounded in the foot by shrapnel and was sent to a civilian hospital in Mürzzuschlag, Austria, where he remained until September 19, 1944. German records found after the war indicate that Bitzinger, Baker, Lottman, Johnson, and Black were sent on to POW camps. Still, there were no records regarding Lieutenants Donoghue, Hogan, and Roettger, or Corporal Diaz.

An RAF pilot later said that he saw Donoghue's name on medical records in a Budapest hospital, while a British paratrooper reported that he saw Diaz in Stalag Luft IV. However, neither man was ever repatriated to Allied control. Meanwhile, the status of Hogan and

Roettger seems to have been more ominous. Sergeant Baker said both officers carried .45-caliber pistols and ammunition with them on the aircraft and stated that if their capture were imminent, they would use their weapons to escape by force. While Baker was in the hospital being treated for his wounds, he met an Austrian physician named Gangl, who was kind and claimed to be part of the Austrian resistance. Gangl even smuggled food and cigarettes to Baker and the other American patients in Baker's ward, an act for which he would have been executed if the Germans found out. Gangl told Baker that shortly after he was captured, German authorities told the doctor that two American officers had killed some civilians while evading capture. Both officers were caught shortly after that and executed via firing squad by the Gestapo for the murder of these civilians. While Gangl did not know these officers' names, Baker always suspected they were Hogan and Roettger.

An investigation by authorities from the American Graves Registration Command conducted in the vicinity of Frankenfels, Austria, after the war finally provided more conclusive information on the fates of Lieutenants Donoghue, Hogan, and Roettger, and Corporal Diaz. The investigating team interviewed the men who had gone to the crash site, recovered the bodies of four men, and buried them in the village cemetery. These local men said there were no identification tags or papers found on any of the bodies, so they assumed German military personnel who had visited the site the day before had taken them. However, when the American team disinterred the remains, they found the identification tags for Lieutenants Donoghue and Hogan. Since only four men from the crew were unaccounted for, it was assumed that the other two sets of remains belonged to Lieutenant Roettger and Corporal Diaz. Apparently they were unable to bail out and were killed in the crash of the aircraft.[43]

Having decimated the 724th and 725th flights, the Germans attacked the planes in the group's lead flight from the 726th. The aircraft in the flight's number five position, Lieutenant Harvey Clapp's *Kings High*, took the brunt of the German fighter assault. Eyewitnesses reported that the cannon fire from the Fw 190s caused the number two engine to catch fire while severely damaging the left aileron, right rudder, ball turret, and tail turret. The ball turret gunner, Corporal Manual Sanchez, was wounded in the foot and climbed out of the tur-

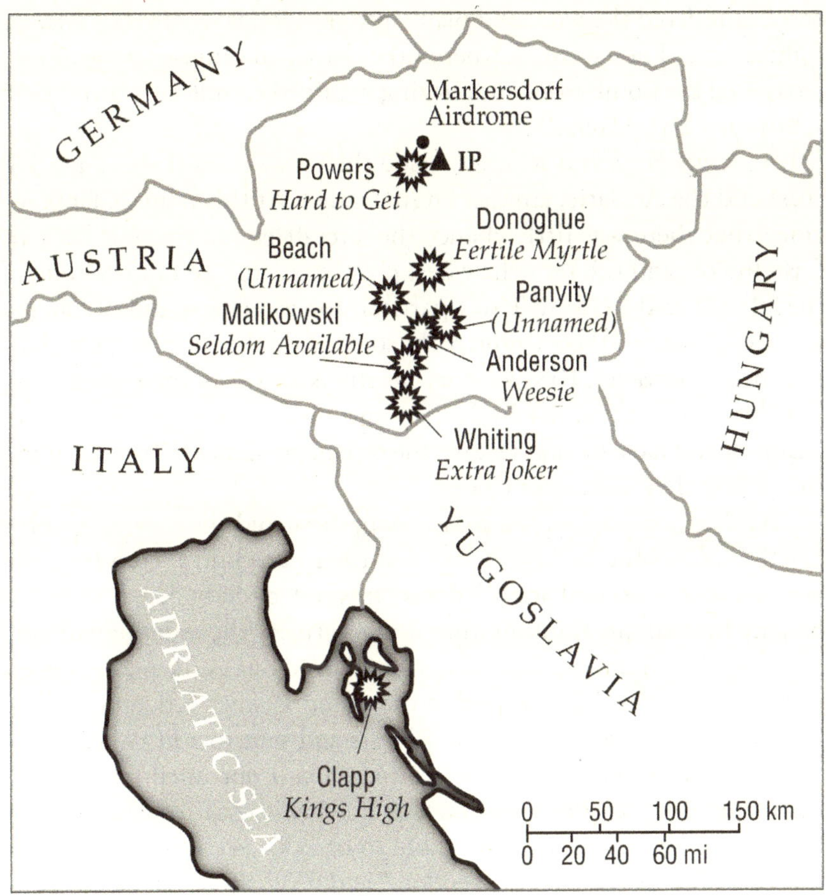

Locations of 451st Bomb Group aircraft lost during the Markersdorf mission.

ret. Even though his foot had nearly been shot off, he made his way to one of the waist guns where his fire downed two Fw 190s.[44]

After three minutes of the aircraft maintaining straight and level flight, the damage to the rudders caused it to fall sideways in a twenty- to thirty-degree bank for about three thousand feet before Clapp and his copilot, Lieutenant Chester Ennis, could get control. However, while eyewitnesses reported seeing parachutes as the aircraft went down before falling out of sight, the crew of *Kings High* did not immediately bail out. While the aircraft was "badly shot up," Clapp and Ennis dived the wounded plane into the clouds where the German fighters could not see it, feathered the damaged number two engine, jettisoned the bomb load, and, having regained complete control, flew south into Yugoslavia.[45]

As *Kings High* and its crew made their way toward the Yugoslav coast and the Adriatic, another engine failed. At this point, Clapp decided that there was little chance the aircraft would make it back to Castelluccio and thought their best chance was to bail out over one of the islands still held by Tito's partisan forces. The island of Cherso was the closest to their flight path, so it made the most sense to bail out there. However, Krk, another nearby island only three miles east of Cherso, was occupied by Italian and German troops. Therefore, Clapp would have to wait to give the order and signal to bail out until they knew they were over Cherso.[46]

As they approached the coast, Clapp first told the crew to be prepared for a bailout so they should don their parachutes. However, the nose gunner, Corporal John Pilcher, misunderstood Clapp's order to prepare for bailout, thinking that it was actually the order to bail out. He opened the nose gear door hatch and bailed out as the plane crossed over Krk. As a result, he landed in the water between Krk and Cherso, where he was rescued by Italian soldiers and sent to a POW camp.[47]

The remainder of the crew waited to bail out until Clapp gave them the order as they overflew the northeast coast of Cherso. The wounded Corporal Sanchez was able to bail out even though his foot was "hanging by the Achilles tendon," and he was wearing two tourniquets. When he landed safely on Cherso, he cut off the damaged foot and threw it away. The remainder of the crew landed in their parachutes nearby, and Lieutenant Ennis did his best to care for Sanchez over the next six days while they awaited rescue. The partisans on the island notified Allied authorities that the crew of *Kings High* was there with them, and they eventually sent a Catalina amphibious aircraft to pick them up. Corporal Sanchez survived his ordeal and was awarded the Silver Star.[48]

As the surviving elements of the 451st formation prepared for the bomb run, the German fighters did not let up in their attacks. However, the gunners from the group were steadily inflicting heavy losses on the aggressive German fighters. By the time they reached the target, sixteen enemy planes were confirmed as destroyed, with eight

Bombs from the 451st Bomb Group explode on the Markersdorf aircraft factory. In addition to damaging the factory, the mission was successful in another major priority: to draw off German fighter opposition from other bomb raids. (*National Archives*)

more probable.[49] But amid the furious German fighter attacks, a critical navigational error emerged as the wing formation arrived at the IP: the lead formation from the 484th Bomb Group was heading in the wrong direction. Lieutenant Byers, the 451st's group navigator, realized something was wrong and informed Colonel Eaton over the intercom that the "484th had not properly identified the target and were about to head for a vacant field or some other place." Eaton trusted Byers's navigation skills and told him, "Hang on as long as you can, but peel off when our turning to the correct target becomes jeopardized." Byers acknowledged these orders, and after several minutes, the 484th seemed to be heading somewhere southwest of the target. Byers directed the 451st formation to turn to 030°, which would take it to the correct location of the Markersdorf Airdrome. This new heading was forty-five degrees off from the planned bomb run heading of 345°, but it would not adversely impact the ability to hit the target. The 484th, meanwhile, continued—having not been attacked by a single German fighter or lost a single aircraft—to drop its bombs on the wrong target.[50]

With the 451st properly headed for the target, the group's lead bombardier, Lieutenant Hughes, identified the airdrome through his Norden bombsight, took control of the aircraft, sighted an aimpoint on the southwest corner of the airdrome, and released his bombs. As the fragmentation bombs began to fall from Walkey's plane, the remaining bombers in the 726th's flight toggled off their bombs as well. The rest of the squadron flights followed a similar approach, with the flight lead aiming and dropping its bombs, and the other aircraft in each flight dropping their bombs based on the lead aircraft's bomb release. Luckily, the 461st did not follow the 484th but instead followed the 451st's lead to also bomb the correct target.[51]

As the 451st's formation turned off the bomb run, the Germans began the third phase of their attacks. This series of attacks lasted only five minutes, during which the enemy lost two more fighters destroyed with two more hit and damaged. This final phase of their attacks also had one very curious aspect. As the bomber formation turned off the target, a B-17 escorted by two Fw 190s pulled in behind the bombers. It had a white tail and black swastikas on its wings, clearly identifying it as a captured American aircraft. This B-17 began firing on the rear of the bomber formation. However, as soon as one of the 451st tail turret gunners hit the B-17 and damaged one of its engines, it turned away and flew off to the north.[52]

About this time, a second group of P-51s assigned to escort the group after the bomb run arrived on the scene, and the German fighters broke off their attacks. But those attacks had taken a terrible toll on the 451st. It was estimated that as many as forty-five fighters had attacked the formation, shooting down eight B-24s in only about twenty-five minutes.[53] This was tragically ironic because, as Sergeant Lindley Miller from George Tudor's crew later noted, only a few days before the Markersdorf mission, intelligence had said "the Luftwaffe was through because of gas shortages." Many of the bombers that had survived the attacks were also hit and damaged. On the *Thunder Mug*, flown by George Tudor, there were over 150 holes in the aircraft, most of them from 20mm cannon fire. One fuel tank had been punctured by enemy shells, and one of the rudders was damaged. Miller later said, "Our whole waist was shattered, and a whole section was blown out next to the ball turret. It was a miracle none of us were hit." *Thunder Mug* would limp home to Castelluccio, where Tudor made a successful crash landing.[54]

The postmission reconnaissance photos of the Markersdorf Airdrome showed that most of the 451st's bombs struck the southwest corner of the airfield and then progressed diagonally across to the hangar line on the north side. At the same time, one string of bombs hit starting in the middle of the airfield and going east just beyond the field's perimeter. While twenty Bf 109s could be seen in the photos, only five were probably destroyed, with five more damaged. In his Daily Operations Report for August 23, Colonel Eaton stated, "Mission successful but costly."[55] The diversion tactic the Fifteenth Air Force had devised for the mission was also successful. The 451st seemed to have absorbed the entire German fighter response, as there was no German fighter opposition to the other Fifteenth Air Force bomb groups that attacked high-priority targets in the Vienna area.

While the attack on the Markersdorf Airdrome had been costly for the 451st, it seems to have been a tipping point for the Luftwaffe. While the intelligence estimates stating that the Luftwaffe was "through" were not in evidence on August 23, the scale of its losses that day regarding aircraft and pilots was severe. Those losses, combined with real fuel shortages, the damage being done to the Luftwaffe in the skies over Germany, and the ability of American fighters to escort the Fifteenth Air Force's bombers on long-range missions led to a virtual end of the fighter threat to the 451st in the months that followed the Markersdorf mission. A review of the group's operations summaries from August 24 through January 1945 shows that only one mission had any fighter response from the Luftwaffe.

On October 2, 1944, the 451st was awarded its third Distinguished Unit Citation, for the Markersdorf Airdrome mission of August 23, 1944. The citation read:

> Displaying outstanding courage, professional skill and fortitude, the gallant crews battled their way through the overwhelming enemy opposition to the target, where, under continued heavy opposition, they completed a highly successful bombing run. Through

their superior ability to maintain a tight protective formation and to direct heavy defensive fire against the fierce attacks of the enemy, the Group accounted for twenty-nine (29) enemy aircraft destroyed or damaged in the air.

By the outstanding courage, professional skill, and unwavering determination of the combat crews, together with the superior technical skill and devotion to duty of the ground personnel, the 451st Bombardment Group has upheld the highest traditions of the Military Service, thereby reflecting great credit upon themselves and the Armed Forces of the United States of America.[56]

Chapter Seven

Mission Five Zero

Fifty missions were the holy grail for all the 451st Bomb Group's aircrews. Surviving fifty missions meant you could rotate back to the United States, and the war was over for you. Because of this, by late summer and fall 1944, the 451st was experiencing a regular and increasing shift in personnel as aircrews completed their fiftieth missions, entitling them to go home. In September 1944 alone, 125 officers and men left the group, and 168 arrived. At first, an individual or aircrew completing their fiftieth mission was a somewhat rare and celebrated event. However, as the war continued and more missions were flown, an aircrew member achieving his fiftieth mission became a regular occurrence. Of course, since all aircrews had enlisted for the duration of the war, going home did not mean leaving one's uniform behind for civilian life. Still, rotating back to the United States meant you would get leave to go home to see your family, and best of all, the Germans would no longer be trying to kill you.

Because completing the fiftieth mission was so important to the aircrews, some organizations established a policy regarding how a crew was assigned to its fiftieth and final mission. One of those organizations was the 727th Bomb Squadron, which created a process whereby, once you had finished your forty-ninth mission, the aircraft commander for each crew was allowed to choose their final combat mission. While the aircraft commander was given plenty of time to make the selection, he still had to be at least somewhat diligent about the selection process.[1]

One of the men from the 727th who was faced with deciding on the last mission was Harold Thompson. His crew had completed its forty-ninth mission in late October, and he immediately began the process to select number fifty. Every afternoon, he would go to the squadron operations office to see what orders it had received for the next day's mission. If the orders indicated something too challenging, he would decline to be assigned to that mission and return the next day to check again. Finally, on November 5, 1944, Thompson found the right mission. The next day, November 6, the 451st would mount two missions, a large one going to Vienna and a small nine-plane sortie to bomb the transformer station outside Bolzano in northern Italy. The Bolzano mission would be only six hours long; no fighter threat was expected, and little heavy AAA was defending the target. If you were looking for a milk run at this stage in the war, this was it.[2]

The next morning, Thompson's crew boarded the new aircraft they had been flying since September, *Sloppy But Safe*. The name came from the aircraft's initial check flight when it first arrived at the 727th. That day, the aircraft's pilot reported issues with the flight controls, which he said seemed a bit "sloppy." The crew chief and his men checked the airplane to see what might have caused the problem but could not find anything wrong. So they recorded in the maintenance log that while the flight controls might seem "sloppy," the aircraft was safe to fly. When Thompson and his crew first read that entry in the maintenance log, they immediately called it *Sloppy But Safe*. Thompson's nose turret gunner, Sergeant Gordon Snyder, had been a commercial artist in civilian life, so he painted the name on the right side of the nose section alongside a topless female figure hanging her wet clothes out to dry on a clothesline.[3]

Lieutenant Harold Thompson, front row, center, and his crew gather for a final photograph as they wait to start their journey home in November 1944. (*Author*)

The mission to Bolzano went as planned; the target was severely damaged, and all nine aircraft made it safely back to Castelluccio, although a formation from the 461st that had followed the 451st planes had taken some heavy fire from the few AAA batteries around the target. Thompson and his crew were outprocessed a week later for their return to the United States. As they awaited transportation to Naples, where they would board a troop transport headed for Boston, Thompson handed his camera to a bystander. He and his crew posed for a final photograph before they headed home. Not surprisingly, it turned out to be a photo of a delighted group of young men.[4]

The mission to Markersdorf on August 23, 1944, was mission number 109 for the 451st, and many more would follow. The targets continued to be of the same type: oil facilities, rail infrastructure, and aircraft manufacturing plants. However, from September 10–22, the group was tasked to fly supplies to France for the tactical air forces and the 7th Army, which was advancing north up the Rhone River valley. Three missions flew to the airfield in Lyon, while five more went to Bron.[5] These proved to be a welcome respite from the endless stream of combat bombing missions. The missions were flown through Allied-controlled airspace at altitudes low enough that no one even had to wear their oxygen masks. And because there was no threat from the enemy, the crews also did not have to wear helmets or flak vests. It was almost like a cross-country flight back in the United States.

However, the strange nature of these supply missions caused several headaches for the ground crews. Each aircraft was loaded with 55-gallon drums of gasoline in the waist compartment, and the ground crews were told to remove all the bomb hoists from the aircraft. Late on the night of September 7, Karl Eichhorn and the armaments ground crew from the 726th were awakened at 11:30 PM and told to remove ball turrets and load twelve, five-hundred-pound bombs each onto nine aircraft. No one had ever removed a ball turret, so they had to devise procedures to do so. Their efforts quickly stopped when they realized that because of the plane's low ground clearance, the ball turret on a B-24 could not be removed unless the aircraft was lifted up on hydraulic jacks. The crew chiefs found the needed jacks, and each plane was lifted up enough to remove the turrets from the belly of each of the nine planes. Eichhorn and the others finished the job around 6:30 AM, but then they were told to perform the same job on two more aircraft. On September 11, the planes from the 726th began ferrying the gasoline and bombs to France.[6]

Of course, despite the lack of enemy threats on these supply missions, it was still possible to have a minor crisis now and then. Harold Thompson was flying one of the supply missions with another pilot riding along as his copilot. The weather was beautiful, and from five thousand feet, they enjoyed sightseeing in the beautiful French countryside. Suddenly, however, the number three engine failed. As Thompson scrambled to determine what had happened, he looked over at his substitute copilot, who had pushed his seat back and crossed his legs for comfort. But in doing so, he had inadvertently kicked the switch for the number three engine, causing it to stop in midflight. The engine was restarted, and nothing more was said about it. That is, nothing more was said until after the war. The substitute copilot later became the chief operations officer for a major airline, and whenever he saw Thompson at a reunion, he begged him not to tell this story lest his airline pilots find out their boss had done something so stupid.[7]

After the resupply missions were complete, the group resumed the deadly business of bombing occupied Europe.

The continuing rotations from duty also applied to the 451st's commander, Colonel Eaton. The colonel had flown his fiftieth mission on September 13, 1944, and the Army Air Force decided it was time for him to perform other duties. On October 6, Eaton left for a new assignment in Britain and was replaced by Lieutenant Colonel James Knapp, who had been commander of the 461st. Under Knapp's leadership, the 451st flew mission 176 before the end of the year. On February 24, 1945, the group reached the milestone of its two hundredth mission. The group's last mission came on April 26, 1945, when it bombed the rail marshaling yards at Sachsenburg, Austria. For the men of the 451st, the war was over at last.[8]

Late that evening, word came down to group headquarters that the 451st would receive a POM inspection within the next two weeks. This was essentially the same inspection it had received back at Fairmont in fall 1943. This time, everyone wondered if it meant they would go home or perhaps be sent to the Pacific theater.[9]

The group was tasked to fly new combat missions on April 30 and May 1, but both were canceled. Then, on May 8, Germany surrendered, and the war in Europe was over. The 451st was assigned to fly a special "Victory Flight" mission for the Fifteenth Air Force commander, General Twining, that cruised over the Italian countryside. All around Castelluccio, the men celebrated and were also ordered to turn in their .45-caliber pistols lest someone get accidentally shot amid the revelry.[10]

The next day, May 9, the ground crews were ordered to start getting the planes ready to leave, although no one knew where the aircraft and the group would be going. The preparation process included removing all the ammunition and machine guns from each aircraft, coating each gun with heavy oil, and packing them away for shipment. Two days later, the armament sections in each squadron were told to remove and pack all the remaining ammunition and to clean, oil, and pack all their tools. It was then that the rumors began to spread that the 451st was not headed for the Pacific but was going back to the United States, which, for some unknown reason, the Army Air Force had decided to call the "Zone of the Interior."[11]

On May 14, the Fifteenth Air Force conducted the POM inspection of the 451st and declared it ready to proceed. Two days later, the group's men finally learned they would head home. After that, things began to move quickly, but not quickly enough for men who wanted to get home badly. One man from the 726th wrote in his journal on May 21, "The whole Group will be gone in less than two weeks, we think. It seems that we will never get started. I want to see my wife and baby, and all my loved ones."[12] On May 23, just nine days after the POM was complete, the first aircraft departed, using almost the same route they had traveled during the initial deployment in November and December 1943. Half of the aircraft and crews started back that day, and the others steadily departed after that.

On May 27, Sergeant Clyde Phifer, a nose turret gunner in the 726th, and his crew, led by pilot Lieutenant Edward Shimanski, took off at 10:30 AM. When they loaded the aircraft, the crew's adopted pet, a dog they had named Queenie, tried to board with them, something she had never done before. The last Phifer saw of her was behind the aircraft as it taxied out. She watched the crew leave as the propeller blast covered her with sand and dust. Seeing her sadly standing there, Phifer said, "I'm not ashamed to say I cried."

Phifer's plane flew to Gioia del Colle and onto Marrakech, Morocco, the next day. That night, as Phifer sat on the wing of the aircraft writing in his journal, he recalled that another nose gunner in the plane had been blinded when the nose turret was hit by enemy fire. Further, as he looked around him, he could not help but notice that the surface of the wing on which he was sitting was covered with aluminum patches where enemy 20mm cannon fire and shrapnel from German flak had ripped holes in it.

On May 30, around 8:30 AM, Shimanski lifted the plane carrying Phifer and the rest of the crew off the runway at Marrakech before landing in Senegal, French West Africa, nine hours later. They picked up two passengers and took off the next morning for Natal, Brazil, where they landed at about 2:00 PM local time. During the initial deployment in 1943, Natal was packed with aircraft transiting the field, and nothing had changed since then. Four days passed before Shimanski, his crew, and passengers could continue their journey. They departed on June 4 for Atkinson Field in British Guiana, en route to Borinquen Field, Puerto Rico, where they landed on June 5. After a one-day delay, they struck out for Hunter Army Airfield in Savannah, Georgia, where they returned to the United States.

Most of the 451st's planes and crews followed a similar path before eventually arriving at Kingman Army Airfield, Arizona, where the aircraft were parked amid hundreds of other planes recently returned from the European theater. In many cases, saying farewell to their planes was an occasion for tears. From Kingman, most of the group's B-24s would eventually be flown to various contractor facilities where they would be disassembled and turned into scrap metal—a sad and ignominious end for aircraft that had served their crews and their country with such distinction.[13]

While the return of the aircraft and aircrews mainly occurred without incident, there was one tragic event. While the initial deployment of the group in 1943 had gone without any losses, one aircraft flown by Lieutenant William Silliman from the 725th was lost during the return trip with all aboard. Silliman, his crew, and two passengers had made it to Mallard Field in Dakar on the evening of June 3. They took off the next morning for their flight across the Atlantic to Natal. The aircraft took off from Runway 030 on the morning of June 4 with no apparent difficulties. However, things quickly went very wrong. When only about one hundred feet off the ground, the plane was seen making a slow left turn while losing altitude before crashing into the Atlantic and exploding on impact. Only one body from the plane was ever recovered, that of Sergeant William Geller. Silliman and the rest of the crew were lost forever in the waters of the Atlantic. Their names are now inscribed on the "Wall of the Missing" at the North African American Cemetery in Carthage, Tunisia.[14]

Meanwhile, back at Castelluccio, the ground echelon had been tearing down tents, cleaning up, and packing everything for shipping. On May 23, it got a seventy-two-hour notice to prepare to be shipped out. The men quickly "finished tearing up all the woodwork in the tents and hauled all the scrap lumber to the supply building." Next, they dismantled a few of the stone buildings, leaving only the officers' and enlisted men's clubs, maintenance garages, supply buildings, and engineering and armaments shops, which, with the tents gone, became the only places for the men to sleep.[15]

Once the task of breaking down the facilities at Castelluccio was complete, the ground echelon began making its way to Naples, where the troop ship USS *General Meigs*, awaited it. On June 4, the ship was loaded with more than six thousand men, mostly personnel from the Fifteenth Air Force and 5th Army, which, along with the British Eighth Army, had been fighting its way up the Italian peninsula since September 1943. At 4:00 PM, the *Meigs* weighed anchor and set sail for Newport News, Virginia, from where the ground echelon of the 451st had departed aboard the SS *John Pillsbury* in December 1943. With no U-boats to worry about, the *Meigs* could sail in a straight line and not zigzag while cruising along at a brisk speed of twenty-two knots.[16]

It took ten days to transit the Mediterranean and Atlantic, but at 10:30 AM on June 14, the coast of Virginia came into sight. Many men said it was the "sweetest sight they had seen" in over eighteen months. As the ship docked, they also could not help but notice all the pretty girls who had come down to the docks to greet them. That night, a train took them back to Camp Patrick Henry, where much of the food they dined on had not been canned or reconstituted from some odious powder. Among these items was fresh milk, which they had not seen since leaving for Italy.[17]

After a brief stay at Camp Patrick Henry, the men received orders that sent them to camps closer to their homes of record, where they would be processed for either a reassignment or discharge. Most men who had chosen to stay in uniform were given thirty days leave to go home to see their families. After that leave, in which most had the opportunity to sleep in a real bed and eat decent food, those still on duty were sent to Dow Army Airfield in Bangor, Maine, which had become the new home of the 451st Bomb Group. But when they arrived, they found that there was not a single bomber in sight, and the group had been placed under the command of the Air Transport Command. By the end of July 1945, it was all too apparent that the group would be broken up. A few months later, on September 26, 1945, the last commander of the 451st Bomb Group, Major William McGuire, accepted the orders to deactivate the group, which would now fade into history.[18]

During almost nineteen months of overseas duty, the 451st Bomb Group had dropped an estimated thirteen thousand tons of bombs on enemy targets. The group had been assigned 280 aircraft, of which 112 were lost in action, and an estimated eight thousand men were assigned during the group's existence.[19]

The 451st had built a well-deserved reputation for excellence and perseverance in the worst of aerial combat conditions. That reputation came from the courage and dedication of its men and was paid for at a terrible price, no more so than on the three missions for which the group received its Distinguished Unit Citations: Regensburg on February 25, 1944, Ploesti on April 5, 1944, and Markersdorf on August 23, 1944.

The brave men who flew for the 451st have almost all left us. In a poem about the 451st, Bob Karstensen wrote:

The die is cast, the bell has rung, the parade has ended, its finale sung.
The engines have "shut down" one by one; the cockpit is empty, its job now done.

AFTERWORD

Following the war, a few men who were part of the 451st Bomb Group's story and even those who served in the Luftwaffe continued in military service, but most returned to civilian life. Here are brief biographies of those whose experiences or postwar writings influenced this volume.

James Atkinson. Following his release from a POW camp, Atkinson returned to the United States and began taking classes at the University of Alabama to become a physician. He married in June 1946 and began studies at the Tulane University School of Medicine in 1948. Atkinson enjoyed a highly successful medical career as an obstetrician and gynecologist, which included becoming a founding member and first Chief of Staff of Women's Hospital in Baton Rouge, Louisiana, a facility that pioneered the care of women and newborns under his leadership. He retired from medicine in 1981 and was an active member of the 451st Bomb Group Association until his death in August 2008 at eighty-five.[1]

James Beane. Upon returning to the United States after liberation from his POW camp, Beane attended the Commanding General Staff School at Fort Leavenworth, Kansas. He was subsequently assigned to Albuquerque, New Mexico, as a provost marshal. He was then sent to Albrook Field, Panama, where he served as an executive officer. After leaving active duty and transferring to the reserves, he was a mercenary of sorts, ferrying aircraft to the fledgling Israeli Air Force. When the Korean War broke out, he was recalled to active duty. He spent one year with Strategic Air Command in Topeka, Kansas, and another year in Korea as the wing inspector of the 17th Bomb Wing. After he returned from Korea, he returned to civilian life. Still, he remained in the Air Force Reserve until he retired as a lieutenant colonel. Beane was a supervisor with the Kern County Welfare Department in Bakersfield, California, until his retirement. He died October 9, 1972, at fifty-seven.[2]

Robert Eaton. After leaving the 451st, Eaton served as Deputy Director of Operations at Army Air Force Headquarters, Europe, until the war's end. Following the war, he remained in the military, first serving in various positions at the Pentagon from 1945 to 1953, where he was promoted to brigadier general in 1950. From 1953 to 1955, General Eaton was commander of NATO Air Forces Southeastern Europe, 6th Allied Tactical Air Force, headquartered in Izmir, Turkey. In 1955, he became commander of the 10th Air Force, Selfridge Air Force Base, Michigan. Eaton served in that capacity until 1959, when he returned to the Pentagon as assistant chief of staff Reserve Forces, USAF. He retired with thirty years of service in 1961. Following his retirement, Eaton was National Commander of the American Legion from 1973–74. He died in April 1993 and was buried at Arlington National Cemetery. Upon his death, Bob Karstensen, a wartime member of the 451st, wrote of his former commander:

> I hope someday, when my time draws near, I will hear my good Colonel say, "Circle once more, boys, our flight's not quite full. Let's make room for this lost lonely stray."
>
> We'll miss you, my Colonel, though it's hard to believe, for your rules on training still ring. Just leave a slot open as you fly on by, and we'll tuck it right under your wing.[3]

Karl Eichhorn. Eichhorn returned to Ohio and enrolled at Ohio State University, where he received an undergraduate degree in engineering physics and a graduate degree in physics. He was married in 1965 and became an engineering manager for TRW Systems, working on the Minuteman Missile program at Cape Canaveral. He left TRW in 1970 and opened his own business, a camping store called The Wilderness Shop. He became a member of the Audubon Society and Sierra Club. Eichhorn died in November 2017 at ninety and was buried at Cape Canaveral National Cemetery.[4]

Karl Rammelt. Rammelt, the Luftwaffe fighter pilot who led the attack on the B-24s of the 727th Squadron during the mission to Ploesti, was severely wounded on December 23, 1944, by machine-gun fire from a B-24 and did not fly again. At the war's conclusion, he was credited with forty-six confirmed victories, eleven of which were heavy bombers like the B-24. In 1956, Rammelt became part of the new Luftwaffe of West Germany, the West German Federal Defense Forces air arm. He retired as an Oberstleutnant, the equivalent of an American lieutenant colonel. He died in May 2009 at ninety-four.[5]

Lloyd Ryan. Ryan remained on active duty following the war and served in the Korean War. He rose to the rank of colonel before retiring in December 1963 after twenty-two years of service in the Army Air Force and US Air Force. He moved to San Diego, California, after he retired and lived there until his death in May 2004 at eighty-six. He was buried in Fort Rosecrans National Cemetery in San Diego.[6]

Harold Thompson. After his return to the United States in November 1944, Thompson was assigned to fly C-54 transports at Charleston Army Air Field until his discharge in 1945. Following active duty, he returned to farming in Ohio, married in 1949, and started a family. However, having joined the Air Force Reserve following the war, he was recalled to active duty during the Korean War in 1953 and served as a B-29 instructor pilot at Randolph Air Force Base, Texas. When the Korean War ended, he elected to remain on active duty. He served in various positions, including a return to combat, flying C-123K transports in Vietnam from 1968–1969 when he was forty-six. He retired as a lieutenant colonel in May 1970, having been awarded two Distinguished Flying Crosses, one for a mission with the 451st in October 1944 and another for his combat service in Vietnam. He eventually started his own home design and building firm in San Antonio. In November 2022, he reached one hundred and was the last surviving member of his B-24 crew. He died in March 2023 and was buried at Fort Sam Houston National Cemetery, Texas.[7]

George Tudor. Tudor flew his last mission on October 7, 1944, and returned to the United States in December 1944 via a hospital ship. Soon after his discharge, Tudor embarked on a new career by joining American Airlines, where he would spend the next thirty-three years. In August 1948, he married Jane Pattison. Over the following years, they welcomed two children to their Massachusetts home, born in 1957 and 1959. Tudor retired as a captain from American Airlines in 1977 and subsequently designed a home, moving to Maine in 1978. He enjoyed piloting his boat, the *Extra Joker II*, on the Damariscotta River during his leisure time there. Throughout his retirement, Tudor remained actively involved in the 451st Bomb Group Association, attending reunions from 1980 until he died in April 2010 at ninety-two. Known for his generosity, Tudor regularly contributed to various causes.[8]

Lewis Williams. The pilot of *The Jolly Roger* returned from a Romanian POW camp and remained in the reserves before returning to active duty in the Air Force in 1947. Williams served as chief of flight test at Kelly Air Force Base, San Antonio, flying B-36s and other aircraft. In 1954, he went to Santiago, Chile, as a maintenance adviser to the country's air force. He returned from Chile to take command of the Strategic Air Command's 28th Bomb Wing at Ellsworth Air Force Base, South Dakota, which had just received its first B-52 bombers. In 1959, Williams moved to Strategic Air Command Headquarters in Omaha, Nebraska, before going to Warner-Robins Air Force Base, Georgia, as director of materiel. He went to Vietnam in 1966 as base commander at Tan Sun Nhut Air Base, Saigon, returning to Kelly Air Force Base in 1967 to be chief, Jet Engine Division, and retired in 1972. During his military career, Williams received the Silver Star, Legion of Merit, Bronze Star, Purple Heart, Air Medal with four clusters, Chilean Order of Merit, and Vietnamese Medal of Honor. He died in San Antonio in April 2011 at ninety and was buried at Fort Sam Houston National Cemetery.[9]

NOTES

Preface

1. Franklin D. Roosevelt, Exec. Order No. 9075, *Authorizing and Directing the Secretary of War to Issue Citations in the Name of the President of the United States to Army Units for Outstanding Performance in Action*, February 26, 1942, American Presidency Project, accessed March 29, 2024, https://www.presidency.ucsb.edu/node/210791.

Chapter 1: Creating a Heavy Bomber Group

1. Lloyd Ryan, "Captain Lloyd Ryan's Early Diary and Remembrances from Overseas," *Ad Lib*, no. 35 (Spring/Summer 2002), 451st Bomb Group Publication, 8.
2. Draft Card for Lloyd Murlin Ryan, National Archives and Records Administration, St. Louis, WWII Draft Registration Cards for Kansas, 10/16/1940–03/31/1947, Records of the Selective Service System, 147, box 333; Army Enlistment Record for Lloyd M. Ryan, National Archives and Records Administration, College Park, MD; Electronic Army Serial Number Merged File, 1938-1946, National Archives Identifier (NAID): 1263923, Records of the National Archives and Records Administration, Washington, DC, 1789–ca. 2007, Record Group 64, box 02712, reel 128; *Suburban News*, July 2, 1942, Merriam, KS.
3. Ryan, "Early Diary," 8.
4. Ryan, "Early Diary," 8.
5. The astrodome was a small glass bubble that allowed the navigator to see the sun or stars using his sextant.
6. Ryan, "Early Diary," 8.
7. Richard K. Smith, "Marston Mat," *Air Force Magazine*, April 1989, 84. The nickname "Marston Mat" came from Marston, North Carolina, adjacent to Camp Mackall airfield where the material was first used.

8. Al Schutt, *History of the 451st Bombardment Group (H)*, https://451st.org/ History/History.html, 1.
9. Shutt, *History of the 451st*, 1; Maurer Maurer, ed., *Air Force Combat Units of World War II* (Washington, DC: Office of Air Force History, 1961), 325-326.
10. Shutt, *History of the 451st*, 1.
11. Shutt, *History of the 451st*, 2.
12. William Atkinson, *The Jolly Roger: An Airman's Tale of Survival in World War II*, 2nd. ed. (Sulphur, LA: Wise Publications, 2023), 139.
13. US Air Force, "Major General Robert E. L. Eaton," accessed February 10, 2024, https://www.af.mil/About-Us/Biographies/Display/Article/107175/major-general-robert-el-eaton.
14. Mike Hill, *The 451st Bomb Group in World War II: A Pictorial History* (Atglen, PA: Schiffer Military History, 2001), 8.
15. Shutt, *History of the 451st*, 2.
16. Shutt, *History of the 451st*, 2.
17. Shutt, *History of the 451st*, 2; Technical Order No. 03-1-46, *Index of Army-Navy Aeronautical Equipment-Miscellaneous* (Indianapolis: Success P&L, 1945), 155.
18. Shutt, *History of the 451st*, 2.
19. Hill, *451st Bomb Group*, 9.
20. Shutt, *History of the 451st*, 2-3.
21. Shutt, *History of the 451st*, 3-4.
22. Shutt, *History of the 451st*, 3.
23. Karl F. Eichhorn Jr., National Archives and Records Administration, College Park, MD; Electronic Army Serial Number Merged File, 1938–1946, NAID: 1263923; Records of the National Archives and Records Administration, Washington, DC, 1789–ca. 2007; Record Group 64, box 09655, reel 27.
24. Karl F. Eichhorn Jr., "The Wartime Journal of Karl Eichhorn (726th)," *Ad Lib*, no. 17 (Winter 1988), 451st Bomb Group Publication, 18-19.
25. Shutt, *History of the 451st*, 3.
26. Karl F. Eichhorn Jr., "The Wartime Journal of Karl Eichhorn (726th)," *Ad Lib*, no. 18 (Fall 1989), 451st Bomb Group Publication, 10.
27. Hill, *451st Bomb Group*, 10.
28. Shutt, *History of the 451st*, 3.
29. Shutt, *History of the 451st*, 3.
30. Shutt, *History of the 451st*, 3; Hill, *451st Bomb Group*, 11-12.
31. Eichhorn, "Wartime Journal," *Ad Lib*, no. 18, 10.
32. Lieutenant Colonel James Bishop Beane, "Personal Memoirs," private collection, transcribed from audiotape by Justine Beane Bradford, 1970, 21.
33. Beane, "Personal Memoirs," 23.
34. Shutt, *History of the 451st*, 4.
35. Shutt, *History of the 451st*, 4; Eichhorn, *Ad Lib*, no. 18, 11.
36. Atkinson, *Jolly Roger*, 138-139.
37. Eichhorn, *Ad Lib*, no. 18, 11.

38. Eichhorn, *Ad Lib*, no. 18, 11-12.
39. Shutt, *History of the 451st*, 5.
40. Shutt, *History of the 451st*, 5-6.
41. Beane, "Personal Memoirs," 26.
42. Eichhorn, *Ad Lib*, no. 18, 12.
43. Eichhorn, *Ad Lib*, no. 18, 12.
44. Eichhorn, *Ad Lib*, no. 18, 13.
45. Eichhorn, *Ad Lib*, no. 18, 13.
46. Atkinson, *Jolly Roger*, 142.
47. Atkinson, *Jolly Roger*, 145-146.
48. Atkinson, *Jolly Roger*, 145-146.
49. Shutt, *History of the 451st*, 6-7.
50. Shutt, *History of the 451st*, 7-8.
51. Shutt, *History of the 451st*, 8-10
52. Shutt, *History of the 451st*, 8-9.
53. Shutt, *History of the 451st*, 9-10.
54. Jarvis D. Anderson, "Roaming with the 451st," *Ad Lib*, no. 39 (Winter 2004, 2005), 451st Bomb Group Publication, 29.
55. Eichhorn, *Ad Lib*, no. 18, 14.
56. Anderson, "Roaming," 14.
57. Eichhorn, *Ad Lib*, no. 18, 14.
58. Eichhorn, *Ad Lib*, no. 18, 14-15.
59. Eichhorn, *Ad Lib*, no. 18, 15.
60. Andrew Pendleton, interview, December 2023, YouTube, accessed April 3, 2024, https://www.youtube.com/watch?v=U9wyEwdWv4E.
61. Pendleton interview.
62. Shutt, *History of the 451st*, 10; Sedgefield D. Hill, ed., *The "Fight'n" 451st Bombardment Group* (Paducah, KY: Turner, 1990), 21.
63. Shutt, *History of the 451st*, 10.

Chapter 2: The "Flying Boxcar"

1. Harold Thompson, conversations with the author.
2. Thomas A. Manning, *History of Air Education and Training Command, 1942–2002* (Randolph Air Force Base, TX: Office of History and Research, 2005), 341.
3. The rest of this section about Harold Thompson's flight training is based on his conversations with the author.
4. Beane, "Personal Memoirs," 11.
5. Letter from Aviation Cadet Examining Center, Cleveland, Ohio, to Harold T. Thompson, dated December 12, 1942, author's personal collection; Aviation Cadet Graduation Certificate for Harold T. Thompson, issued at Brooks Field, Texas, November 3, 1943, author's personal collection.
6. Manning, *History of Air Education*, 6.
7. Manning, *History of Air Education*, 6, 16.

8. George McGovern, quoted in Stephen E. Ambrose, *The Wild Blue: The Men and Boys Who Flew the B-24s over Germany 1944–1945* (New York: Simon & Schuster, 2011), 68.
9. Ambrose, *Wild Blue*, 70.
10. Beane, "Personal Memoirs," 12.
11. Thomas P. Reynolds, *Belle of the Brawl: A Biographical Memoir of Walter Malone Baskin* (Paducah, KY: Turner Publishing, 1996), 18.
12. Ambrose, *Wild Blue*, 80-81; *Pilot Training Manual for the B-24 Liberator, Army Manual No. 50-12* (Winston-Salem, NC: AAF Headquarters, Office of Flying Safety, 1945), 25.
13. *Pilot Training Manual for the B-24 Liberator*, 6.
14. Ambrose, *Wild Blue*, 81; Tom Faulkner, *Flying with the Fifteenth Air Force: A B-24 Pilot's Missions from Italy during World War II* (Denton: University of North Texas Press, 2018), 54.
15. Wesley Frank Craven and James Lea Cate, eds., *The Army Air Forces in World War II,* vol. 6, *Men and Planes* (Chicago: University of Chicago Press for the Office of Air Force History, 1955), 206-207.
16. Bert Kinsey and Rock Rozak, *B-24 Liberator in Detail & Scale* (Detail & Scale Publications, 2023), 9-10.
17. Alan Griffith, *Consolidated Mess: An Illustrated Guide to Nose-Turreted B-24 Production Variants in USAAF Combat Service* (Sandomierz, Poland: Stratus sp.j., 2018), 12.
18. Griffith, *Consolidated Mess*, 12.
19. *Pilot Training Manual for the B-24 Liberator*, 23.
20. Griffith, *Consolidated Mess*, 12.
21. Reuben Fleet, quoted in Ambrose, *Wild Blue*, 22.
22. Ambrose, *Wild Blue*, 80.
23. Craven and Cate, *Army Air Forces*, 6:207.
24. Ambrose, *Wild Blue*, 77-78.
25. *Pilot Training Manual for the B-24 Liberator*, 4.
26. *Pilot Training Manual for the B-24 Liberator*, 4-5.
27. Thompson conversations; "Citation Accompanying Award of the Distinguished Flying Cross to Harold T. Thompson," November 1944, author's personal collection.
28. Craven and Cate, *Army Air Forces*, 6:312.
29. Barrett Tillman, *Forgotten Fifteenth: The Daring Airmen Who Crippled Hitler's War Machine* (Washington, DC: Regnery History, 2014), 9.
30. Tillman, *Forgotten Fifteenth,* 9; Ambrose, *Wild Blue*, 79-80; *Flight Manual: B-24D Aircraft*, Consolidated Aircraft, September 1942, 25.
31. Kinzey and Rozak, *B-24 Liberator*, 43; Mantelli Brown, *Consolidated B-24 Liberator*, book 2 of *Aircraft of World War II* (Le Grau-du-Roi, France: R.E.I. Editions, 2015), 34.
32. Kinzey and Rozak, *B-24 Liberator*, 43.
33. Kinzey and Rozak, *B-24 Liberator*, 52-54.

34. Kinzey and Rozak, *B-24 Liberator*, 49; Tillman, *Forgotten Fifteenth*, 89.
35. Thomas Childers, *Wings of Morning: The Story of the Last American Bomber Shot Down over Germany in World War II* (Reading, MA: Addison-Wesley, 1995), 21.
36. Childers, *Wings of Morning*, 22-23.
37. Ambrose, *Wild Blue*, 95-96; Childers, *Wings of Morning*, 24-25.
38. Thompson conversations.
39. Ambrose, *Wild Blue*, 80.
40. The descriptions in the next six paragraphs of the crew members' jobs are based on *Pilot Training Manual for the B-24 Liberator*, 6-7, 13-14, 16.
41. The discussion of fuzes in the next three paragraphs is based on Karl F. Eichhorn Jr., "Karl Eichhorn's 726th Journal," *Ad Lib*, no. 20 (Summer 1991), 451st Bomb Group (H) Publication, 10.
42. *Pilot Training Manual for the B-24 Liberator*, 17.
43. Burl D. Harmon, *Combat Missions: Flying the B-24 Liberator Bomber out of Manduria, Italy, 450th Bomb Group, 720th Squadron, WWII* (Pennsauken Township, NJ: BookBaby Publishers, 2022), 39.
44. *Pilot Training Manual for the B-24 Liberator*, 18-19.
45. *Pilot Training Manual for the B-24 Liberator*, 212.
46. Ambrose, *Wild Blue*, 82.
47. *Flight Manual: B-24D Aircraft*, 48.
48. Lieutenant "Pep" Petrocine, interview by Elaine Stahlman Jurs, 398th Bomb Group Annual Reunion, Phoenix, November 2007, 398th Bomb Group Memorial Association, accessed February 17, 2024, http://www.398th.org/History/Veterans/Voices/Transcriptions/Interview_Petrocine_Pep.html#PP_Feathering; Faulkner, *Flying with the Fifteenth Air Force*, 51.
49. *Flight Manual: B-24D Aircraft*, 13.
50. Ambrose, *Wild Blue*, 79-80.
51. *Flight Manual: B-24D Aircraft*, 13-14.
52. *Flight Manual: B-24D Aircraft*, 14.
53. *B-24 Pilot Training Manual*, 68; *Flight Manual: B-24D*, 14.
54. *Flight Manual: B-24D*, 15-16.
55. *Flight Manual: B-24D*, 16-17.

Chapter 3: War in the Air

1. *Bombardier's Information File (BIF)* (Washington DC: US War Department, Army Air Force, March 1945), 95.
2. *Bombardier's Information File*, 99.
3. *Bombardier's Information File*, 134, 141.
4. *Bombardier's Information File*, 134.
5. Malcom Gladwell, *The Bomber Mafia: A Dream, a Temptation, and the Longest Night of the Second World War* (New York: Little, Brown, 2021), 34.
6. Gladwell, *Bomber Mafia*, 51-52; John T. Correll, "Daylight Precision Bombing," *Air & Space Forces Magazine* 91, no. 10 (October 2008): 1-5.

7. Kenneth Walker, "Driving Home the Bombardment Attack," *Coast Artillery Journal* 73, no. 4 (October 1930): 328-340, cited in Phil Haun, *Lectures of the Air Corps Tactical School and American Strategic Bombing in World War II (Aviation & Air Power)* (Lexington: University Press of Kentucky, 2019), 90-91.
8. Haun, *Lectures*, 91-93.
9. Correll, "Daylight Precision Bombing," 1-5.
10. *German Antiaircraft Artillery, Special Series No. 10, M18 461,* February 8, 1943 (Washington, DC: US War Department, Military Intelligence Services, 1943), 19.
11. Correll, "Daylight Precision Bombing," 1.
12. Correll, "Daylight Precision Bombing," 3.
13. Chris McNab, *Fighting from the Heavens: Tactics and Training of USAAF Bomber Crews, 1941–45* (Havertown, PA: Casemate, 2023), 7.
14. *TM E9-369A: German 88-mm Antiaircraft Gun Materiel—Technical Manual* (Washington, DC: US War Department, 1943), 2; Thompson conversations.
15. Beane, "Personal Memoirs," 39.
16. *German Antiaircraft Artillery*, 2-3, 78.
17. *German Antiaircraft Artillery*, 82, 88, 107.
18. "Chaff" is the term for thousands of thin strips of aluminum that bombers dropped to blind or confuse enemy radar.
19. Kevin A. Mahoney, *Fifteenth Air Force against the Axis: Combat Missions over Europe during World War II* (Toronto: Scarecrow Press, 2013), 601-602.
20. McNab, *Fighting*, 268-269.
21. The next three paragraphs are based on Robert Forsyth, "Luftwaffe vs Mighty Eighth: The Battle to Stop US bombers," Key.Aero, accessed February 20, 2024, https://www.key.aero/article/luftwaffe-vs-mighty-eighth-battle-stop-us-bombers, July 15, 2022.
22. Beane, "Personal Memoirs," 37.
23. Martin C. Windrow, *The Messerschmidt Bf 110* (London: Profile Publications, 1965), 3-8.
24. Mantelli Brown, *Junkers Ju 88*, book 22 of *Aircraft of World War II* (Le Grau-du-Roi, France: R.E.I. Editions, 2015), 20.
25. This excerpt and the next four paragraphs are based on Forsyth, "Luftwaffe."
26. Roger A. Freeman, *The Mighty Eighth War Manual* (Beverly, MA: Motorbooks International, 1991), 37.
27. *B-24 Pilot Training Manual*, 234.
28. Robert S. Capps, *Flying Colt: Liberator Pilot in Italy* (Hamilton, ON: Manor House, 1997), 102.
29. Capps, *Flying Colt*, 104.
30. Capps, *Flying Colt*, 107, 397.
31. From *Bombardier's Information File*, in McNab, *Fighting*, 270-272; Charles Haltom, "Closer Look at Regensburg Mission," *Ad Lib*, no. 35 (Spring/Summer 2002), 451st Bomb Group Publication, 4.

32. *Air Power History, Vol. I* (Washington, DC: Air Force Historical Foundation, 2003), 33-35.
33. Mahoney, *Fifteenth Air Force*, 607.
34. Tillman, *Forgotten Fifteenth*, 61-62.
35. Mahoney, *Fifteenth Air Force*, 607-608.
36. Mahoney, *Fifteenth Air Force*, 608-609.
37. Mahoney, *Fifteenth Air Force*, 599.
38. Mahoney, *Fifteenth Air Force*, 599.
39. McNab, *Fighting*, 112.
40. McNab, *Fighting*, 112-113.
41. McNab, *Fighting*, 113.
42. McNab, *Fighting*, 114-115.
43. *B-24 Pilot Training Manual*, 232.
44. McNab, *Fighting*, 61; *B-24 Pilot Training Manual*, 232-233.
45. Mahoney, *Fifteenth Air Force*, 600.
46. Mahoney, *Fifteenth Air Force*, 600.
47. Thompson conversations.
48. Mahoney, *Fifteenth Air Force*, 600.
49. Faulkner, *Flying with the Fifteenth Air Force*, 101.
50. Missing Air Crew Reports (MACRs) of the US Army Air Forces, 1942–1947, National Archives and Records Administration, Washington, DC, 2008, 1.
51. Thompson conversations.
52. Thompson conversations.

Chapter 4: "Big Week"

1. Roger McCollester, "Raid on Regensburg," *Flight Journal* (December 2001): 46.
2. McCollester, "Raid," 46.
3. McCollester, "Raid," 46.
4. Wesley Frank Craven and James Lea Cate, eds., *The Army Air Forces in World War II*, vol. 3, *Europe: ARGUMENT to V-E Day, January 1944 to May 1945* (Chicago: University of Chicago Press for the Office of Air Force History, 1951), 30.
5. Shutt, *History of the 451st*, 10.
6. Atkinson, *Jolly Roger*, 199.
7. Atkinson, *Jolly Roger*, 200.
8. Thompson conversations.
9. Shutt, *History of the 451st*, 10; Atkinson, *Jolly Roger*, 204.
10. Atkinson, *Jolly Roger*, 206; Shutt, *History of the 451st*, 10.
11. Shutt, *History of the 451st*, 10; *Mission Summary for the First 200 Missions,* Headquarters, 451st Bombardment Group (H), Office of the Intelligence Officer, APO 520 US Army, February 24, 1945, 1.
12. Craven and Cate, *Army Air Forces*, 3:30.
13. Craven and Cate, *Army Air Forces*, 3:30.
14. Craven and Cate, *Army Air Forces*, 3:36.

15. McCollester, "Raid," 45-46, 49.
16. Craven and Cate, *Army Air Forces,* 3:37; Daily Operations Report, February 22, 1944, 451st Bombardment Group, 1-2.
17. Craven and Cate, *Army Air Forces*, 3:37; Daily Operations Report, February 22, 1944, 1-2.
18. Craven and Cate, *Army Air Forces*, 3:39; Daily Operations Report, February 23, 1944, 1-2.
19. Eichhorn, "726th Journal," 12.
20. Craven and Cate, *Army Air Forces*, 3:41; Douglas C. Dildy, *"Big Week" 1944: Operation Argument and the Breaking of the Jagdwaffe* (Oxford, UK: Osprey, 2022), 2352-2355.
21. Craven and Cate, *Army Air Forces*, 3:41; Dildy, *"Big Week,"* 2355-2363.
22. *Mission Summary, 25 February 1944*, 451st Bombardment Group, 1; McCollester, "Raid," 46.
23. *Mission Summary, 25 February 1944*, 1; McCollester, "Raid," 46.
24. McCollester, "Raid," 45.
25. McCollester, "Raid," 46.
26. Atkinson, *Jolly Roger*, 216.
27. Atkinson, *Jolly Roger*, 216-217.
28. McCollester, "Raid," 47-48; Atkinson, *Jolly Roger*, 217-218.
29. McCollester, "Raid," 48; "Narrative History of Regensburg, Germany, Mission #10," *Ad Lib* (January 1982), 451st Bomb Group Publication, 4.
30. "Narrative History of Regensburg," *Ad Lib* (January 1982), 4.
31. McCollester, "Raid," 48;
32. McCollester, "Raid," 48.
33. Haltom, "Closer Look," 4.
34. Atkinson, *Jolly Roger*, 218.
35. Atkinson, *Jolly Roger*, 219-220.
36. Atkinson, *Jolly Roger*, 220. The items contained in escape and evasion kits remained almost the same well into the late twentieth century.
37. Atkinson, *Jolly Roger*, 220.
38. Atkinson, *Jolly Roger*, 222; *Pilot Training Manual for the B-24 Liberator*, 35, 74.
39. Atkinson, *Jolly Roger*, 223.
40. Atkinson, *Jolly Roger*, 223.
41. Dildy, *"Big Week,"* 2355-2363.
42. Dildy, *"Big Week,"* 2367.
43. US World War II Army Enlistment Records, National Archives and Records Administration, College Park, MD; Electronic Army Serial Number Merged File, 1938–1946, NAID: 1263923, Records of the National Archives and Records Administration, Washington, DC, 1789–ca. 2007, Record Group 64, box 02712, reel 128; James F. Thompson, "Clarifications, References and Updates," *Ad Lib*, no. 36 (Winter/Spring 2003), 451st Bomb Group Publication, 27.

44. Missing Air Crew Report (MACR) for Aircraft 42-7765, 1944, 1945, National Archives and Records Administration, Washington, DC. In 2018, Sergeant Duran's remains were found buried in a Slovenian churchyard, positively identified, and returned to his family for burial. *Army Times*, Washington, DC, June 6, 2018.
45. Statement by Sergeant Corbin McPherson, Missing Air Crew Report (MACR) for Aircraft 42-52167, 1944, 1945, National Archives and Records Administration, Washington, DC, 6.
46. Statement by Lieutenant James Boornazian, MACR for Aircraft 42-52167, 7; Statement by Lieutenant Harold Adams, MACR for Aircraft 42-52167, 25.
47. McPherson statement, MACR for Aircraft 42-52167, 6.
48. Boornazian statement, MACR for Aircraft 42-52167, 7.
49. Information from Lieutenant George Strickner, MACR for Aircraft 42-52167, 28.
50. Boornazian statement, MACR for Aircraft 42-52167, 7.
51. Edi Šelhaus, *Evasion and Repatriation: Slovene Partisans and Rescued American Airmen in World War II* (Manhattan, KS: Sunflower University Press, 1993), 5.
52. Notes by Captain Robert Grabb, MACR for Aircraft 42-52167, 42.
53. "Narrative History," 6; "Statement by SSgt Israel Willig," 724th Bombardment Squadron (H), 451st Bombardment Group (H), APO 520 US Army, March 14, 1944, Missing Air Crew Report (MACR) for Aircraft 42-52101, National Archives and Records Administration, Washington, DC, 2.
54. Ryan, "Early Diary," 10; "Statement by TSgt Benneville E. Rhoads," 725th Bomb Squadron, Missing Air Crew Report (MACR) for Aircraft 42-52168, National Archives and Records Administration, Washington, DC, 1944, 1945, 2; "Statement by TSgt Henry W. Dieter," 725th Bomb Squadron, MACR 42-52168, 3.
55. Casualty Information Report for the Adjutant General's Office, Headquarters, AAF Redistribution Station No. 2, Miami Beach, June 17, 1944, Missing Air Crew Report (MACR) for Aircraft 42-77388, National Archives and Records Administration, Washington, DC, 1944, 1945, 7-8; "Statement by 2nd Lieutenant George E. Dewey," Michel Field, NY, MACR 42-77388, 20-22; "Eyewitness Statement," Edward F. McGoldrick, MACR 42-77388, 12; "Eyewitness Statement," 2nd Lieutenant Albert L. Roemer, MACR 42-77388, 13.
56. Dewey statement, MACR 42-77388, 20-22.
57. Casualty Report, Sergeant John Chamberlain, MACR 42-77388, 28-31; "Statement or Report of Interview with Recovered Personnel," 2nd Lieutenant George E. Dewey, MACR 42-77388, 20-21.
58. Casualty Questionnaire, 2nd Lieutenant George Dewy, MACR 42-77388, 25.
59. Missing Air Crew Report (MACR) for Aircraft 41-29244, National Archives and Records Administration, Washington, DC, 1944, 1945, 2.
60. McCollester, "Raid," 50.
61. Haltom, "Closer Look," 4; McCollester, "Raid," 50; Craven and Cate, *Army Air Forces*, 3:42.
62. Ryan, "Early Diary," 10; Atkinson, *Jolly Roger*, 50; Daily Operations Report, February 25, 1944, 451st Bombardment Group (H), February 26, 1944, 2.

63. Ryan, "Early Diary," 10; Atkinson, *Jolly Roger*, 50.
64. This paragraph and the next three are based on Haltom, "Closer Look," 4.
65. "The 'Big Week': 449th Missions of 'Big Week'—February 20–25, 1944," 449th Bomb Group Association, accessed February 15, 2024, https://449th.com/the-big-week.
66. Dildy, *"Big Week,* 2392-2393.
67. "Narrative History," 5.
68. Craven and Cate, *Army Air Forces*, 3:42; Ryan, "Early Diary," 10.
69. Commendation of Unit, Headquarters 47th Bomb Wing, 23 April 1944.

Chapter 5: The Oil Campaign Renewed

1. Atkinson, *Jolly Roger*, 265; John Weal, *Jagdgeschwader 51 'Mölders' (Aviation Elite Units)* (Oxford, UK: Osprey, 2006), 201-202.
2. Atkinson, *Jolly Roger*, 274.
3. Atkinson, *Jolly Roger*, 274.
4. Schutt, *History of the 451st*, 11.
5. Eichhorn, "726th Journal," 13.
6. Eichhorn, "726th Journal," 13.
7. Schutt, *History of the 451st*, 11.
8. Mahoney, *Fifteenth Air Force*, 22; Tillman, *Forgotten Fifteenth*, 84.
9. Tillman, *Forgotten Fifteenth*, 84.
10. Steven J. Zaloga, *The Oil Campaign 1944–45: Draining the Wehrmacht's Lifeblood,* Air Campaign Book 30 (Oxford, UK: Osprey, 2022), 48-49.
11. Craven and Cate, *Army Air Forces*, 3:173.
12. Craven and Cate, *Army Air Forces*, 3:173-174; Tillman, *Forgotten Fifteenth*, 85.
13. Tillman, *Forgotten Fifteenth*, 86; Jay A. Stout, *Fortress Ploesti: The Campaign to Destroy Hitler's Oil Supply* (Havertown, PA: Casemate, 2003), 156.
14. Tillman, *Forgotten Fifteenth*, 86.
15. Atkinson, *Jolly Roger*, 260, 263; Robert Stone in "P.R.O. Does Major Job for 724th C.O.: Beane," *Ad Lib*, no. 20 (Summer 1991), 451st Bomb Group Publication, 20-21.
16. Atkinson, *Jolly Roger*, 260-261.
17. Atkinson, *Jolly Roger*, 261-262.
18. Atkinson, *Jolly Roger*, 262-263.
19. Robert Stone, quoted in "P.R.O. Does Major Job for 724th C.O.: Beane," *Ad Lib*, no. 20, 21.
20. Atkinson, *Jolly Roger*, 267; Schutt, *History of the 451st*, 11.
21. Atkinson, *Jolly Roger*, 267-268.
22. Stout, *Fortress Ploesti*, 139-140.
23. Roger Johnston in "P.R.O. Does Major Job for 724th C.O.: Beane," *Ad Lib*, no. 20, 22.
24. Robert Stone in "P.R.O. Does Major Job for 724th C.O.: Beane," *Ad Lib*, no. 20, 21; Robert L. Stone to Dr. Justine Beane Bradford, March 20, 2002, Dr. Bradford's personal collection.

25. Weal, *Jagdgeschwader 51*, 197.
26. Stout, *Fortress Ploesti*, 140.
27. Robert Stone quoted in *Ad Lib,* no. 20, 21; Roger Johnston quoted in *Ad Lib*, no. 20, 22.
28. This paragraph and the next 20 are based on Atkinson, *Jolly Roger*, 263-301.
29. Atkinson, *Jolly Roger*, 299-300.
30. "Declaration by Gheorghe Ctanoiu, Sergiu Nicolescu, Mircea Rosulescu, Ioan Coserennu, and C-tin Brandabur," Missing Air Crew Report (MACR) for Aircraft 42-52081, National Archives and Records Administration, Washington, DC, 1944, 1945, 14; "Investigation to Determine the Battle Casualty Status," 2616th Investigating Detachment (OVHD), APO 520, US Army, January 31, 1945, MACR for Aircraft 42-52081, 16.
31. "Individual Casualty Questionnaire for Stennis, William C.," Missing Air Crew Report (MACR) for Aircraft 42-7720, National Archives and Records Administration, Washington, DC, 1944, 1945, 12.
32. "Individual Casualty Questionnaire for Burge, Arthur P.," MACR for Aircraft 42-7720, 2.
33. "Casualty Questionnaire," TSgt James Bennett, MACR for Aircraft 42-7720, 27.
34. "Individual Casualty Questionnaire for Burge, Arthur P.," MACR for Aircraft 42-7720, 2.
35. "Casualty Questionnaire," 1st Lt. Robert R. Blaschke, MACR for Aircraft 42-7720, 5, 11.
36. "Individual Casualty Questionnaire for Carrol, Wylie C.," MACR for Aircraft 42-7720, 4.
37. "Casualty Questionnaire, 1st Lt. Robert J. Berg," Missing Air Crew Report (MACR) for Aircraft 42-6442, National Archives and Records Administration, Washington, DC, 1944, 1945, 11; Atkinson, *Jolly Roger*, 277-278.
38. "Individual Casualty Questionnaire for Smith, Dale W.," MACR for Aircraft 42-6442, 8.
39. "Individual Casualty Questionnaire for Wahl, Harold R.," MACR for Aircraft 42-6442, 10.
40. "Individual Casualty Questionnaire for Smith, Dale W.," MACR for Aircraft 42-6442, 13.
41. "Casualty Questionnaire, 1st Lt. Robert J. Berg," MACR for Aircraft 42-6442, 11.
42. "Casualty Questionnaire, Alan R. May," MACR for Aircraft 42-6442, 27; "Casualty Questionnaire, MSgt Harold W. Shireman," MACR for Aircraft 42-6442, 21.
43. "Individual Casualty Questionnaire for Brownell, Claremont D.," MACR for Aircraft 42-6442, 22; "Individual Casualty Questionnaire for Smith, Dale W.," MACR for Aircraft 42-6442, 23.
44. Missing Air Crew Report (MACR) for Aircraft 42-5103, National Archives and Records Administration, Washington, DC, 1944.
45. MACR for Aircraft 42-5103.
46. Atkinson, *Jolly Roger*, 278.

47. Stout, *Fortress Ploesti*, 141.

48. Roger Johnston in "P.R.O. Does Major Job for 7124th C.O.: Beane," *Ad Lib*, no. 20, 22; Stout, *Fortress Ploesti*, 141.

49. John C. Bounds, "S/Sgt John C. Bounds Recalls," *Ad Lib*, no. 41 (Winter/Spring 2005/2006), 451st Bomb Group Publication, 18; Roger Stone in "P.R.O. Does Major Job for 7124th C.O.: Beane," *Ad Lib,* no. 20, 21; Roger Johnston in "P.R.O. Does Major Job for 7124th C.O.: Beane," *Ad Lib*, no. 20, 22.

50. Roger Stone in "P.R.O. Does Major Job for 7124th C.O.: Beane," *Ad Lib*, no. 20, 21; Roger Johnston in "P.R.O. Does Major Job for 7124th C.O.: Beane," *Ad Lib*, no. 20, 22.

51. Roger Stone in "P.R.O. Does Major Job for 7124th C.O.: Beane," *Ad Lib*, no. 20, 21; Roger Johnston in "P.R.O. Does Major Job for 7124th C.O.: Beane," *Ad Lib*, no. 20, 22.

52. Roger Johnston in "P.R.O. Does Major Job for 7124th C.O.: Beane," *Ad Lib*, no. 20, 22.

53. Bennie Hayman in "P.R.O. Does Major Job for 7124th C.O.: Beane," *Ad Lib*, no. 20, 23.

54. John Steurer in "P.R.O. Does Major Job for 7124th C.O.: Beane," *Ad Lib*, no. 20, 22.

55. Roger Stone in "P.R.O. Does Major Job for 7124th C.O.: Beane," *Ad Lib,* no. 20, 21; Tillman, *Forgotten Fifteenth*, 45.

56. Roger Stone in "P.R.O. Does Major Job for 7124th C.O.: Beane," *Ad Lib*, no. 20, 21.

57. Daily Operations Report April 5, 1944, 451st Bombardment Group (H), April 6, 1944; Stout, *Fortress Ploesti*, 142.

58. "451st Bomb Group Receives Two Unit Citations," public affairs release, 451st Bombardment Group (H), September 3, 1944.

Chapter 6: Overwhelming Opposition

1. "George E. Tudor," *Lincoln County News* (Newcastle, ME), April 30, 2010, accessed February 24, 2024, https://lcnme.com/obituaries/george-e-tudor/.

2. Mission flimsy, August 23, 1944, 451st Bombardment Group Association, accessed February 1, 2024, https://451st.org/Missions/Mission%20Flimsies/451st%20BG%20Pilot%20Flimsies/440823.JPG; George Tudor, "Saga of the Extra Joker," 725th Bomb Squadron, Markersdorf 75th Anniversary, 451st Bomb Group, August 2019, accessed February 10, 2024, https://www.facebook.com/groups/451stbg/permalink/2383229095046982.

3. Tudor, "Saga"; Winson Jones, "Win Jones and the Markersdorf Airdrome Mission of 23 August 1944," speech at the 2017 451st Bomb Group Reunion, New Orleans, YouTube, https://www.youtube.com/watch?v=cj3ougnPUCU, 3:53-4:17.

4. Tudor, "Saga."

5. Tudor, "Saga."

6. Lindley Miller, "Tech Sergeant Lindley Miller's Missions," *Ad Lib*, no. 41, 17; Tudor, "Saga."
7. Karl Eichhorn, "Karl Eichhorn's 726th Journal," *Ad Lib*, no. 21 (Winter 1991), 451st Bomb Group Publication, 11-12; "Castelluccio," Abandoned Forgotten & Little Known Airfields in Europe, accessed February 10, 2024, https://www.forgottenairfields.com/airfield-castelluccio-562.html.
8. Schutt, *History of the 451st*, 11-12; Eichhorn, *Ad Lib*, no. 21, 11-12.
9. Eichhorn, *Ad Lib,* no. 21, 11-12.
10. Schutt, *History of the 451st*, 11.
11. *Mission Summary for the First 200 Missions*, February 24, 1945.
12. Mahoney, *Fifteenth Air Force*, 130.
13. "Markersdorf," Abandoned Forgotten & Little Known Airfields in Europe, accessed February 1, 2024, https://forgottenairfields.com/airfield-markersdorf-51.html; Henry deZeng IV, *Luftwaffe Airfields 1935-45, Austria (1937 Borders)*, https://www.ww2.dk/lwairfields.html, 20-21.
14. "3rd Group DUC Reviewed," *Ad Lib,* no. 9 (undated), 451st Bomb Group Publication, 1; Operations Order No. 142, 22 August 1944, Headquarters, 49th Bombardment Wing (H), APO 520, US Army, National Archives and Records Administration.
15. "3rd Group DUC Reviewed," *Ad Lib,* no. 9, 4; Operations Order No. 142.
16. Tudor, "Saga"; "3rd Group DUC Reviewed," *Ad Lib*, no. 9, 3; "Intelligence Annex 'A,'" Operations Order No. 142.
17. Mission Flimsy, August 23, 1944.
18. General Robert E. L. Eaton, "General Eaton Amends Markersdorf Raid," *Ad Lib,* no. 10 (1983), 451st Bomb Group Publication, 1.
19. Eaton, "General Eaton Amends," *Ad Lib*, no. 10, 1.
20. Tudor, "Saga."
21. Tudor, "Saga."
22. Kurt Rieder and Rick Brown, *Stab & IV. (Sturm)/JG 3 Angriffsformation am 23. August 1944*, 451st Bomb Group Association, Facebook, August 2019; "Intelligence Annex 'A,'" Operations Order No. 142.
23. "3rd Group DUC Reviewed," *Ad Lib*, no. 9, 1, 3.
24. Eaton, "General Eaton Amends," *Ad Lib*, no. 10, 1; "3rd Group DUC Reviewed," *Ad Lib,* no. 9, 1.
25. "3rd Group DUC Reviewed," *Ad Lib*, no. 9, 3; Eaton, "General Eaton Amends," *Ad Lib,* no. 10, 2.
26. Eaton, "General Eaton Amends," *Ad Lib*, no. 10, 2.
27. "3rd Group DUC Reviewed," *Ad Lib*, no. 9, 3.
28. "3rd Group DUC Reviewed," *Ad Lib*, no. 9, 3.
29. Tudor, "Saga."
30. Miller, "Tech Sergeant," *Ad Lib*, no. 41, 17.
31. "German Status Report, ME 2015," Missing Air Crew Report (MACR) for Aircraft 42-78171, National Archives and Records Administration, Washington, DC,

1944-1945, 10; Report on Shoot-Down of Aircraft (German), Casualty No. KSU-2015, MACR for Aircraft 42-78171, 14-17; Miller, "Tech Sergeant," *Ad Lib*, no. 41, 17.

32. Missing Air Crew Report (MACR) for Aircraft 42-7763, National Archives and Records Administration, Washington, DC, 1944-1945.

33. MACR for Aircraft 42-7763.

34. Missing Air Crew Report (MACR) for Aircraft 44-40196, National Archives and Records Administration, Washington, DC, 1944-1945.

35. Thompson conversations.

36. This paragraph and the next three are based on Missing Air Crew Report (MACR) for Aircraft 42-78523, National Archives and Records Administration, Washington, DC, 1944-1945.

37. This paragraph and the next three are based on Missing Air Crew Report (MACR) for Aircraft 42-51729, National Archives and Records Administration, Washington, DC, 1944, 1945.

38. Dulag Lufts were facilities where new prisoners were processed before being sent to a permanent POW camp.

39. This paragraph and the next four are based on "23.08.1944, 724th Bombardment Squadron (H) B-24J 42-51729 2nd Lt. Robert L Beach," *Archive Report: US Forces, 1941–1945,* Aircrew Remembered, accessed August 6, 2024, https://aircrewremembered.com/beach-robert.html.

40. MACR for Aircraft 42-51729.

41. This paragraph and the next three are based on Missing Air Crew Report (MACR) for Aircraft 42-78471, National Archives and Records Administration, Washington, DC, 1944, 1945.

42. MACR for Aircraft 42-78471.

43. "AG 704 DEAD 10 January 1949, MEMORANDUM FOR: Officer in Charge, Casualty Section Personnel, Actions Branch, AGO, SUBJECT: Reports of Death," cited in "A Cousin's Search for Answers—Finds Them & Shares Them," *Ad Lib*, no. 30 (Fall/Winter 1998), 451st Bomb Group (H) Publication, 5-7.

44. Missing Air Crew Report (MACR) for Aircraft 42-51334, National Archives and Records Administration, Washington, DC, 1944, 1945; Chester H. Ennis, "The Individual Picture, 20 August 1983," *Ad Lib*, no. 10, 3.

45. Ennis, "Individual Picture," *Ad Lib*, no. 10, 3; Harvey S. Clapp quoted in "Individual Picture," *Ad Lib,* no. 10, 3.

46. Clapp, "Individual Picture," *Ad Lib*, no. 10, 3.

47. Comment by Bob Karstensen, editor, "Individual Picture," *Ad Lib*, no. 10, 3.

48. Ennis, "Individual Picture," *Ad Lib*, no. 10, 3.

49. "3rd Group DUC Reviewed," *Ad Lib*, no. 9, 4.

50. Eaton, "General Eaton Amends," *Ad Lib*, no. 10, 1-2; "3rd Group DUC Reviewed," *Ad Lib,* no. 9, 3.

51. "3rd Group DUC Reviewed," *Ad Lib*, no. 9, 3.

52. "3rd Group DUC Reviewed," *Ad Lib*, no. 9, 3.

53. "3rd Group DUC Reviewed," *Ad Lib*, no. 9, 3.
54. Miller, "Tech Sergeant," *Ad Lib*, no. 44, 17.
55. Robert E. L. Eaton, Colonel, Air Corps, Commanding, Daily Operations Report, August 23, 1944, 451st Bombardment Group.
56. "3rd Group DUC Reviewed," *Ad Lib*, no. 9, 4.

Chapter 7: Mission Five Zero

1. Thompson conversations.
2. Thompson conversations; Statistical Summary, Week Ending 11 November 1944, 451st Bombardment Group (H), APO 520, US Army, 4.
3. Thompson conversations.
4. Thompson conversations.
5. Schutt, *History of the 451st*, 18; *Mission Summary for the First 200 Missions*, 3.
6. Eichhorn, "Karl Eichhorn's 726th Journal," *Ad Lib*, no. 22 (Spring 1993), 451st Bomb Group (H) Publication, 16.
7. Thompson conversations.
8. Schutt, *History of the 451st*, 19; *Mission Summary for the First 200 Missions*, 5-6.
9. Hill, *451st Bomb Group*, 72.
10. Hill, *451st Bomb Group*, 72.
11. Eichhorn, "726th Journal," *Ad Lib*, no. 22, 14; Schutt, *History of the 451st*, 37.
12. This paragraph and the next three are based on Clyde W. Phifer, "My Overseas Tour (Concluding Chapter)," *Ad Lib*, no. 43 (Winter 2007), 451st Bomb Group (H) Publication, 10.
13. Hill, *451st Bomb Group*, 73.
14. "More on the 1Lt William Silliman Incident (Crash off Coast of North Africa on Way Home)," *Ad Lib*, no. 34 (Fall 2001), 451st Bomb Group (H) Publication, 11; "Silliman Crash Still Evokes Memories," *Ad Lib,* no. 25 (Spring/Summer 2002), 451st Bomb Group Publication, 17; Schutt, *History of the 451st*, 37.
15. Karl Eichhorn, "Karl Eichhorn's 726th Journal," *Ad Lib*, no. 23 (Summer 1993), 451st Bomb Group Publication, 14.
16. Hill, *451st Bomb Group*, 73.
17. Hill, *451st Bomb Group*, 73; Schutt, *History of the 451st*, 37.
18. Hill, *451st Bomb Group*, 73; Schutt, *History of the 451st*, 37.
19. Schutt, *History of the 451st*, 37; 451st Aircraft Spreadsheet, accessed February 1, 2024, https://451st.org/Aircraft/pdfs/451st%20Aircraft%20Spreadsheet%20as%20of%20Aug%202019.pdf.

Afterword

1. Atkinson, *Jolly Roger*, 492, 494-496.
2. Beane, *Personal Memoirs*, 40; email from James Beane's daughter, Justine Beane Bradford, April 5, 2024.
3. "M/General Robert E. L. Eaton Succumbs," *Ad Lib,* no. 23 (Summer 1993), 451st Bomb Group (H) Publication, 1-3.

4. Jenny Henke, "It's Not Nice to Fool Mother Nature," *Florida Today* (Cocoa), September 7, 1974, 1D; Hubert Griggs Jr., "Karl Eichhorn Started a Camping Business," *Orlando Sentinel*, July 31, 1977, 96.

5. Atkinson, *Jolly Roger*, 501.

6. *U.S. Veterans Gravesites, ca. 1775–2006*, National Cemetery Administration (Lehi, UT: Ancestry.com Operations, 2006).

7. Author's personal information.

8. Biographical information provided by George Tudor's son, Jonathon Tudor, March 2, 2024.

9. *U.S. Military Registers, 1862–1985, Army and Air Force, 1948, Vol. 2* (Lehi, UT: Ancestry.com Operations, 2013), 502; *Find a Grave Index, 1600s–Current, 2012* (Lehi, UT: Ancestry.com Operations, 2013).

BIBLIOGRAPHY

Air Power History, Vol. I. Washington, DC: Air Force Historical Foundation, 2003.

Ambrose, Stephen E. *The Wild Blue: The Men and Boys Who Flew the B-24s over Germany 1944–1945*. New York: Simon & Schuster, 2011.

Anderson, Jarvis D. "Roaming with the 451st." *Ad Lib*, no. 39 (Winter 2004, 2005). 451st Bomb Group Publication.

Army Enlistment Records, 1789–ca. 2007. National Archives and Records Administration, College Park, MD.

Atkinson, William. *The Jolly Roger: An Airman's Tale of Survival in World War II*. 2nd ed. Sulphur, LA: Wise Publications, 2023.

Beane, Lieutenant Colonel James Bishop. "Personal Memoirs." Private collection. Transcribed from audiotape by Justine Beane Bradford, 1970.

"The 'Big Week': 449th Missions of 'Big Week'—February 20–25, 1944." 449th Bomb Group Association. Accessed February 15, 2024. https://449th.com/the-big-week.

Bombardier's Information File (BIF). Washington, DC: US War Department, Army Air Force, March 1945.

Bowman, Martin W. *The USAAF Handbook, 1939–1945*. Mechanicsburg, PA: Stackpole, 1997.

Brown, Mantelli. *Consolidated B-24 Liberator*. Book 2 of *Aircraft of World War II*. Le Grau-du-Roi, France: R.E.I. Editions, 2015.

Brown, Mantelli. *Junkers Ju 88*. Book 22 of *Aircraft of World War II*. Le Grau-du-Roi, France: R.E.I. Editions, 2015.

Capps, Robert S. *Flying Colt: Liberator Pilot in Italy*. Hamilton, ON: Manor House, 1997.

"Castelluccio." Abandoned Forgotten & Little Known Airfields in Europe. https://www.forgottenairfields.com/airfield-castelluccio-562.html.

Childers, Thomas. *Wings of Morning: The Story of the Last American Bomber Shot Down over Germany in World War II*. Reading, MA: Addison-Wesley, 1995.

Commendation of Unit. Headquarters, 47th Bomb Wing, April 23, 1944.

Correll, John T. "Daylight Precision Bombing." *Air & Space Forces Magazine* 91, no. 10 (October 2008).

Craven, Wesley Frank, and James Lea Cate, eds. *The Army Air Force in World War II.* Vol. 3, *Europe: ARGUMENT to V-E Day, January 1944 to May 1945*. Chicago: University of Chicago Press for the Office of Air Force History, 1951.

Craven, Wesley Frank, and James Lea Cate, eds. *The Army Air Forces in World War II.* Vol. 6, *Men and Planes*. Chicago: University of Chicago Press for the Office of Air Force History, 1955.

Daily Operations Report, February 22, 1944. 451st Bombardment Group (H), February 23, 1944.

Daily Operations Report, February, 25, 1944. 451st Bombardment Group (H), February 26, 1944.

Daily Operations Report, April 5, 1944. 451st Bombardment Group (H), April 6, 1944.

DeZeng, Henry, IV. *Luftwaffe Airfields 1935–45, Austria (1937 Borders)*, https://www.ww2.dk/lwairfields.html.

Dildy, Douglas C. *"Big Week" 1944: Operation Argument and the Breaking of the Jagdwaffe*. Oxford, UK: Osprey, 2022.

Eaton, Robert E. L. Daily Operations Report for August 23, 1944. 451st Bombardment Group (H). Robert E. L. Eaton, Colonel, Air Corps, Commanding, August 24, 1944.

Eaton, Robert E. L. "General Eaton Amends Markersdorf Raid," *Ad Lib*, no. 10 (1983). 451st Bomb Group Publication.

Eichhorn, Karl F., Jr. "Karl Eichhorn's 726th Journal." *Ad Lib,* no. 20 (Summer 1991). 451st Bomb Group (H) Publication.

Eichhorn, Karl F., Jr. "Karl Eichhorn's 726th Journal." *Ad Lib*, no. 21 (Winter 1991). 451st Bomb Group Publication.

Eichhorn, Karl F., Jr. "Karl Eichhorn's 726th Journal." *Ad Lib*, no. 22 (Spring 1993). 451st Bomb Group Publication.

Eichhorn, Karl F., Jr. "Karl Eichhorn's 726th Journal." *Ad Lib*, no. 23 (Summer 1993). 451st Bomb Group Publication.

Eichhorn, Karl F., Jr. "The Wartime Journal of Karl Eichhorn (726th)." *Ad Lib,* no. 17 (Winter 1988). 451st Bomb Group Publication.

Eichhorn, Karl F., Jr. "The Wartime Journal of Karl Eichhorn (726th)." *Ad Lib*, no. 18 (Fall 1989). 451st Bomb Group Publication.

Faulkner, Tom. *Flying with the Fifteenth Air Force: A B-24 Pilot's Missions from Italy during World War II*. Denton: University of North Texas Press, 2018.

Find a Grave Index, 1600s–Current, 2012 (Lehi, UT: Ancestry.com Operations, 2013).

Flight Manual: B-24D Aircraft. Consolidated Aircraft, September 1942.

Forsyth, Robert. "Luftwaffe vs Mighty Eighth: The Battle to Stop US Bombers." Key.Aero. July 15, 2022. https://www.key.aero/article/luftwaffe-vs-mighty-eighth-battle-stop-us-bombers.

451st Aircraft Spreadsheet. Accessed February 1, 2024. https://451st.org/Aircraft/pdfs/451st%20Aircraft%20Spreadsheet%20as%20of%20Aug%202019.pdf.

"451st Bomb Group Receives Two Unit Citations." Public affairs release. 451st Bombardment Group (H), September 3,1944.

Freeman, Roger A. *The Mighty Eighth War Manual*. Beverly, MA: Motorbooks International, 1991.

German Antiaircraft Artillery, Special Series No. 10, M18 461, February 8, 1943. Washington, DC: US War Department, Military Intelligence Services, 1943.

Gladwell, Malcolm. *The Bomber Mafia: A Dream, a Temptation, and the Longest Night of the Second World War*. New York: Little, Brown, 2021.

Griffith, Alan. *Consolidated Mess: An Illustrated Guide to Nose-Turreted B-24 Production Variants in USAAF Combat Service*. Sandomierz, Poland: Stratus sp.j., 2018.

Haltom, Charles. "Closer Look at Regensburg Mission," *Ad Lib*, no. 35 (Spring/Summer 2002). 451st Bomb Group Publication.

Harmon, Burl D. *Combat Missions: Flying the B-24 Liberator Bomber out of Manduria, Italy, 450th Bomb Group, 720th Squadron, WWII*. Pennsauken Township, NJ: BookBaby Publishers, 2022.

Haun, Phil. *Lectures of the Air Corps Tactical School and American Strategic Bombing in World War II (Aviation & Air Power)*. Lexington: University Press of Kentucky, 2019.

Hill, Mike. *The 451st Bomb Group in World War II: A Pictorial History*. Atglen, PA: Schiffer Military History, 2001.

Hill, Sedgefield D., ed. *"The Fight'n" 451st Bombardment Group*. Paducah, KY: Turner, 1990.

Intelligence Annex "A" for Operations Order No. 142, 22 August 1944. 451st Bombardment Group (H), August 22, 1944.

Jones, Winson. "Win Jones and the Markersdorf Airdrome Mission of 23 August 1944." Speech at the 2017 451st Bomb Group Reunion, New Orleans. YouTube. https://www.youtube.com/watch?v=cj3ougnPUCU.

Kinsey, Bert, and Rock Rozak. *B-24 Liberator in Detail & Scale*. Detail & Scale Publications, 2023, Kindle.

Lieutenant "Pep" Petrocine. Interview by Elaine Stahlman Jurs. 398th Bomb Group Annual Reunion, Phoenix, November 2007. 398th Bomb Group Memorial Association. Accessed February 17, 2024. http://www.398th.org/History/Veterans/Voices/Transcriptions/Interview_Petrocine_Pep.html#PP_Feathering.

Mahoney, Kevin A. *Fifteenth Air Force against the Axis: Combat Missions over Europe during World War II*. Toronto: Scarecrow Press, 2013.

Manning, Thomas A. *History of Air Education and Training Command, 1942–2002*. Randolph Air Force Base, TX: Office of History and Research, 2005.

"Markersdorf." Abandoned Forgotten & Little Known Airfields in Europe. Accessed February 1, 2024. https://forgottenairfields.com/airfield-markersdorf-51.htm.

Maurer, Maurer, ed. *Air Force Combat Units of World War II*. Washington, DC: Office of Air Force History, 1961.

McCollester, Roger. "Raid on Regensburg." *Flight Journal* (December 2001): 44-51.

McNab, Chris. *Fighting from the Heavens: Tactics and Training of USAAF Bomber Crews, 1941–45*. Havertown, PA: Casemate, 2023.

"M/General Robert E. L. Eaton Succumbs." *Ad Lib*, no. 23 (Summer 1993). 451st Bomb Group (H) Publication.

Miller, Lindley. "Tech Sergeant Lindley Miller's Missions." *Ad Lib*, no. 41 (Winter/Spring 2005/2006). 451st Bomb Group Publication.

Missing Air Crew Report (MACR) for Aircraft 41-29244. National Archives and Records Administration, Washington, DC, 1944, 1945.

Missing Air Crew Report (MACR) for Aircraft 42-5103. National Archives and Records Administration, Washington, DC, 1944, 1945.

Missing Air Crew Report (MACR) for Aircraft 42-51334. National Archives and Records Administration, Washington, DC, 1944, 1945.

Missing Air Crew Report (MACR) for Aircraft 42-51729. National Archives and Records Administration, Washington, DC, 1944, 1945.

Missing Air Crew Report (MACR) for Aircraft 42-52081. National Archives and Records Administration, Washington, DC, 1944, 1945.

Missing Air Crew Report (MACR) for Aircraft 42-52101. National Archives and Records Administration, Washington, DC, 1944, 1945.

Missing Air Crew Report (MACR) for Aircraft 42-52167, National Archives and Records Administration, Washington, DC, 1944, 1945.

Missing Air Crew Report (MACR) for Aircraft 42-52168. National Archives and Records Administration, Washington, DC, 1944, 1945.

Missing Air Crew Report (MACR) for Aircraft 42-6442. National Archives and Records Administration, Washington, DC, 1944, 1945.

Missing Air Crew Report (MACR) for Aircraft 42-7720. National Archives and Records Administration, Washington, DC, 1944, 1945.

Missing Air Crew Report (MACR) for Aircraft 42-7763. National Archives and Records Administration, Washington, DC, 1944, 1945.

Missing Air Crew Report (MACR) for Aircraft 42-7765. National Archives and Records Administration, Washington, DC, 1944, 1945.

Missing Air Crew Report (MACR) for Aircraft 42-77388. National Archives and Records Administration, Washington, DC, 1944, 1945.

Missing Air Crew Report (MACR) for Aircraft 42-78171. National Archives and Records Administration, Washington, DC, 1944, 1945.

Missing Air Crew Report (MACR) for Aircraft 42-78471. National Archives and Records Administration, Washington, DC, 1944, 1945.

Missing Air Crew Report (MACR) for Aircraft 42-78523. National Archives and Records Administration, Washington, DC, 1944, 1945.

Missing Air Crew Report (MACR) for Aircraft 44-40196. National Archives and Records Administration, Washington, DC, 1944, 1945.

Missing Air Crew Reports (MACRs) of the US Army Air Forces, 1942–1947, National Archives and Records Administration, Washington, DC, 2008.

Mission flimsy. August 23, 1944. 451st Bombardment Group Association. Accessed February 1, 2024. https://451st.org/Missions/Mission/20Flimsies/451st/20BG/20Pilot/20Flimsies/440823.JPG.

Mission Summary. February 25, 1944. 451st Bombardment Group (H), 1944.

Mission Summary for the First 200 Missions. Headquarters, 451st Bombardment Group (H), Office of the Intelligence Officer, APO 520 US Army, February 24, 1945.

"More on the 1Lt William Silliman Incident (Crash off Coast of North Africa on Way Home)." *Ad Lib*, no. 34 (Fall 2001). 451st Bomb Group (H) Publication.

"Narrative History of Regensburg, Germany, Mission #10." *Ad Lib* (January 1982). 451st Bomb Group Publication.

Operations Order No. 142. August 22, 1944. Headquarters, 49th Bombardment Wing (H), APO 520, US Army. National Archives and Records Administration.

Pendleton, Andrew. Interview. December 2023. YouTube, https://www.youtube.com/watch?v=U9wyEwdWv4E.

Phifer, Clyde W. "My Overseas Tour (Concluding Chapter)." *Ad Lib*, no. 43 (Winter 2007). 451st Bomb Group (H) Publication.

Pilot Training Manual for the B-24 Liberator, Army Manual No. 50-12. Winston-Salem, NC: AAF Headquarters, Office of Flying Safety, 1945.

"P.R.O. Does Major Job for 724th C.O.: Beane." *Ad Lib*, no. 20 (Summer 1991). 451st Bomb Group Publication, 1991.

Records of the Selective Service System. *WWII Draft Registration Cards.* National Archives and Records Administration, St. Louis.

Reynolds, Thomas P. *Belle of the Brawl: A Biographical Memoir of Walter Malone Baskin.* Paducah, KY: Turner Publishing, 1996.

Rieder, Kurt, and Rick Brown. *Stab & IV. (Sturm)/JG 3 Angriffsformation am 23. August 1944*. 451st Bomb Group Association. Facebook, August 2019.

Roosevelt, Franklin D. Exec. Order No. 9075, *Authorizing and Directing the Secretary of War to Issue Citations in the Name of the President of the United States to Army Units for Outstanding Performance in Action*, February 26, 1942. American Presidency Project. https://www.presidency.ucsb.edu/node/210791.

Ryan, Lloyd. "Captain Lloyd Ryan's Early Diary and Remembrances from Overseas." *Ad Lib*, no. 35 (Spring/Summer 2002). 451st Bomb Group Publication.

Schutt, Al. *History of the 451st Bombardment Group (H)*. https://451st.org/History/History.html.

Šelhaus, Edi. *Evasion and Repatriation: Slovene Partisans and Rescued American Airmen in World War II*. Manhattan, KS: Sunflower University Press, 1993.

"Silliman Crash Still Evokes Memories." *Ad Lib*, no. 25 (Spring/Summer 2002). 451st Bomb Group Publication.

Smith, Richard K. "Marston Mat." *Air Force Magazine,* April 1989.

Statistical Summary, Week Ending 11 November 1944. 451st Bombardment Group (H), APO 520, US Army, 1944.

Stone, Robert. Letter to Dr. Justine Beane Bradford, March 20, 2002.

Stout, Jay A. *Fortress Ploesti: The Campaign to Destroy Hitler's Oil Supply*. Havertown, PA: Casemate, 2003.

Technical Order No. 03-1-46. *Index of Army-Navy Aeronautical Equipment-Miscellaneous*. Indianapolis: Success P&L, 1945.

"3rd Group DUC Reviewed," *Ad Lib*, no. 9 (undated). 451st Bomb Group Publication.

Thompson, Harold. Conversations with the author.

Thompson, James F. "Clarifications, References and Updates," *Ad Lib*, no. 36 (Winter/Spring 2003). 451st Bomb Group Publication.

Tillman, Barrett. *Forgotten Fifteenth: The Daring Airmen Who Crippled Hitler's War Machine*. Washington, DC: Regnery History, 2014.

TM E9-369A: German 88-mm Antiaircraft Gun Materiel—Technical Manual. Washington, DC: US War Department, 1943.

Tudor, George. "Saga of the Extra Joker." 725th Bomb Squadron, Markersdorf 75th Anniversary, 451st Bomb Group, August 2019. Accessed February 10, 2024. https://www.facebook.com/groups/451stbg/permalink/2383229095046982.

"23.08.1944, 724th Bombardment Squadron (H) B-24J 42-51729 2nd Lt. Robert L Beach." *Archive Report: US Forces, 1941–1945*. Aircrew Remembered. Accessed August 6, 2024. https://aircrewremembered.com/beach-robert.html.

US Air Force. "Major General Robert E. L. Eaton." https://www.af.mil/About-Us/Biographies/Display/Article/ 107175/major-general-robert-el-eaton.

U.S. Military Registers, 1862–1985, Army and Air Force, 1948, Vol. 2. Lehi, UT: Ancestry.com Operations, 2013.

U.S. Veterans Gravesites, ca.1775–2006. National Cemetery Administration. Lehi, UT: Ancestry.com Operations, 2006.

Weal, John. *Jagdgeschwader 51 'Mölders' (Aviation Elite Units)*. Oxford, UK: Osprey, 2006.

Zaloga, Steven J. *The Oil Campaign 1944–45: Draining the Wehrmacht's Lifeblood.* Air Campaign Book 30. Oxford, UK: Osprey, 2022.

ACKNOWLEDGMENTS

I sincerely thank those who assisted me in bringing the story of the 451st Bomb Group to life. Among these are the 451st Bomb Group Association and its manager, Jonathon Tudor. Jonathan provided critical information and pointed the way toward many historical data sources. One of the best of these sources was the *Ad Lib*, a newsletter whose original namesake was the daily newspaper printed by the 451st during World War II. The postwar version was written and printed by the 451st Bomb Group Association from about 1991–2005 and distributed to veterans of the 451st and their families. Many issues of the *Ad Lib* contained first-hand accounts of the three missions described in this book and details about life in southern Italy during the war. Quite frankly, I could not have written this book without the information from issues of the *Ad Lib*.

I must also offer my thanks to family members of veterans of the 451st, whom I could contact via the 451st Bomb Group Association's Facebook page. These include Justine Beane Bradford, William Atkinson, and Michael Rousch. Further, I must thank the many members of that Facebook page who encouraged me when I posted information about the writing of this book.

Lastly, I thank my publisher, Bruce H. Franklin, and his very able and helpful staff at Westholme Publishing. Without their professionalism and skills, this book would not exist. They continue to be an absolute joy to work with.

INDEX